CONTENTS

GOVERNMENT DOESN'T WANT YOU TO KNOW THIS

CHANDRACHUR GHOSE | ANUJ DHAR

Vitasta

Published by
Renu Kaul Verma
Vitasta Publishing Pvt Ltd
2/15, Ansari Road, Daryaganj
New Delhi - 110 002
info@vitastapublishing.com

ISBN 978-81-949640-5-6

First Edition 2021
Third Reprint 2024

MRP ₹399

Edited by Manjula Lal
Cover by Koushik Banerjee
Layout by Somesh Kumar Mishra
Printed at Chaman Enterprises

ONE

THE DEAD END

IN THE SUMMER of 2004, the answer to the question whether or not Subhas Chandra Bose was alive, long after his reported death, seemed at hand. An inquiry constituted by the Atal Bihari Vajpayee government following a court order was reaching its logical conclusion. The ground zero of sorts for this seminal event was Kolkata's Mahajati Sadan, an impressive edifice built in the 1930s at the initiative of Netaji himself. Inside the building was a posh auditorium dominated by an old table in the middle, with an archaic judge's chair behind it. Lying on the table were five sealed packages containing yet-to-be disclosed DNA and handwriting reports, which were to furnish the clincher in modern India's most twisted political mystery.

A suited man wearing large square eyeglasses sat on the chair, preparing to unseal the packages. He looked around at the few mediapersons and others who had come to attend this special public hearing. For nearly five years, former Supreme Court judge Manoj Mukherjee had assiduously investigated all the possible theories of Netaji's fate. To his experienced eye, the dots of the official plane crash theory were not connecting. Evidence for it was not direct and, at that, riddled with far too many contradictions and loopholes. The testimonies of those who had by their own claims witnessed Bose's horrifying end in Taipei city were crammed with inconsistencies, which shouldn't have been there if they were being truthful.

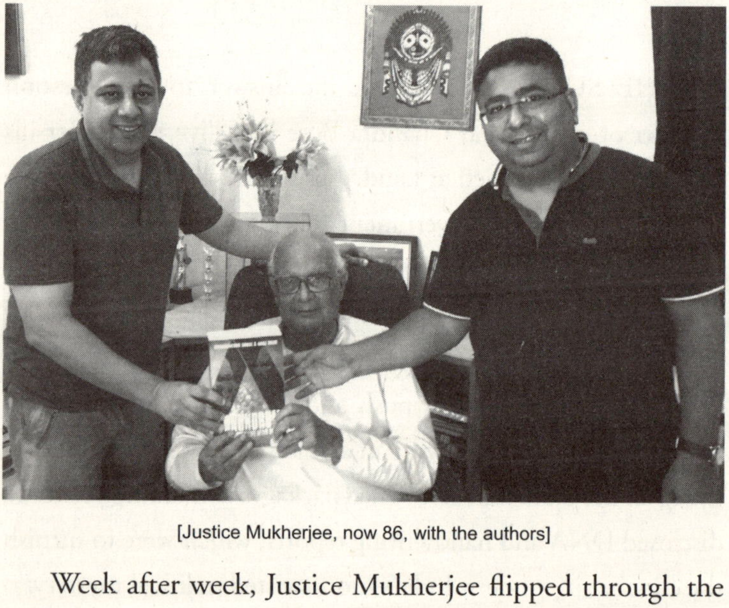

[Justice Mukherjee, now 86, with the authors]

Week after week, Justice Mukherjee flipped through the yellowing vintage records of their sworn statements dating back to the 1950s and 70s. All but one of the witnesses, mostly Japanese, were long dead. Fortunately though, the 'star witness' to the death of Bose had testified before his commission—and given him reason not to believe his word.

As he spoke slowly but clearly, former army doctor Taneyoshi Yoshimi left little doubt that his ninety plus years had not dented his mental agility. Yet, like on previous occasions, he contradicted what he had said earlier. If contradicting himself was not enough, when cornered by Mukherjee, the doctor accepted that he had issued a fake death certificate for Bose. This he had done in 1988, at the behest of a 'researcher' helping the Government of India to lend credence to the official version.

Right from the start of his inquiry, Mukherjee became increasingly uncomfortable with the top officials and ministers in New Delhi. Their body language reeked of resentment of his inquiry, which they seemed to accord only grudging acceptance. The commission had been set up after a Public Interest Litigation (PIL) was filed in the Calcutta High Court, where, then Chief Justice Prabha Shankar Mishra found the government counsel unsure of the official air crash theory floated by the Japanese at the close of World War II. The court deduced in its 30 April 1998 order that in spite of the finding of two previous inquiries in the 1950s and 1970s (set up by the Nehru and Indira governments under public pressure) that Bose had come to an untimely end in 1945, deep down, the Government doubted if this was true. The court therefore ordered the Government to 'launch a vigorous enquiry…for the purpose of giving an end to the controversy'.

When he took charge of the commission of inquiry thus established, Mukherjee thought the sailing would be smooth as the BJP was in power, not Congress—widely believed to be unsympathetic towards Bose. But his hopes began to be dashed quite early. Doordarshan and Akashvani wouldn't even give coverage to his inquiry. Mukherjee complained to Information & Broadcasting Minister Arun Jaitley after failing to elicit any response from the Prasar Bharati head. Not that it changed anything. Non-cooperation and delayed responses from the government's side became the norm.

Far more disturbing was the concealment of vital documents. In 2003, Mukherjee visited London in search of relevant records in the British archives. Indian High Commission officials extended the usual courtesies to him but were not willing to go the extra mile in helping him. Mukherjee turned to his London-based younger brother, an influential man in the corporate sector. At Mukherjee's request, House of Lords member Peter Archer communicated with Alexander Irvine, the then Lord Chancellor, the Keeper of Public Records. Irvine drew Archer's attention to two recently declassified files.

At the British National Archives, Mukherjee rummaged through one of the files of 1950s vintage. Events from the days when he was a young lawyer flashed in his mind's eye as Mukherjee sifted through the pages. On the face of rising public demand, the otherwise unwilling Jawaharlal Nehru government had been compelled to form a committee headed by Shah Nawaz Khan, a former INA officer who joined the Congress and had become a minister by the time the inquiry ended. The committee wanted to check facts at Taipei, the site of the air crash. Since India did not have diplomatic relations with Taiwan, the Ministry of External Affairs approached the British High Commission.

Andrew Franklin, the British Consul in Tamsui, Taiwan, reported to the Foreign Office in London on 10 July 1956: 'It will be seen that most of the witnesses the Indian authorities requested us to obtain evidence from, have either died, disappeared or know nothing'. Old Japanese records, said to be that of Subhas Bose, actually turned out to be of a Japanese soldier. A municipal bureau clerk who had supposedly seen 'Bose's body' prior to issuing the cremation permit in 1945 clarified that all he saw was a body, 'packed in powdered lime, swathed in white cloth' with 'only the eyes, the nose and the lips' visible. The clerk had added: 'We were not acquainted with Bose in his lifetime; it therefore follows that we could not identify him after his death.'

At the end of the file, Mukherjee found a damming record. It stated that not one, but five copies of the British/Taiwanese report had been promptly handed over to New Delhi. The judge closed the archives file, leaned back, reflecting on the reason why the Government back home should have kept this secret from him.

POL. B/24

OFFICE OF THE HIGH COMMISSIONER
FOR THE UNITED KINGDOM,
6 TEES JANUARY MARG,
NEW DELHI.

10th August, 1956.

I delivered to the Indian Ministry of External Affairs yesterday afternoon five copies of the translation of the letter from the Governor of Formosa together with the police report and cremation certificate. I also gave them the two copies of the letter in Chinese.

[The National Archives, Kew]

The Government's mala fide intentions were further exposed when Mukherjee sought to understand from them the reasons why a Prime Minister's Office (PMO) file, said to be Nehru's master file on the death of Bose, was destroyed in 1972 along with a bunch of irrelevant files. The Manual of Official Procedure in force at that time stipulated that the files of historical importance, especially those relating to issues agitating the public mind, would be kept in office for 25 years and then sent to the National Archives. If that was not reason enough to call the destruction illegal, it happened at a time when the GD Khosla Commission was functioning. So you have an inquiry going on and rather than hand over the file to its own Commission, the Government shredded it. Why?

File No.	Subject	
12(219)/56-PM	Monetary Reward to the workers of Sindhri Fertilizer Factory.	-do-
12(223)/56-PM	Coal Miners - New Housing Scheme for-	-do-
12(225)/56-PM	Indian Delegation to H.R.H. the Duke of Edinburgh's Conference on the social responsibility of Industry.	-do-
12(226)/56-PM	Investigation into the circumstances leading to the death of Shri Subhash Chander Bose.	-do-
12(229)/56-PM	Loan of Rs. 1.45 crores granted by the U.P. Govt. to M/S Sahu Jain Ltd. for a Soda Ash and Ammonium Chloride factory in U.P. - objection raised by the Central Govt. about ~~his grant of~~ -	-do-

[Ref to file destruction. Source: PMO. Obtained under RTI]

Mukherjee pressed for an explanation. He was given the runaround. Despite several reminders, he was not even sent the rule book governing the destruction of official records in the relevant period. He pursued the matter further with the PMO, the Ministry of Home Affairs (MHA) and the Ministry of External Affairs (MEA). The MEA lobbed the matter into the PMO's court, the MHA clammed up and the PMO sent a reply which did not address his queries. Later, a Director at the PMO stated that the destroyed file contained agenda paper/Cabinet decision regarding its destruction, and the same could be obtained from the Cabinet Secretariat 'since records of Cabinet proceedings are kept permanently' there. But a Home Ministry affidavit speaking for the

Cabinet Secretariat claimed that the Secretariat did not have in its possession any files/papers concerning Bose's fate. Mukherjee concluded that the government's dilly-dallying was deliberate.

More jolts came when the former judge tried to find out the facts in Taiwan. Starting 2001, he began pressing the MEA to seek relevant information from there. In June 2003, the MEA told the Commission that no 'relevant' documents were available in Taiwan. But the very next month the Commission learned from a journalist (co-author of this book) of his correspondence with the Taiwanese government. Taipei Mayor Dr Ying Jo Ma's office stated, 'According to the historical documents in Taipei city archives, there is no such record of a plane crash in Taipei on that day'. Taiwan's Minister of Transportation and Communications Lin Ling-San emailed that a thorough analysis of the records left by the Japanese showed that there had been only one major air crash during that period. An American C-47 transporter carrying about 26 released POWs had crashed around 200 nautical miles from Taipei. That was in September 1945. There was 'no evidence' to show that any plane carrying Subhas Bose had ever crashed in or around Taipei between August 14 and October 25 of 1945.

After being tipped off by the journalist, the Commission wrote to the Taiwanese authorities, who were, unlike Government of India officials, prompt in forwarding the same information. Actually, the fact that the Commission had got in touch with Taiwan government riled Indian bureaucrats. The MEA peevishly told the Commission, 'Any information required to be obtained from Taiwan may be referred to the Ministry'. The explanation was that 'We do not recognise "Republic of China" or "Taiwan" and hence we do not have any official dealing with them'. In 2003 a foreign newspaper reported about India's secret military ties with Taiwan. It was no secret that a Taiwanese representative office existed in New Delhi to maintain bilateral ties between the two nations.

By April 2004, the MEA had made it clear to Justice Mukherjee that it did not want him to visit Taiwan. Mukherjee sought time from the minister, Yashwant Sinha, who said he would be available only after the general elections in May that the BJP hoped to win on the basis of their 'India Shining' campaign.

While all this was happening over the basic thrust of the inquiry, Mukherjee was simultaneously applying his mind to the other theories of Netaji's disappearance. He followed up on what was, and remains till date for many, India's most sinister conspiracy theory—that Subhas Bose was in Russia after he was reported to have died. And that sometime in the early 1950s, he was liquidated in a gulag there on Joseph Stalin's order, at the prodding of New Delhi—which did not want Bose back in India. By 2014, the judge had in front of him credible statements backed by intelligence records to show that the Russia theory had something going for it.

Lt General Saburo Isoda, who had worked out Bose's last known movements, had accepted before Khosla Commission that Bose was on his way to Soviet Russia so that he could continue his struggle for India's independence. It appears that Mahatma Gandhi also knew of Bose's presence in Soviet Russia. Several months after the 'Taipei air crash', a letter was written to celebrated American journalist and Gandhi's biographer Louis Fischer on Gandhi's behalf by his secretary. 'If Bose comes with the help of Russia neither Gandhiji nor the Congress will be able to reason with the country,' it chillingly read. The judge couldn't utilise it as evidence, but there it was.

As in the case of Taiwan, the Government's response to Justice Mukherjee's repeated pleas to let his Commission visit Russia reeked of apathy. They kept making up excuses, the Commission officials thought. A genuine desire to help an inquiry engaged in trying to ascertain the fate of a front-ranking freedom fighter was completely missing.

Yet another claim that had caught Justice Mukherjee's attention was the most unlikely of all the theories. It held that Bose had died neither in Taipei nor somewhere in Siberia, but he actually returned to India in the guise of a sanyasi and died in Ayodhya in 1985 at the ripe old age of 88. Mukherjee's interest in this angle was kindled by a bulky court document. It was a descriptive inventory of the sanyasi's belongings prepared under an order of the Allahabad High Court in response to a writ petition filed by a niece of Subhas Chandra Bose. How could Mukherjee, who had served the same court as its chief justice in the 1990s, not take a look at it?

Lalita Bose came in the picture only after the death of the mostly unseen holy man. Commotion was building up in Uttar Pradesh as local media and others were making claims that he was Subhas Bose in disguise. They called him 'Gumnami Baba', since no one knew the name of the mysterious man. Lalita made her own enquiries, questioned his followers, and, rather incredulously, concluded that the claim was true. Tears flowing from her eyes, she admitted as much before many. She told *The Pioneer* in April 1986 that her father Suresh (Subhas' elder brother) used to confabulate with a rustic-looking visitor from Basti (where Gumnami Baba lived in the 1960s) to take messages from 'Subi'—which is what Subhas' older siblings called him. She rued the fact that she did not believe her father in his living years. She went on to tell *Hindustan Times* that the sanyasi was 'the same age, size and colour as Netaji. His accent was Bengali. His notes on books in English and Bengali looked like the writing of Netaji'.

When her attempts to get the matter properly inquired into were stonewalled by the authorities in UP, Lalita Bose filed a suit in the state's High Court. She submitted that as Netaji's niece she had rightful claim to the belongings left by Gumnami Baba, if he was found to be Netaji.

Giving the matter the due attention that the state government had not, Justices SS Ahmad and GB Singh announced an interim relief on the first day of the hearing. The state government was called upon to file a counter affidavit explaining their stand 'within six weeks'. (They would not do it for thirteen years!) The Faizabad District Magistrate was ordered to oversee the preparation of an elaborate inventory recording details of the items, letters, books, etc. found from the rented accommodation occupied by Gumnami Baba at 'Ram Bhawan' in the Civil Lines area of the city. The process of cataloguing stretched from 23 March 1986 to 23 April 1987, covering 2,673 items.

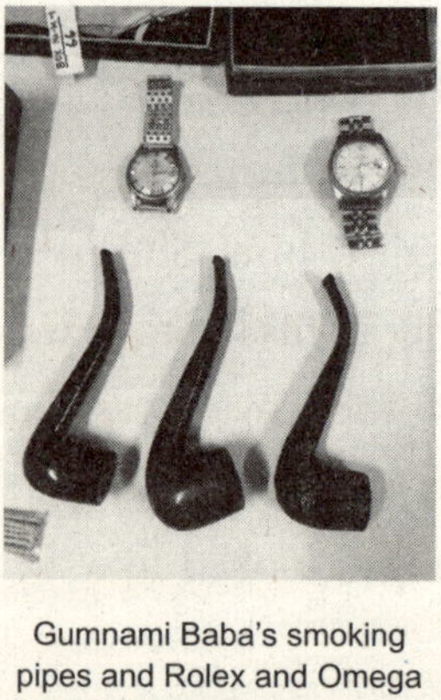

Gumnami Baba's smoking pipes and Rolex and Omega Gold watches. Subhas Bose's mother had presented him an Omega Gold watch

Justice Mukherjee found the details in the inventory astonishing. Just the collection of the holy man's books was sufficient to show that he was an extremely erudite Bengali. Nearly half his collection comprised Bengali books, English came a close second, followed by books written in Hindi and Sanskrit. The range of topics of the books was bewildering. Only someone with the highest level of intellect and intense curiosity to obtain knowledge would be a keen reader of books on classic literature, philosophy, unabridged scriptures in Sanskrit, homeopathy, ayurveda, occult and paranormal, cookery, physical exercise, India's freedom struggle, children's literature, history, politics, grammar, etc. Nothing seemed beyond the realm of his interest. In addition, from the RSS mouthpiece *Organiser* to *Time* magazine, he lapped up a variety of magazines. And of course, his special interest seemed to be contemporary research on the life and work of Subhas Bose.

George Washington, who was considered to be a significant book collector of his time, had his Mount Vernon estate in Virginia to accommodate his collection of an estimated 1,200 volumes. Gumnami Baba's nearly 1,000 books and over 500 periodicals were all stashed in a room measuring not more than 300 square feet.

Among the authors whose works he collected were Shakespeare, Walter Scott, Alexandre Dumas and Charles Dickens. If the volumes of Will Durant's *The Story of Civilization* held his attention (he wrote comments on the margins), he was equally enamoured with the works of Alexander Solzhenitsyn. He read Aldous Huxley, Andrei Sakharov and Nietzsche. What was a holy man doing in Ayodhya reading PG Wodehouse?

Among the Bengali books, the complete works and single volume editions of Sarat Chandra Chattopadhyay,

Rabindra Rachanabali (the collected works of Tagore), the novels of Bankim Chandra Chattopadhyay, works of Ishwar Chandra Vidyasagar, Tarashankar Bandhopadhyay and poet Rajani Kanta Sen featured most prominently. Multiple copies of the multi-volume translation of Mahabharata by Kaliprasanna Singha were present too. Among the other favourites were Balai Chand Mukhopadhyay, and Bibhuti Bhushan Bandopadhyay. These would be the staple of a well-read Bengali intellectual who lived in the first half of twentieth century Calcutta.

Quite a few books that he possessed were interesting for their subject matter. Among them were *International Military Tribunal for the Far East: Dissentient Judgment of Justice Radha Binod Pal*—which he had underlined at several places. Then there were Dr RC Majumdar's epic *The History of the Freedom Movement in India*, Leonard Mosley's *The Last Days of the British Raj*, Peter Sengar's *Moscow's Hand in India*, Rajni Mukherjee's *Moscow's Shadow over West Bengal*, Sita Ram Goyal's *Nehru's Fatal Friendship* and Solzhenitsyn's *The Gulag Archipelago*—which detailed life in forced labour camps in Soviet Russia.

His interest aroused, Justice Mukherjee looked for items which could have evidentiary value. He found letters from old revolutionaries and INA veterans, or their kin, to the holy man, indicating that they considered him to be Subhas Bose and kept him informed on matters and developments relating to him. They secretly observed the holy man's birthday each 23rd January at sharp 12.15 pm, (the date and time of Netaji's birth) either paying him a visit or celebrating in Calcutta. Pictures were taken of such functions in Calcutta and sent to him. Mukherjee's eyebrows curled up in amazement.

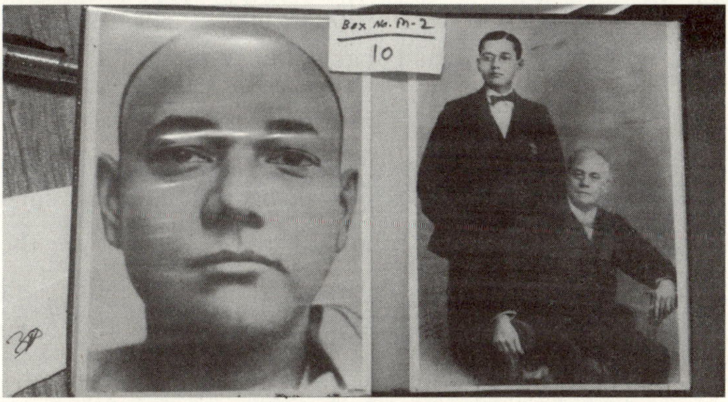

[Several pictures of Netaji and his parents were found in Ram Bhawan]

As the inquiry proceeded, Mukherjee examined on and off the record some of the living followers of Gumnami Baba and found them quite credible for the most part, especially those who had also met Netaji. They believed that they saw or conversed with Netaji long after he was declared dead.

With both eyewitness accounts and documentary evidence buttressing the Netaji link, Mukherjee started contemplating the next logical step. The tantalising possibility that Gumnami Baba was Netaji meant the Taipei air crash and Russia execution theories wouldn't hold true. If

Netaji was alive and in India in the 1970s and 80s, there was no way he could have died in either of these places.

There was no picture of Gumnami Baba, for he never allowed anyone to click him. Getting into fingerprinting was tricky but handwriting and DNA tests were feasible. In November 2001, Mukherjee visited Faizabad District Magistrate's office to personally examine the witnesses in UP and view Gumnami Baba's belongings lying sealed in the district treasury as the court order had stipulated. In the presence of mediapersons, he selected some 700 items, mostly letters and books, to be taken to the Commission's office in Kolkata. Most important among them were the specimens of Gumnami Baba's writings in English and Bengali and a matchbox containing a few teeth, said to be his. These samples went to two government laboratories each. One independent handwriting expert was also hired. One by one, all the reports arrived in sealed covers.

Mukherjee opened all the reports at the same time in Mahajati Sadan on 23 June 2004.

The report of Dr SK Mandal, senior scientific officer at the Forensic Science Laboratory, Kolkata, stated that the handwriting in English and Bengali did not match Subhas Bose's.

The report from Amar Singh and ML Sharma, the bosses at the Government Examiner of Questioned Documents (GEQD), Shimla, stated that the handwriting in English did not match Subhas Bose's.

The report from B Lal Kapoor, former GEQD chief and independence expert, stated that the handwritings in English and Bengali were a complete match with Subhas Bose's.

Mukherjee then turned to DNA test reports.

The report from the Centre for DNA Fingerprinting and Diagnostics (CDFD) in Hyderabad said that two out of seven teeth made available to them were 'subjected to DNA isolation, and DNA fingerprinting profiles were prepared'. The same were then matched with the DNA obtained from blood samples given by Subhas Bose's relatives. This report was inconclusive as the teeth 'did not yield DNA suitable for complete analysis'.

The remaining five teeth were examined by Kolkata-based Central Forensic Science Laboratory (CFSL), Ministry of Home Affairs. The CFSL concluded that 'the individual source of the teeth does not belong to either maternal or paternal DNA lineage of Netaji Subhas Chandra Bose'.

Two hours after the Commission's hearing, the Press Trust of India flashed the news report: 'A DNA test conducted on the teeth allegedly of one Gumnami Baba has disproved claims that the Faizabad-based ascetic was Netaji Subhas Chandra Bose in disguise, Justice MK Mukherjee Commission of inquiry said today.'

So, it seemed that the rumour that Gumnami Baba was Netaji, despite all the interesting coincidences, was just a legend.

TWO

TIPPING POINT

JUSTICE MANOJ MUKHERJEE'S troubles were compounded with the return to power of the Congress party in May 2004. True to their image of not being sympathetic towards matters relating to Subhas Bose, the new dispensation did not take long to send clear signals that they did not approve of the inquiry. Feeling offended, Mukherjee had to issue a veiled threat publicly in October that year. He said he was ready to submit his report on the basis of the inquiry carried out till that time 'if the Centre did not cooperate with the probe panel'. The Home Ministry, under which the Commission functioned, was coming in the way of his Taiwan visit and had posed certain objectionable queries to the judge. 'It is humiliating for the Commission to reply to the queries,' Mukherjee said.

The Government was slowly tightening the screws on

him. One of the earliest decisions taken by the Cabinet Committee of Political Affairs, theoretically working under Prime Minister Dr Manmohan Singh, was to effectively tell Mukherjee to stop his inquiry. In November 2004, Finance Minister P Chidambaram roared before a disinterested and clueless media that 'no further extension' will be given to the inquiry beyond May 2005. Home Minister Shivraj Patil rubbed in the message personally. Mukherjee entered his spacious office in North Block to find the old Gandhi family loyalist looking somewhat angrily at him. Not even asked to sit down, Mukherjee was given a dressing down. 'Mr Patil is learnt to have opined that the inquiry had gone on for "too long", and that "too much money" has been spent on it,' *The Pioneer* reported. This was the unkindest cut as Mukherjee, out of deference to the freedom fighter's memory, was drawing only one rupee as pay.

Interventions by Dr Murli Manohar Joshi, George Fernandes and others, however, led to the extension of the Commission's tenure beyond May 2005. Dr Joshi pressed the need for the Commission to visit Russia in a letter to Prime Minister Dr Manmohan Singh. The Government of the Russian Federation needed to be approached 'at the highest level,' he underscored.

The trips to Russia and Taiwan materialised somehow. In Russia, Mukherjee drew a blank as he could not visit the all-important security and intelligence related archives

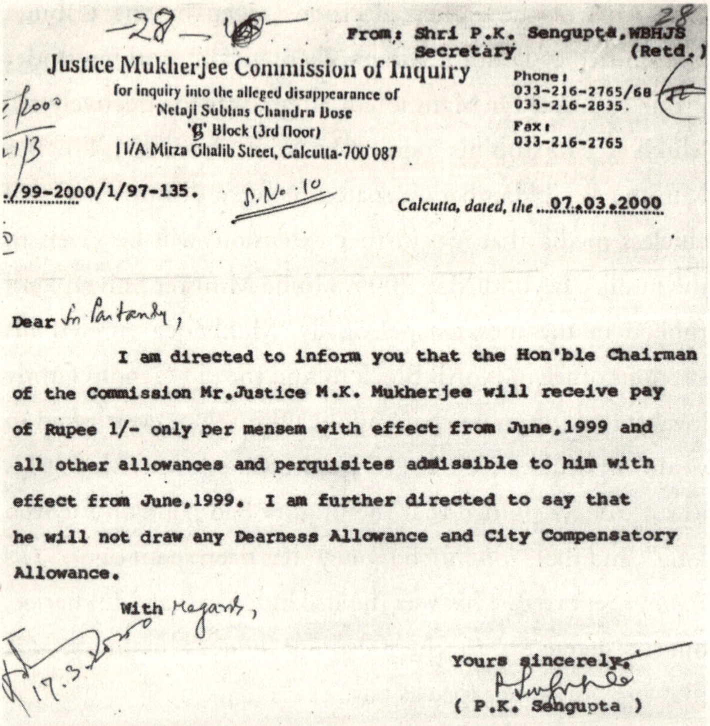

From: Shri P.K. Sengupta, WBHJS
Secretary (Retd.)

Justice Mukherjee Commission of Inquiry
for inquiry into the alleged disappearance of
Netaji Subhas Chandra Bose
'G' Block (3rd floor)
11/A Mirza Ghalib Street, Calcutta-700 087

Phone:
033-216-2765/68
033-216-2835.
Fax:
033-216-2765

./99-2000/1/97-135.

Calcutta, dated, the 07.03.2000

Dear

I am directed to inform you that the Hon'ble Chairman of the Commission Mr. Justice M.K. Mukherjee will receive pay of Rupee 1/- only per mensem with effect from June, 1999 and all other allowances and perquisites admissible to him with effect from June, 1999. I am further directed to say that he will not draw any Dearness Allowance and City Compensatory Allowance.

With Regards,

Yours sincerely,
(P.K. Sengupta)

[Letter from Mukherjee Commission stating that the judge would charge only Rs 1]

which could have held the information sought by him. Our government had no interest in approaching the Russians even at the middle level, forget the highest.

At Omsk in Siberia, the state archive authorities produced two volumes containing the names of persons sent to the various concentration camps in the Soviet years. There was no mention of Bose in the enormous volumes, they said. The archive director told Mukherjee that since all visiting foreigners in Stalin's era were required to register themselves with the authorities, documents about Bose must exist in Russian archives if he had indeed come to the USSR and 'used his real name'. (Bose had actually entered Russia in 1941 using another name.) But if Bose had come incognito, or been assigned a pseudonym, no record was expected to be found. It was a classic chicken and egg situation: You can't get the records unless you have the assigned name, and you can't get the assigned name unless you have the records.

The visit to Taiwan was far more fruitful. In January 2005, top officials in Taipei confirmed to Mukherjee that as far as they knew, there had been no crash and Bose had not died or been cremated in their country.

BBC NEWS

Watch One-Minute World News

News Front Page
Africa
Americas
Asia-Pacific
Europe
Middle East
South Asia
UK
Business
Health
Science & Environment
Technology
Entertainment
Also in the news

Last Updated: Friday, 4 February, 2005, 13:00 GMT

E-mail this to a friend | Printable version

Taiwan rejects Bose crash theory

By Subir Bhaumik
BBC News, Calcutta

The Taiwanes authorities have said Indian independence fighter Subhash Chandra Bose could not have died in a plane crash in the country.

Subhas Chandra Bose did not live to see Indian independence

Many believe the nationalist leader was killed in a plane crash in the capital, Taipei on 18 August, 1945.

Taiwan has now told a Indian investigation that there were no plane crashes at Taipei between 14 August and 20 September

For proof, Mukherjee requested Sean Hsu of Foreign Ministry for cremation records for the period during which Bose had allegedly died. Hsu said it would be done within a fortnight. Ruefully, Mukherjee thought back to the obstructionist ways of the Indians and the Japanese when he had requested the same records from them. The Japanese told MEA that they had tried their best to find out the documents relating to cremation permits as required by Mukherjee, but could not locate anything. 'You may understand how difficult it is to find out nearly half a century old documents,' was the lame excuse from the Japanese foreign office.

In a matter of a few days, the Taiwanese couriered to the Commission what could be considered the holy grail of the Netaji air crash mystery: The 1945 register from the old crematorium of Taipei city. The Japanese-era record was comprehensive and meticulous. It listed details of about 273 persons—Japanese, Chinese, British—cremated or buried in Taipei between 17 and 27 August 1945. When they were probing the death of Bose back in the 1940s, British investigators really wanted to lay their hands on these records. Colonel GD Anderson of Combined Services Detailed Interrogation Centre (CSDIC) had observed that many inquiries into Bose's death at that time relied 'solely upon the oral testimony of some witnesses without caring to search for the relevant records', such as those from the Taipei city crematorium, 'to test the veracity of their assertion'.

Mukherjee accomplished what Anderson could not. A meticulous study of the register showed that neither Subhas Bose nor others reported dead in the alleged crash were cremated in Taipei during this period. The finding was backed by other records and accounts on record. The story of Netaji's cremation in Taiwan was a red herring and so was the story of the air crash.

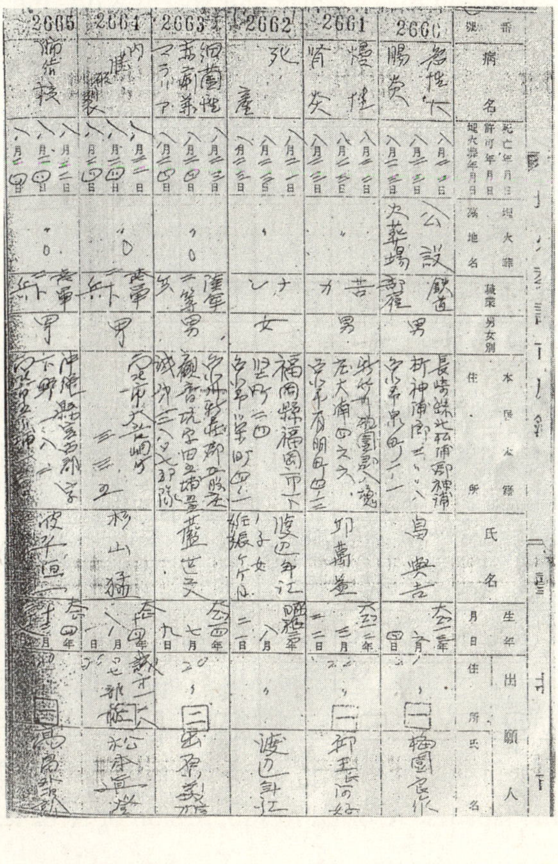

[A page from the cremation register]

When Mukherjee began writing his final report, he was acutely aware of its implications irrespective of what the Government did with it. 'I don't care if they put it in a dustbin,' he is said to have privately commented during that period. Limiting himself to the core points—whether or not Bose had died in the alleged air crash and if not, when and where did he actually die—he went about outlining his findings based on the evidence. His style was dry and to the point, written in legalese. This was a complete contrast to the flowery rhetoric that made GD Khosla's report eminently readable. Mukherjee wrote that recording a firm finding by merely 'treating the oral evidence of the eyewitness about Netaji's death and cremation as axiomatically true would be *non sequitur* and over-simplification of and a superficial approach to this complex issue'. Contemporary official records, he added, could provide the best corroborative evidence. He emphasised that he would not accept the evidence of the eyewitnesses on face value unless it cleared the two basic litmus tests of appreciation of evidence. One, probability and, second, the aphoristic saying, 'Men may lie but circumstances do not.'

Mukherjee went on to elucidate that robust circumstantial evidence showed that a secret plan was contrived to send Bose to the Soviet Union and that this was not possible without Japanese support. As they planted the fake story of Bose's death, the Japanese resorted to suppression of facts, leading to contradictions and loopholes in the evidence. Mukherjee's main conclusion in his report was that Bose succeeded in evading the Allied forces and the camouflage of air crash and cremation was created by the Japanese. But whether or not Bose landed in landed in Russia or elsewhere 'cannot be answered for dearth of evidence'.

On 8 November 2005, a Commission official presented the report to Home Minister Shivraj Patil. Mukherjee was not well, and he also had no desire to meet Patil again. The official handed over the sealed report to the minister, who asked for the conclusion. He did not respond when told that the official theory was rejected. The Intelligence Bureau must have briefed him beforehand. The Commission official later said the look on Patil's face was of resentment.

The report also gave considerable attention to the Gumnami Baba angle. While accepting that there was 'no reason for not acting or relying upon the evidence' of certain witnesses who had seen both Netaji and the holy man, Mukherjee discussed the stumbling blocks. He summarised the negative findings of the DNA/handwriting experts and concluded that there was no 'clinching evidence' to prove that Gumnami Baba was Netaji.

On 18 May 2006, the Mukherjee Commission report was placed before Parliament with a single-page Memorandum of Action Taken by the Home Ministry that contained no explanation. The Government arbitrarily rejected the main finding that Subhas had not died in Taiwan. In the ensuing discussion, Home Minister Patil stated that air crash theory held true, as was proven by the Khosla Commission and Shah Nawaz Committee previously. There was some commotion in Parliament and there were some media reports criticising the government action, but with this development the Netaji death mystery matter was put to rest. So it seemed.

The revival of the issue in subsequent years has to do with the activities of a group called 'Mission Netaji' comprising the authors and friends. We started making use of the Right to Information Act, enacted in 2005, to extract information relating to Netaji. Our efforts received support of the members of the Bose family, given that most of them wholeheartedly supported Mukherjee's findings. In a letter to Prime Minister Manmohan Singh, Netaji's nephew and Member of Parliament Subrata Bose not only underlined that the whole family stood behind the Mukherjee report but also took swipes against those few family members with links to Congress party who did not.

In 2010, the UPA government was compelled by the Central Information Commission to undertake the largest declassification exercise as a result of Mission Netaji's transparency activism. That was only the tip of the iceberg. Although the government would never give the correct number of classified files, we knew that there were much more. Mission Netaji-Bose family joint action took the form

SUBRATA BOSE
Member of Parliament
(Lok Sabha)

15, North Avenue,
New Delhi -110001
Tel. : 011-23093806

1/385, Gariahat Road South,
Jodhpur Park, Kolkata -700068
Tel. : 033-24734598
Mobile : 9830011421

30-May-06

Hon'ble Dr. Manmohan Singh
Prime Minister
Government of India
New Delhi

Dear Dr. Manmohan Singhji,

I enclose a copy of the Press statement released by 43 members of Netaji Subhas Chandra Bose's family at the Media Conference held by them in Kolkata on 26th May ,2006 on the subject of Justice M K Mukerjee Commission of Inquiry's Report on the alleged disappearance of Netaji Subhas Chandra Bose in August, 1945 and the Government of India's Action taken Report on the same, which were placed in Parliament on 17-05-06,for your kind perusal.

You will please find from the aforesaid Press Statement that we have demanded that the Commission's Report be accepted by the Government of India, withdrawing or amending the A.T.R. placed in the Parliament on 17-05-06.

I like to draw your attention to the fact that Smt. Krishna Bose, widow of Late Dr. Sisir Kumar Bose and former M.P. as also her children are not signatories to the said Press Statement and the said Press Statement reflect the considered views of more than overwhelming number of the Bose family members, who are alive today.

I may also point out to you that both Late Dr. Sisir Kumar Bose and Smt. Krishna Bose, when invited by the Mukerjee Commission of Inquiry to depose before it, wrote back stating that they had in their possession absolutely no knowledge and information relating to the alleged death of Netaji in an air-crash on 18-08-1945 and hence wished to be excused by the Commission from appearing before it. It is strange that having admitted in writing (which is in the record of the Commission) that they had no knowledge or information on the related matter, they have chosen to air their views in public contrary to the written admissions made by them in the recent past.

I trust that you will, after giving due thought to the demand of 43members of the Bose Family, will accept the same and act accordingly.

With kind regards,

Yours sincerely,

Subrata Bose

Ack. being put up separately.

Enclos: as above

[National Archives, New Delhi]

of marches and press conferences and so slowly over a period of time the ground was prepared for what was going to be the most sensational event in the history of the Netaji mystery.

Four years of chasing the Home Ministry by the authors

led to the declassification of over 10,000 pages in 2010. These papers were then sent to the National Archives in 2012 and opened to reseràchers in late 2014. Among the heaps of thousands of papers the authors found records revealing that after Independence, people related to Netaji, his kin and others, were subjected to surveillance at the behest of the Intelligence Bureau. It was evident that the Government did not believe that Bose was dead and were on the lookout for leads about him, hence the snooping on those who were believed to be close to him or could have information the Government needed.

The controversy raked up a massive media storm, which in turn prompted Mamata Banerjee and Narendra Modi governments to release nearly 400 more secret files. While releasing the tranche of records from state intelligence files in September 2015, Mamata Banerjee became the first chief minister of Bengal to make a public announcement that upon the reading of the files, it was clear that Netaji did not die in 1945 and was alive after that. The family members put a seal on this. Niece Chitra Ghosh told *The Times of India,* 'Nehru…knew that the plane crash was a hoax and feared that Netaji was confabulating with his family from abroad'. Her cousin Dr DN Bose added: 'I am surprised to find that police continued to snoop on the Bose family till 1971. This makes me believe that the Government wasn't sure about Netaji's whereabouts till then.' Another nephew suggested that the snooping continued till 1984.

The Bose family began getting calls from the PMO. Within days, Prime Minister Narendra Modi himself announced that he was going to meet the delegation led by the family members in October. At this point, certain members of the Bose family became so overwhelmed by the sudden importance thrust on them that they began steering the case in their own way, sidelining Mission Netaji. We wanted to corner the Government on the snooping matter, seek a proper inquiry about it. But paranoia gripped the family members

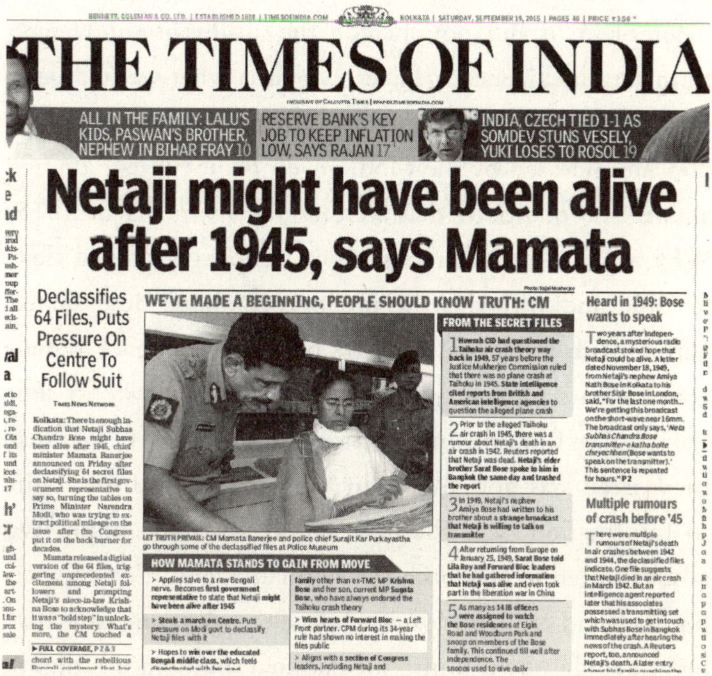

BENNETT, COLEMAN & CO. LTD. | ESTABLISHED 1838 | TIMESOFINDIA.COM | KOLKATA | SATURDAY, SEPTEMBER 19, 2015 | PAGES 40 | PRICE ₹3.50

THE TIMES OF INDIA

ALL IN THE FAMILY: LALU'S KIDS, PASWAN'S BROTHER, NEPHEW IN BIHAR FRAY 10

RESERVE BANK'S KEY JOB TO KEEP INFLATION LOW, SAYS RAJAN 17

INDIA, CZECH TIED 1-1 AS SOMDEV STUNS VESELY, YUKI LOSES TO ROSOL 19

Netaji might have been alive after 1945, says Mamata

Declassifies 64 Files, Puts Pressure On Centre To Follow Suit

Times News Network

Kolkata: There is enough indication that Netaji Subhas Chandra Bose might have been alive after 1945, chief minister Mamata Banerjee announced on Friday after declassifying 64 secret files on Netaji. She is the first government representative to say so, turning the tables on Prime Minister Narendra Modi, who was trying to extract political mileage on the issue after the Congress put it on the back burner for decades.

Mamata released a digital version of the 64 files, triggering unprecedented excitement among Netaji followers and prompting Netaji's niece-in-law Krishna Bose to acknowledge that it was a "bold step" in unlocking the mystery. What's more, the CM touched a

▶ FULL COVERAGE, P 2 & 3

chord with the rebellious

WE'VE MADE A BEGINNING, PEOPLE SHOULD KNOW TRUTH: CM

LET TRUTH PREVAIL: CM Mamata Banerjee and police chief Surajit Kar Purkayastha go through some of the declassified files at Police Museum

HOW MAMATA STANDS TO GAIN FROM MOVE

> Applies salve to a raw Bengali nerve. Becomes **first government representative** to state that Netaji **might have been alive after 1945**

> **Steals a march on Centre.** Puts pressure on Modi govt to declassify Netaji files with it

> Hopes to **win over the educated Bengali middle class**, which feels

family other than ex-TMC MP **Krishna Bose** and her son, current MP **Sugata Bose**, who have always endorsed the Taihoku crash theory

> **Wins hearts of Forward Bloc** — a Left Front partner. CPM during its 34-year rule had shown no interest in making the files public

> Aligns with a **section of Congress** leaders, including Netaji and

FROM THE SECRET FILES

1 **Howrah CID had questioned the Taihoku air crash theory way back in 1949**, 57 years before the Justice Mukherjee Commission ruled that there was no plane crash at Taihoku in 1945. **State intelligence cited reports from British and American intelligence agencies** to question the alleged plane crash

2 Prior to the alleged Taihoku air crash in 1945, there was a rumour about Netaji's death in an air crash in 1942. Reuters reported that Netaji was dead. **Netaji's elder brother Sarat Bose spoke to him in Bangkok the same day and trashed the report**

3 In 1949, Netaji's nephew Amiya Bose had written to his brother about a **strange broadcast that Netaji is willing to talk on transmitter**

4 After returning from Europe on January 25, 1949, **Sarat Bose told Lila Roy and Forward Bloc leaders that he had gathered information that Netaji was alive** and even took part in the liberation war in China

5 As many as **14 IB officers were assigned to watch the Bose residences** at Elgin Road and Woodburn Park and snoop on members of the Bose family. This continued till well after Independence. The snoops used to give daily

Heard in 1949: Bose wants to speak

Two years after independence, a mysterious radio broadcast stoked hope that Netaji could be alive. A letter dated November 18, 1949, from Netaji's nephew Amiya Nath Bose in Kolkata to his brother Sisir Bose in London, said, "For the last one month... We're getting this broadcast on the short-wave near 16mm. The broadcast only says, '*Neta Subhas Chandra Bose transmitter-e katha bolte cheyechhen*' (Bose wants to speak on the transmitter).' This sentence is repeated for hours." **P 2**

Multiple rumours of crash before '45

There were multiple rumours of Netaji's death in air crashes between 1942 and 1944, the declassified files indicate. One file suggests that Netaji died in an air crash in March 1942. But an intelligence agent reported later that his associates possessed a transmitting set which was used to get in touch with Subhas Bose in Bangkok immediately after hearing the news of the crash. A Reuters report, too, announced Netaji's death. A later entry who, in spite of calling for such an inquiry, eventually shelved the idea. They were wary of our stand on the Gumnami Baba matter, which we wanted to get sorted out.

While Mission Netaji members were present in the meeting with Prime Minister Modi and also in January 2016 when the first set of files were released at the National Archives, the entire show was run by Government in consultation with the Bose family members. Many of our friends were annoyed and did not want to be present but we thought that not to be a part of it was not a wise thing to do.

As it turned out, the declassification drive was incomplete. It did not include the all-important records from the intelligence agencies, which is what we had been demanding to be released first and foremost. That's why the 303 files released by the Modi government till date do not answer the questions that were raging in media in 2015: Why was surveillance mounted on people considered close to Bose and why was the intelligence about Bose shared with British intelligence by the post-Independence Indian government? On our part, we tried the RTI way to seek clarification from the Intelligence Bureau, but were told that the bureau was not covered by the provisions of the Right to Information Act. The Bose family remained mum. We advised them to approach the Human Rights Commission but they had suddenly lost interest in the snooping issue that had catapulated them into the national spotlight overnight.

The reason why the Bose family members turned their back on the snooping issue, and as such gave the government an escape route, had to do with the spectre of Gumnami Baba. The family did not want this 'dead' matter to come back to life as the probability of Netaji living decades after his reported death did not fit in the worldview of most family members, who subscribed to the 'liquidation in Russia' theory at that time. We also noted that the family was not talking straight on the issue and feigning ignorance. After all, it was one of them, Lalita Bose, who had ignited the fuse.

Though we worked as a team, tension was brewing between the Bose family and Mission Netaji members over the Gumnami Baba issue. At the centre of this tussle was Justice Mukherjee, silently leading his retired life in Salt Lake area of Kolkata. Praised to the skies by the Boses after his report came out in 2006, the same retired judge later became a sort of bugbear to the family as it began trickling out that in his personal view there was more to the Gumnami Baba matter than met the eye.

Things came to head in 2010, four years after the government's dismissal of his core finding in his report that Subhas never perished in any air crash. A man of few words who did not socialise much and hardly ever spoke to media, Mukherjee could not hold back his feelings during a casual discussion while a documentary was being filmed. This was inadvertently recorded. A portion from this recording was then shown in the media. The authors chanced to see the entire recording. Blasting the central government in language he could not have used in his report, Mukherjee could be heard hinting at a forensic fraud. He asserted more than once that he was '100 per cent sure' that Gumnami Baba was Subhas Bose, adding that he was not able to prove it due to the government's shenanigans and non-cooperation by members of the Bose family.

THREE

A SHAM EXPOSED

ON THE HEELS of Justice Mukherjee's sensational off-the-record admission, another dramatic development brought the Gumnami Baba matter back to the headlines in the year 2013. The Allahabad High Court pronounced a judgment on the PILs filed in 1986 by Lalita Bose (who had died before she could depose before the Mukherjee Commission) and another one by Shakti Singh, in whose house, Ram Bhawan in Ayodhya, Gumnami Baba had lived last from 1983 to 1985.

The court surveyed the entire matter and agreed, 'There appears to be no room for doubt that there was substantial oral and documentary evidence which prima facie makes out a case for scientific investigation with regard to the identity of late Gumnami Baba'. Co-author of this book Anuj Dhar was singled out for praise as the court order stated that his efforts (in previous books) to find out the truth about Netaji 'seem to be genuine and based on relevant material' and that both the state and central governments should have looked into the issues raised by him 'to remove doubts with regard to Gumnami Baba by holding appropriate enquiry'.

Stating that the 'materials and belongings of Gumnami Baba are national assets and must be protected for future generations', the court directed that they be moved to a local museum. The court also suggested that an inquiry 'consisting of a team of experts and higher officers, headed by a retired judge of High Court' be set up to ascertain the identity of Gumnami Baba, 'treated as Netaji by a substantial section of public'. In other words, the High Court saw some merit in the claims that the holy man could have been Netaji. This was no longer a crazy conspiracy theory.

As for the negative DNA test, the court pointed out that the assumption that the teeth examined were actually of Gumnami Baba was not backed by proper evidence. The court also stated that the Mukherjee Commission did not meticulously examine the Baba's belongings. 'Even little doubt with regard to the veracity of teeth will compel a man of common prudence not to ignore the oral and other documentary evidence, that too when there was difference of opinion with regard to handwriting of Netaji compared by the experts,' the court order read.

The state government led by the Samajwadi Party's

Akhilesh Yadav quietly opposed the court's directive on the inquiry, careful not to create a public controversy. The central government, as expected, remained totally silent, as if the matter pertained to someone who was of no consequence. Come to think of it, right from the very start, New Delhi chose to sidestep this matter. It did not respond to media outcries, court case or UP Assembly discussions in the 1980s when the government was being beseeched by Lalita Bose and others to get a proper inquiry done. This is possibly because of total disinterest, or fear.

The first time the matter was raised in Parliament was in March 1988. Ratnakar Pandey, a Gandhi family loyalist, asked in the Rajya Sabha who the Baba really was in view of the claims that he was Netaji. In response, then Deputy Home Minister, the clear-headed, Harvard-educated P Chidambaram assured: 'The information is being collected and will be placed before the House.' It never was. Nearly ten years later, in response to a similar question in the Lok Sabha, the same response was parroted.

The authors have not come across anything outlining the government's response to these two questions in any of the files declassified by the Modi government. This is when there are several papers and even files among the declassified lot dealing with all sorts of parliamentary questions raised at different points in time from the 1950s onwards concerning Netaji and the issue of his disappearance. As per a declassified file, following an appeal to then Prime Minister IK Gujral, the Home Ministry, in 1997, asked the UP Home Department to have 'this matter investigated' and inform both MHA as well as the Prime Minister's Office. The Home Department was told to treat this as an 'urgent matter'. The UP government must have responded but there is nothing more in the declassified files.

In March 2013, an adjournment notice was moved in the UP Assembly by about a dozen MLAs, demanding the inquiry to ascertain Gumnami Baba's identity. In the discussion that followed, leaders of all political parties sank their differences—a feat that one doesn't see too often in Uttar Pradesh—and put across their views in a most dignified way.

In February 2016, when matters relating to Netaji were making headlines because of declassification drive of the Modi government, Mission Netaji members, the Netaji family members who were backing us and Shakti Singh met then UP Chief Minister Akhilesh Singh Yadav with the request to commence the inquiry. By this time, the state government had partially complied with the HC order to display Gumnami Baba's belongings in a museum by deciding them to send them to Ayodhya's Ram Katha Museum. We told the Chief Minister that this made it all the more necessary to establish his identity as so much public money was being incurred on his belongings. The young

CM gave us a patient hearing, but remarkably never uttered a word about the fact that his government had contested the court's suggestion for an inquiry.

[Netaji kin and Mission Netaji members at UP CM's residence. Pic: CMO, UP]

Official UP cabinet records accessed under the RTI Act by fellow Mission Netaji member and author Sayak Sen reveal that the state government had no plan to carry out any inquiry. They were most content with a perfunctory and inconclusive police inquiry conducted in 1985. Then, for reasons which are not apparent in the official records, the state government changed its stand. In June 2016, announcement was made to set up a one-man commission under Vishnu Sahai, a retired judge of the Allahabad High Court. The court's suggestion to have experts and higher officers on this panel was ignored. Sahai was already in the news because of his inquiry into the 2013 Muzaffarnagar riots, for which he was criticised in certain sections. 'The Vishnu Sahai Commission serves its political purpose, pinning the blame for the Muzaffarnagar riots on a district officer and exonerating the political leadership,' read a March 2016 report in *The Hindu*.

In his early off-the-record interactions with people interested in the inquiry, Justice Sahai made comments to the effect that his inquiry was about Gumnami Baba and it had nothing to do with Netaji. Like most of the people with no knowledge of this utterly complex matter, he appeared to be generally dismissive of the claims that the man could have been Netaji. Later, as he communicated with the Bose kin opposed to the Gumnami Baba theory, Justice Sahai betrayed his inner feelings. In a Facebook comment, Surya Kumar Bose (famous for making a 180-degree turn on his stand that Netaji was killed in Russia, as the Gumnami Baba issue began having an impact) divulged that Justice Sahai had hinted to him long before his report came out that the holy man was not Netaji.

In view of these circumstances, we decided to give a written submission to the Commission at the time of our deposition as we were not confident that our point of view would be properly heard—so it was better bring it on record. At the very start of this detailed submission, we stated, 'It is the claim of a Netaji link to Gumnami Baba that has prompted the setting up of this commission, and that link must be either nullified or upheld. If upon inquiry it has been ascertained that he was such and such person and his antecedents are verified, the Netaji link will automatically vanish and that aspect of the controversy put to rest'. We also brought to the commission's notice some leads suggesting that DNA tests and handwriting tests were fudged. In all fairness, we also highlighted the points which we at that time thought came in the way of accepting the holy man as Netaji.

After our depositions before the commission we became fully aware that the judge was merely looking for information to fit in the narrative already shaped up in his mind. In December 2017, a very long time before the Sahai commission report was made public by the UP government, we wrote to Chief Minister Yogi Adityanath: 'There is no purpose in having an inquiry led by a former Acting Chief Justice of the Allahabad High Court if it cannot tell us who this man really was,' our neatly printed, lucidly written letter in English stated. It was also signed by Netaji's grandniece Jayanti Rakshit and her brother Arya Bose, both of whom had earlier met CM Yogi as well as Akhilesh Yadav. The meeting received ample coverage in leading media. The CM's office and Yogi themselves had tweeted a picture of that meeting.

In our letter, we asked the Chief Minister to reject the Vishnu Sahai Commission report if it had failed to prove the identity of Gumnami Baba as this would not be in the spirit of the High Court order, which was focused on finding out

[Source: CMO, UP]

who he really was. We reminded Chief Minister Yogi that the one of the reasons assigned by then Home Minister Shivraj Patil for rejecting the Mukherjee Commission report was it was 'inconclusive'—having failed to find out when and where Netaji had really died. What was sauce for the goose must be sauce for the gander. We requested for a Special Investigative Team comprising former intelligence, police, civil officials, researchers, representatives of civil society and media with a view to ending this controversy.

Concerning Justice Vishnu Sahai's 'non-inquiry', we made several points: Justice Sahai, for a start, did not seek evidence from Justice MK Mukherjee to explain why he had stated in 2010 that Gumnami Baba was Netaji. 'It defies logic why Justice Sahai did not approach Justice Mukherjee, who was his senior at both the Allahabad and Bombay High Courts. That the Sahai Commission did not examine Justice Mukherjee on record would be regarded as a great lapse by researchers and general people alike,' we wrote to Yogi.

We did not receive even a routine acknowledgement slip for our letter from the UP CM's office. In contrast, in our quest for truth, whenever we took up matters relating to Netaji with foreigners, they responded well. Howell James, Permanent Secretary, Government Communication, wrote on behalf of the Cabinet Office, United Kingdom, clarifying the position with regard to Bose related records. Phillip Stonehouse, Director of India and South Asia Section in the Department of Foreign Affairs, Government of Australia wrote to inform about the records relating to the United Nations War Crimes Commission. Taiwan's Minister of Transportation and Communications Lin Ling-San was generous enough to detail in a personal email why his country did not believe in the air crash theory.

When America's Central Intelligence Agency (CIA) turned down our request under Freedom of Information (that country's equivalent of America's RTI) for the release of two classified records related to Netaji, we appealed for a review of their decision. Appeal was made that these papers (being held by the agency because their release could harm US interests) should be released for the sake of Bose's admirers all over the world. The CIA was generous enough

CabinetOffice

Howell James CBE
Permanent Secretary, Government Communication

70 Whitehall
London
SW1A 2AS

Telephone 020 7276 0650
Fax 020 7276 0822
E-mail howell.james@cabinet-office.x.gsi.gov.uk

23 October 2006

Anuj Dhar Esq.

Dear Mr. Dhar,

REVIEW OF REQUEST UNDER THE FREEDOM OF INFORMATION ACT 2000

Thank you for your e-mail of 2 October 2006 requesting an internal review of the handling of your Freedom of Information Act request of 31 August. You thought a more vigorous search might yield more information concerning the death of Subhas Chandra Bose.

I have carefully reviewed the handling of your request. A further search has also confirmed that the Cabinet Office does not hold any information relevant to your request.

May I assure you that both your request for an internal review and your original request prompted thorough searches of our records. I am sure you

to duly release those records in response.

Justice Sahai submitted his report in September 2017 to the Yogi Adityanath government. It was made public more than two years later in December 2019, on the last day of the UP Assembly session. The day chosen was 19 December, when UP in general and Lucknow in particular were rocked by anti-CAA protests and riots. In the melee, the Sahai Commission report escaped attention.

The strategy adopted by the Yogi government to release the Sahai Commission report had an uncanny resemblance to the one utilised by the Congress government over the Mukherjee Commission report back in 2006. The Commission of Inquiry Act stipulates release of a report to public within six months of its submission to the authorities. The government chose to release Mukherjee's report eight months later in May 2006, 'at a time when public attention was focused on the anti-quota agitations', according to *India Today*. It was done on 'the last hour on the last day (May 23) of the Budget session for a brief interaction on the report' so that there was little scope for the Opposition to study the report and question the government's arbitrary rejection of it. When some discussions took place in Parliament later, Opposition MPs in both the Houses charged the Government with a cover-up.

Speaking in the Lok Sabha on 3 August, Forward Bloc's Subrata Bose, Netaji's nephew and MP, said he was accusing 'the Government of India of deliberate suppression of facts and information'. He said: 'I accuse the Government for destruction of files and for making files missing which contained relevant information, material information on Netaji Subhas Chandra Bose and his disappearance or, as the Government contends, his so-called death. I accuse the Government of continued non-cooperation with the Commission of Inquiry headed by Justice Mukherjee.'

When we saw the Vishnu Sahai Commission report, we found it was not what it was claimed to be. The bulk of its 450 pages were filled with affidavits of witnesses and deponents, the lengthiest of which were surely the statements of the authors. Shorn of these affidavits, the actual report was about 150 pages, mostly full of procedural details, repetition of arguments and discussion on matters that were not the subject matter of inquiry for the Commission. The 'findings' did not cover not more than 50 pages.

The Commission's 'inquiry' was all about a predetermined, narrow reading of statements of witnesses, records of cross-examinations and selective passages of the Mukherjee Commission report. The records of cross-examination were essentially created by Justice Sahai, who called the witnesses to his chamber to merely answer questions framed by him. So the statements of the witnesses were strictly within the contours drawn by the judge. He gave a long rope to those who had a case against Gumnami Baba being Netaji and, at times, browbeat those who said he was Netaji. The Commission treated as gospel truth statements made by kin of Netaji and others, whose objectivity in this matter is as real as Santa Claus, and disregarded evidence and submissions of those who stated that Gumnami Baba was Netaji on pedantic legalistic grounds.

In our written statement to Justice Sahai, we had discussed at length instances indicating that the state government and central intelligence agencies must be having records about the Gumnami Baba matter. In fact, we provided the Commission a copy of the report of a wishy-washy police inquiry carried out in 1985. Woven around the claim that Gumnami Baba could have been Netaji, the report concluded that 'on inquiry it could not be ascertained as to who was the deceased man'. The report itself referred to inquiry by Intelligence Bureau. The report also stated that the 'state government has been informed of the inquiry conducted by the police in this matter and further instructions of the government are awaited'. These instructions never came.

It was expected of Sahai to summon official records and scrutinise them in view of allegations, levelled by so many, that the government had indulged in cover-up. He did no such thing. He took no action on several such leads provided by us, with proper references. We demonstrated to him that intelligence department of India was on the lookout for Netaji, as widely reported in media, and never denied by Government of India. We even collated and gave to the Commission names of government officials who had handled the Gumnami Baba matter in 1985. In any proper inquiry, their views should have been taken on record. But the Commission did nothing.

Our written submission to the Commission stated that in view of such widespread intelligence activity on anything related to Netaji, it was inconceivable that the intelligence departments never followed up on Gumnami Baba. More so, when Foreign Broadcast Information Service (FBIS)—an open source intelligence gathering component of the CIA which is now called Open Source Center—had not failed to take note of the claims that he was Subhas Bose. One of the annexures to our submission was the copy of the Near East South Asia report No JPRS-NEA-86-040 of FBIS, which referred to the February 1986 claim of mercurial UP politician Raj Narain that Gumnami Baba was Netaji. We beseeched Justice Sahai to summon all records from the state intelligence departments of Uttar Pradesh and West Bengal, the Intelligence Bureau and the Research and Analysis Wing under Section 5 (2) of the Act and if required enforce Section 5 (3) of the Act to obtain such records.

The judge did nothing of the sort.

In our written statement, we stated that several Netaji family members and persons of repute such as Dr Subramanian Swamy have stated on several occasions that Subhas Chandra Bose was killed in Soviet Russia at the behest of India's first Prime Minister and Gumnami Baba was an 'impostor' planted by the Intelligence Bureau to cover-up the matter and confuse the people of India. We urged Justice Sahai to summon Swamy and others, take their views on record and then seek clarification from the IB. The only way to confirm the claim that Gumnami Baba was an impostor set up by IB would be to ask the intelligence agency to respond to the claim. We requested Justice Sahai to seek the response from Director, IB.

The judge did nothing of the sort.

As expected, the Commission concluded that Gumnami Baba's identity could not be established. But he couldn't have been Netaji, of this Justice Sahai was sure. He wrote in his report: 'He was an extraordinary man, the like of whom one very rarely comes across, who chose to die with his identity remaining a mystery.' He admitted that Baba was 'an extraordinarily well-read person' and 'very well-informed about war, politics and current affairs'. He had 'tremendous will-power and self-control' but was 'disillusioned with the state of governance in India'.

Sahai agreed that while there was 'an air of authority in his voice/tone, similar to that in the voice/tone of Netaji Subhas Chandra Bose', Gumnami Baba was not Netaji, but an 'an admirer' of his. In substantiation, on pages 140-41 of his report, Justice Sahai referred to a letter written in 1980 by one 'Bulbul' from Kolkata which was found among the belongings of Gumnami Baba.

In the said letter, Justice Sahai wrote, 'Bulbul has categorically mentioned that "if you come on the date of birthday of Netaji, we will have great pleasure". It is obvious that Gumnami Baba...was not Netaji,' Sahai concluded after going through the letter.

Further, Sahai Commission accepted the claim of journalist Sheetla Singh that Dr Pabitra Mohan Roy, the main follower of Gumnami Baba, had informed this journalist that Baba was not Netaji. This was when Sheetla Singh was found to have cooked up a diversionary conspiracy theory that Gumnami Baba was a fugitive murderer—just on the basis of a letter written to his newspaper by an unidentified person. But the argument about Pabitra was very formidable on the face of it, in view of Roy's antecedents.

A medical doctor by training, Pabitra had followed Subhas Bose to South East Asia for the cause of India's freedom, leaving his wife and young children to fend for themselves. Riding on a Japanese submarine, Roy returned to British ruled India in 1944 as an INA secret service operative. But his mission was doomed by betrayal. A fast-track trial under the Enemy Agents Ordinance against Pabitra, fellow spy Americk Singh Gill and Haridas Mitra, Netaji's kin who had dared to shelter them, commenced in May and by June end their execution orders were out. The sentence was eventually commuted and Roy was released in 1946. Later, in independent India, he was elected to the Bengal Assembly.

Roy was Gumnami Baba's main confidante by all accounts and nearly 85 letters written by him to Baba were listed on the inventory prepared on the orders of the Allahabad High Court. In one of the letters, he wrote to Gumnami Baba: 'I wish to say something—your own words—*You are my intelligence officer*—without fear or favour must act. Now allow me to begin in a similar way. Keeping in mind Ma Kali-Deshmata-Bangajanani-Bharatmata [Mother Bengal-Mother India] and your feet, I wanted to tell you that just like in the past, I still have the same unflinching faith and love-trust; unwavering obedience; total dedication and loyalty towards you.' Does it read like a follower of Netaji writing to another follower, if that's what Gumnami Baba was?

Soon after Justice Sahai's inquiry report was released, it was declared to be full of holes. On 27 December, *Hindustan Times* reported that the Kolkata-based writer of the letter which 'helped' Justice Sahai conclude that Gumnami Baba was not Netaji 'strongly contested the panel's findings'. She said that as far she knew, Gumnami Baba was Netaji only.

Suhita Bhattacharya, nicknamed 'Bulbul' by her freedom fighter father who was a follower of Netaji and then Gumnami Baba, further told *Hindustan Times*: 'The commission should have called me as a witness if it was relying on my letter. I did not appear before the commission on my own as I was not aware about its inquiry and examination of the witnesses. I am surprised and shocked to know that my letter has been used to reach a conclusion on such an important issue.'

On 5 January 2020, Ranendra Mohan Roy, son of Pabitra Mohan Roy, confirmed to *Hindustan Times* that both for his late father and he himself, Gumnami Baba was Netaji himself. Ranendra had himself met Gumnami Baba on several occasions so he was not giving merely his father's view. Like Suhita, Ranendra too was not summoned by the Justice Sahai Commission in the course of the 'inquiry'. Later, talking to the authors, Ranendra said his father was a soldier of Netaji and it is the duty of a solider to obey his general. He said Gumnami Baba, the 'general', told his father to keep his 'lips sealed'. This was the reason Pabitra had dodged the likes of Sheetla Singh in 1985. Singh put his own spin on it to present it as a denial.

Justice Sahai had no desire to get into all these intricacies. The gold standard of proof that Gumnami Baba was not Netaji was hammered home by him in his report over and over again: Mukherjee Commission got the DNA profiling of the teeth of Gumnami Baba and the comparison of handwriting of Gumnami Baba and Netaji and the results were negative. He was being logical and scientific, wasn't he?

Then came a fresh twist. In February 2020, media all over the country began reporting a sensational development. A report in *The Economic Times* read: 'The mystery shrouding the identity of Gumnami Baba, who many claimed was Netaji Subhas Chandra Bose in hiding, has deepened further with CFSL, Kolkata saying the electropherogram of the reclusive sadhu's teeth was not available with it. An electropherogram shows a sequence of data that is produced by an automated DNA sequencing machine and is used for deriving results from genealogical DNA testing.'

The story quoted the mover of RTI application Sayak Sen saying that the disclosure by CFSL has a direct bearing on the finding of Justice Sahai that Gumnami Baba was not Netaji.

'Justice Sahai in his just-released report used the CFSL report to the hilt to reject outright the view that Baba was Netaji.'

Sen underlined that Justice Sahai merely cited Justice Mukherjee Commission's 2005 report in his own report, rather than order a fresh test as demanded by many who appeared before his commission.

'In view of accusations of foul play, I wanted to consult independent DNA experts to verify the test by the CFSL, and hence I filed this RTI application,' said Sen.

FOUR

THE POLITICS OF FORENSICS

CALCUTTA PRESS CLUB witnessed a 'press briefing' like nothing before on 21 February 2019. With hired bouncers keeping an eye on assembled journalists and others, members of the Bose family were all fire and brimstone. An open threat was issued against a National Award-winning filmmaker that his presence in India would become untenable in the near future. The Home Minister was called upon to let loose Intelligence Bureau on Mission Netaji members.

The immediate trigger was the making of *Gumnaami* by Srijit Mukherji on the basis of research by the authors. The movie was to star Bengal superstar Prosenjit Chatterjee as Netaji, including his purported later avatar as Gumnami Baba. The authors were involved in the making of the movie right from the start.

[Authors with Prosenjit Chatterjee on the sets of Gumnaami in Lucknow]

This rattled the Bose family members. Everyone could sense a steep rise in public curiosity about the Gumnami Baba matter which till that time was hardly discussed even on the sidelines in Netaji's home state. Most people dismissed it out of hand, saying it was not possible. With the feature film, a powerful medium that grips the public imagination, this was going to change. The Bose kin, who had all their lives distrusted the government's stand and actions concerning Netaji, vehemently opposed the air crash theory, and worked with Mission Netaji members, underwent an incredible metamorphosis in a matter of weeks. Almost overnight, they became supporters of the air crash theory and the official government position.

In no other Netaji kin was this change more astonishing than Surya Kumar Bose, the Germany-based sophisticated son of Netaji's nephew Amiya Nath Bose. There was a time when Surya used to give the best media bytes on why the air crash theory was not acceptable to his family. In 2013, for instance, he told *Times Now* that an Allied intelligence team which investigated the reported crash in Taiwan came to a 'definite conclusion' that 'there was no trace of any air crash'. Radhabinod Pal, one of the judges at the Tokyo war crimes trial, was shown this file of the Allied intelligence team by one of the American judges. Pal relayed this information to Netaji's elder brother Sarat in the presence of his son Amiya, Surya's father.

Passing on the same information to Sarat and Amiya was *Chicago Tribune*'s Alfred Wagg, who had gone to Taiwan with the Allied team in 1945. Alluding to Netaji's existence long after his reported death, Surya told *Times Now* that in 2013 a former *New York Times* correspondent of British origin asked him, 'Mr Bose, could you tell me, when I came to Japan in 1964 why was MI6 still looking for Subhas Chandra Bose?' Relating this to *Times Now* correspondent, Surya Bose rhetorically asked, 'Now what do you say to that?'

Surya had also contacted the Mukherjee Commission and provided valuable information rubbishing the air crash theory. On 11 September 2003, he wrote that he congratulated Justice Mukherjee for the remarkable progress made 'in spite of all the blockades that have been laid in its path including those by the Government of India'. In March 2001 he expressed displeasure over the attitude of the government over the Top Secret files. 'I therefore feel it is very important that we get hold of other documents before they are destroyed or adverse political pressures are deployed in some way or the other to prevent the truth from surfacing.' He knew back then what the authors realised much later.

Cut to 2019, Surya Bose's state of mind was like the one depicted in the famous Superman Vs Clark Kent fight scene in the 1983 film *Superman III*. Like the superhero, the Bose kin was at war with his former self, as he began distancing himself from his previously held positions. So much so that in time he started slamming Justice Mukherjee for loopholes in his inquiry. Voices from the government side began sounding more and more credible to him—especially with regard to the Gumnami Baba issue.

The Calcutta Press Club 'briefing' happened in this evolving scenario—of Bose family repudiating their own stand on Netaji's fate, seeing the rise in popularity of the Gumnami Baba angle they were totally opposed to. Why they behaved like that became clear subsequently.

At the end of the harangue at the Press Club, the family issued a statement, bearing signatures of Surya Bose and others. The statement charged the authors of running a 'sinister campaign' to prove that Gumnami Baba was Netaji. As if Lalita Bose who went to court in 1986 was our aunt, not theirs! The statement read: 'Central to this outrageous hoax is a photograph of Netaji, doctored to represent an ageing Gumnami Baba with grey beard. This fake has been widely displayed side by side with an actual photograph of Netaji.' For good measure, the statement distributed to mediapersons contained this 'photograph'.

[From the press statement distributed by the Bose family on 21 Feb 2019 at Calcutta Press Club]

And then was outlined the unimpeachable argument in the armoury of the Boses to discredit the Gumnami Baba-Netaji link—the 'irrefutable' forensic evidence:

The Justice Mukherjee Commission of Inquiry 2005 provided conclusive proof through DNA testing at the respected

Central Forensic Laboratory in Kolkata, that there was no match between Netaji and Gumnami Baba. Handwriting comparisons carried out at the same Kolkata laboratory and the Office of the Government Examiner of Questioned Documents in Simla, delivered a similar negative outcome.

'The devil is in the detail,' so goes the old idiom. With regard to the 'doctored' Netaji picture, here are the facts: The following 'picture' of Gumnami Baba has been published in innumerable newspapers, websites and even shown on TV channels for last several years.

This picture is actually an identikit created in 2002 by the online division of *Hindustan Times,* as part of its investigation into the Netaji death controversy (the lead investigator of which was Anuj Dhar). Illustrator Siddharth Ghosh started creating the make-believe image of Gumnami Baba on the basis of the description by a witness who had earlier duly deposed before the Mukherjee Commission. This witness and all others who had seen the holy man stated that he looked exactly like Netaji—but was considerably older.

Ghosh used a picture of Netaji as a base and made changes on it as suggested by the witness who described how the holy man kept his moustache, how thick were his sideburns, etc. The final visual released by *Hindustan Times* showed both the original Netaji picture as well as the artist's impression of Gumnami Baba. This is how it appeared on HT's website. Please read the caption underneath carefully:

Artist's impression of Bhagwanji based on eyewitnesses' accounts. On the left is a late 1930s picture of Netaji Subhas Chandra Bose.

The print edition of *Hindustan Times* on 24 April 2002 carried the same story with Gumnami Baba illustration in a box with the description that it was an 'an artist's impression'.

It was actually the Bose family which doctored the *Hindustan Times* combo image by removing the caption and the name of illustrator from it. Then, they fobbed off their doctored image to media in 2019 with the allegation that Mission Netaji was using this picture to prove Gumnami Baba was Netaji. Truth is, at no point in time did *Hindustan*

Times and Mission Netaji claim that the illustration was Gumnami Baba's actual picture. In none of the books written by the authors, our numerous lectures all over the world, countless Facebook posts and tweets and YouTube videos, we have never ever said or implied or hinted that this was Gumnami Baba's picture—because we have known from Day One that it is an artist's impression based on Netaji's actual picture.

What the Boses did at Calcutta Press Club was part of their psychological war against us, with the singular aim of discrediting the Gumnami Baba-Netaji link by either hook or crook.

This very philosophy of 'hook or crook' guided the government's approach in covering up the Gumnami Baba matter. The best manifestation of this was the unprecedented forensic fraud perpetrated before the Justice Mukherjee Commission. Willy-nilly, Justice Sahai has promoted this fraud, for he ignored the counter-claims pressed before him and did not dig deeper as he was duty-bound to. He can take cover under legalities, but people will be able to see through the charade when the full facts are laid before them.

It is our considered view that Sahai's refusal to examine Mukherjee had to do with the fact that we had ourselves confided in him during our personal meeting that his former senior brother judge had serious doubts about the authenticity of the DNA and handwriting reports furnished to him by government experts. Mukherjee Commission's report, which Sahai quoted all over his report, was replete with instances establishing the mala fides of the government. Mukherjee's off-the-record statement that he was '100 percent sure' that Gumnami Baba was Netaji is freely available on YouTube, proving that deep down Mukhejee disbelieved the claims of forensic experts.

The people of India wanted the truth from Justice Sahai, not legally tenable evasiveness. He had the advantage of running his inquiry at a time when circumstances were far more favourable than they were when Mukherjee conducted his inquiry. If Justice Sahai had gone on to examine Justice Mukherjee as many demanded, he could not have drawn the conclusion he evidently reached before starting his inquiry.

But how, you will ask, can a DNA test be questioned? It is a matter of pure science!

The process of DNA testing is certainly scientific, totally believable and beyond reproach. But it is axiomatically true that political science is the *mother* of all sciences—especially in corrupt societies. The credibility of DNA testing process in India has been called into question over matters that were nowhere as politically volatile as the Netaji mystery. For example, in 2003 three police officers and two doctors were found guilty of fudging the DNA samples of five innocent people killed in the Chattisinghpora massacre of 2,000 in Jammu & Kashmir.

To skip to a recent example, as reported in *The Times of India* on 8 August 2018, the Delhi High 'ordered a CBI probe into the working of the Forensic Science Laboratory (FSL) in the capital after it found shocking irregularities in handling of samples and preparation of reports by the government lab in Rohini'. The court observed that 'FSL had from time to time produced incorrect DNA reports to help the accused, even though the rest of the evidence pointed to their guilt'.

'CBI books FSL deputy director, senior officer for false DNA report to help rape accused'—was the headline of the *Indian Express* story in September 2019 following the CBI inquiry.

Central forensic labs are also not in the league of the labs in the US or Europe that one can take their word as final on issues that have political ramifications. Around 1999, the CFSL performed a DNA test on the remains presumed to be of Paul Wells, a British national kidnapped along with others by terrorists in J&K. According to a report published in *The Independent* of London in January 2000, the J&K Police 'announced that scientists in the Central Forensic Science Laboratories in New Delhi and Calcutta had confirmed through DNA testing of samples of bones and other body parts that this was indeed the body of Mr Wells'. To verify the claims made by the CFSL labs, the British carried out their own tests. The Foreign and Commonwealth Office later announced that 'British police forensic scientists had decided that the remains were neither those of Mr Wells nor of any of the other hostages.'

Asked to choose between the Indian report and the one from London, ordinary citizens like us, fired by patriotism, may want to pick *our* report—but throughout the world, everyone will go with the British report. Even *our* very own elites—politicians, top bureaucrats, soldiers, intellectuals, journalists, spooks, just about everyone—whose children's favourite destination for study, work and permanent domicile is more likely to be London or New York than Mumbai and New Delhi—won't even look at a *desi* report when another one from the West is at hand. That's why every time there is some forensic test involved in some high profile contentious matter in India, the parties involved try to seek opinion from foreign experts as they are regarded not only more learned but also far more credible considering the high corruption levels in India. Remember the recent Sunanda Pushkar case, in which such tests were carried out in the UK and America?

Coming specifically to DNA tests in the Gumnami Baba matter, there are clear-cut circumstantial and scientific reasons to prove that they were fake. As related in a previous chapter, seven teeth believed to be of Gumnami Baba's were sent for testing first at CDFD, Hyderabad and then at CFSL, Kolkata. The CDFD report was inconclusive. The CFSL report dated 11 June 2004 was negative. It was classified as 'Secret' and given to the Mukherjee Commission in a sealed cover. We know it because we have the copies of both the DNA reports in full—obtained from the Ministry of Home Affairs under the Right to Information after considerable effort.

From the morphological examination and analysis of SRY gene, mt DNA (HVS I & HVS II), and Y-STR loci in the forwarded Exhibits 1-10, it can be concluded that forwarded teeth - (Exhibits 2 to 4) belong to a single human aged male individual - (alleged Gumnami Baba). The individual - source of the teeth does not belong to either maternal or paternal DNA lineage of Netaji Subhash Chandra Bose, therefore, can not be of Netaji Subhash Chandra Bose.

The remnants of teeth (Exhibits 1-5) & blood samples (Exhibit 6 -10) are returned in close sealed packet. The impression of specimen seal used in remnant packets is affixed below:

(IMPRESSION OF SPECIMEN SEAL)

11/6/04

(V.K. KASHYAP, *Ph.D.*, FNASc.)
DNA Expert*
DIRECTOR, CFSL, Kolkata

Encls:
i) Photographs: I, II-a, II-b, III & IV
ii) Table - I & II
iii) Appendix - I to V
iv) Annexure I to VI

** C.V. enclosed (Annexure-VII)*

DIRECTOR
Cum-Chemical Examiner
Central Forensic Science Laboratory
Directorate of Forensic Sciences
Ministry of Home Affairs, Govt. of India
Kolkata - 700 014

[Relevant page from CFSL report, signed by its director on 11 June 2004]

Now, here it gets interesting. Six months before Justice Mukherjee received this secret DNA, a story appeared in the No. 1 Bengali daily *Anandabazar Patrika*. The newspaper broke the news that the result of the DNA test had proven that 'Gumnami Baba was by no means Netaji'.

ডিএনএ পরীক্ষায় মার্কিন সেনার কেন্দ্রে আর্জি জানাবে নেতাজি কমিশন

নির্মাল্য মুখোপাধ্যায়

জাপানের রেনকোজি মন্দিরে রাখা দেহাবশেষের ডি এন এ পরীক্ষা করানোর জন্য মার্কিন সেনাবাহিনীর ডি এন এ গবেষণা কেন্দ্রের কাছে সাহায্য চেয়ে ফের যোগাযোগ করবে নেতাজি কমিশন। কমিশনের সচিব পি কে সেনগুপ্ত এখনই বিষয়টি বিশদ ভাবে জানাতে রাজি নন। মঙ্গলবার তিনি বলেন, "এখনই বিস্তারিত ভাবে কিছু বলব না। শুধু এটুকু বলতে পারি যে, সাদ্দাম হুসেন ধরা পড়ার পরে নিশ্চিত ভাবেই ইরাকের পরিস্থিতি বদলাবে। আমরা আশা করি, এর পরে মার্কিন বাহিনীর ডি এন এ গবেষণা কেন্দ্রের সাহায্য পেতে অসুবিধা হবে না।"

কিছু দিন আগেই ওই মার্কিন গবেষণা কেন্দ্রের পক্ষ থেকে কমিশনকে জানিয়ে দেওয়া হয়েছিল, ইরাক নিয়েই তাঁরা ব্যস্ত, তাই দেহাবশেষের ডি এন এ পরীক্ষার ব্যাপারে কোনও ভাবেই সাহায্য করা যাবে না। তার প্রধান দু'টি কারণ ইরাকে মার্কিন সেনার অবস্থিতি এবং সাদ্দাম হুসেনের নিখোঁজ হওয়া। তখনও পর্যন্ত ধরা পড়েননি সাদ্দাম। দু'দিন আগেই ইরাকের তিকরিতে সাদ্দাম পাকড়াও হওয়ায় পরিস্থিতির পরিবর্তন হয়েছে বলে মনে করছে কমিশন। তাই কমিশন মার্কিন বাহিনীর ওই ডি এন এ গবেষণা কেন্দ্রের সঙ্গে নতুন ভাবে যোগাযোগ স্থাপন করতে উদ্যোগী হয়েছে। ধরা পড়ার পরে ওই কেন্দ্রের সাহায্যেই সাদ্দামের পরিচয় নিশ্চিত করতে ডি এন এ পরীক্ষা করিয়েছে মার্কিন বাহিনী।

মার্কিন বাহিনীর ওই ডি এন এ গবেষণা কেন্দ্রের ব্যাপারে কমিশনকে খোলা সার্টিফিকেট দিয়েছে ওই বিষয়ে ভারতের তিন গবেষণা কেন্দ্র— হায়দরাবাদের সি ডি এফ ডি এবং সেন্টার ফর মালিকিউলার বায়োলজি (সি এম বি) এবং কলকাতার সেন্ট্রাল ফরেন্সিক সায়েন্স ল্যাবরেটরি (সি এফ এস এল)। ওই তিন সংস্থার পক্ষ থেকে কমিশনকে জানানো হয়েছে, মার্কিন বাহিনীর ডি এন এ গবেষণাগার বিশ্বের অন্যতম শ্রেষ্ঠ। সেখান থেকে দেহাবশেষের ডি এন এ পরীক্ষা করালে যথার্থ ফলাফল জানা যাবে।

তবে ইউরোপ ও আমেরিকার বিভিন্ন সংস্থার কাছ থেকেও এই ব্যাপারে ইতিবাচক সাড়া পেয়েছে কমিশন। তাদের বিষয়টিও খতিয়ে দেখা হচ্ছে। বার্মিংহ্যাম স্টেট ফরেন্সিক সার্ভিস থেকে ডি এন এ পরীক্ষার দায়িত্ব নেওয়ার জন্য সেখানকার প্রতিনিধিরা ভারতে আসতে আগ্রহী বলে জানানো হয়েছে। ব্রিটেন, জার্মানি থেকেও এই ব্যাপারে আগ্রহ প্রকাশ করে বেশ কয়েকটি চিঠি এসেছে।

চলতি বছরেই দেহাবশেষের ডি এন এ পরীক্ষার কাজ শুরু করতে চায় কমিশন। নেতাজি বলে প্রচারিত উত্তরপ্রদেশের ফৈজাবাদের 'গুমনামি' বাবার ব্যবহৃত জিনিসপত্রের ডি এন এ পরীক্ষায় সুভাষচন্দ্র বসুর সঙ্গে কোনও মিল পায়নি কমিশন। গুমনামি বাবা যে কোনও ভাবেই নেতাজি নন, তা প্রমাণিত হয়ে গিয়েছে। কমিশন ডি এন এ পরীক্ষার জন্য নেতাজির মা প্রভাবতী দেবীর বংশের তিন জনের এবং বাবা জানকীনাথ বসুর বংশের দু'জনের রক্তের নমুনা সংগ্রহ করেছে।

রেনকোজি মন্দিরে রাখা দেহাবশেষের মধ্যে দাঁত এবং কিছু হাড়ের খোঁজ পেয়েছে কমিশন। সেই ছবিও তুলে নিয়ে এসেছে তারা। ডি এন এ বিশেষজ্ঞদের মতে, কেবল ছাই থাকলে ওই দেহাবশেষের কোনও গবেষণামূলক পরীক্ষা করা সম্ভব হত না। কারণ, ছাইয়ের ডি এন পরীক্ষা হয় না।

[The Anandabazar Patrika report of 21 December 2003]

The Mukherjee Commission was functioning when news about the DNA test proving negative was published in December 2003. The Commission regarded the news item as prejudicial 'to the progress of the inquiry' and complained to the Press Council of India. The legal head of *Anandabazar Patrika* responded that the story represented what was 'a scoop in journalistic parlance and they were satisfied about its genuineness'. The legal head submitted that the news published in the paper was substantiated when in June 2004 Justice Mukherjee made the DNA reports public and it became public knowledge that the DNA test was indeed negative.

The Press Council consequently ruled in favour of *Anandabazar Patrika*: 'To say that the press should not publish any information till it is officially released would militate against the spirit of investigative journalism and even to an extent the purpose of journalism.'

Investigative journalism is absolutely fine. Newspaper reports from the early 2000s demonstrate that CFSL, Kolkata was in touch with media over matters relating to Netaji. Reports do get leaked out, findings of commissions reach journalists in advance—but only *after* they have been drafted or the conclusions have been reached. How can one know the conclusion of a DNA test *month*s before it has been ascertained? How could CFSL give ABP the *scoop* that the test was negative when they had yet to start the testing?

Justice Sahai did not think there was anything suspicious in this and so he gave the matter a go-by despite our pleas. The media in Bengal has more or less done the same for another reason. The ABP group is the biggest name in media in Bengal, perhaps the most prestigious employer. So the silence of journalists is understandable. The silence of Government of India is perfectly understandable too. Come to think of it, hell would have broken loose had the matter concerned someone of far more importance to present-day India, say, a terrorism suspect. In that case, media, civil society, top laywers, conscientious citizens all would have fallen like a ton of bricks on the government, screaming around the big cities in India and the world that a 'fake report' has been planted to obstruct justice.

With a view to getting at the truth, the authors took up the CFSL and CDFD reports with the DNA experts who had both professional knowhow to assess them as well as sufficient inside knowledge of the workings of the sarkari labs. Dr Maharshi Krishna Deb, who has worked for leading institutes in India, Germany and the US (Stanford Institute for Stem Cell Biology and Regenerative Medicine, California), took a look at the CDFD report. The lab had examined two out of the seven teeth made available to them. Only one, they claimed, 'yielded DNA which could be partially analysed'. But out of nine loci (location of genes on a chromosome) tested, only three amplified, which was not sufficient to form any opinion. So the CDFD report was inconclusive.

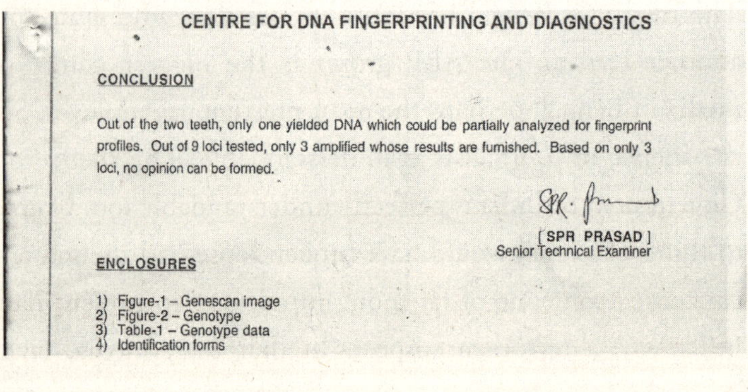

CENTRE FOR DNA FINGERPRINTING AND DIAGNOSTICS

CONCLUSION

Out of the two teeth, only one yielded DNA which could be partially analyzed for fingerprint profiles. Out of 9 loci tested, only 3 amplified whose results are furnished. Based on only 3 loci, no opinion can be formed.

[SPR PRASAD]
Senior Technical Examiner

ENCLOSURES

1) Figure-1 – Genescan image
2) Figure-2 – Genotype
3) Table-1 – Genotype data
4) Identification forms

If that was the case, what prevented CDFD from making use of the third or fourth tooth? Dr Deb felt somewhat amused. The test, to his mind, was 'most likely politically conjugated to truncate its normal inference' for reasons beyond his comprehension. He said that in the report no reason 'has been cited for not being able to amplify other six loci'.

It would be in order here to refer to the October 2017 judgment of the Allahabad High Court in the Aarushi Talwar–Hemraj murder case. Coming down heavily on the CBI for deliberately tampering with a most crucial piece of evidence indicating who could have been the murderer, the court in its order recorded that a pillow was recovered from the house of Krishna, the Talwars' compounder. This pillow bearing some suspicious-looking spots was sent to CDFD, Hyderabad. The lab returned a finding that DNA of Hemraj was found on the pillow. But three years later, CDFD stated that due to a typographic error, it had mistakenly reported this particular finding. The officer who reported this and the finding earlier was the same Senior Technical Examiner who had furnished the Gumnami Baba teeth report!

CDFD's credibility over the Aarushi matter was blown to smithereens in the court order. 'There was no possibility of any mistake creeping into the report,' it stated. What had really happened was that a letter had been mysteriously handed over to CDFD by the CBI's case investigating officer. 'It was virtually suggested by the said letter of the Investigating Officer that there was a typographical error.' The court further said that 'the CDFD Hyderabad simply abided by the cryptic suggestion given by the Investigating Officer on 17.3.2011 and virtually satisfied his requirement.'

So much for scientific testing!

Turning the pages of the 'conclusive' CFSL report, another expert (who works in one of the top government labs and wishes to remain anonymous) noted that a most vital component of it was missing. 'Where is the electropherogram?' we were asked. An electropherogram is a graphical representation of a DNA profile generated by established technical procedures with the help of highly sophisticated equipment. It is on the electropherogram (raw data) that the DNA experts base their findings. While the CDFD report contained an electropherogram, the CFSL report submitted to the Mukherjee Commission had none.

Hence, in 2017 we filed a RTI request seeking 'certified copies of the electropherogram of all the eight analysed Exhibits used during the so-called 'Operation Abhigyan'—the title given to Gumnami Baba test by CFSL. Since CFSL had concluded that Baba was not Netaji—which means he was a nobody—they should have had no hesitation in providing us the electropherogram as nobodies are of no consequence to anyone. As it turned out, CFSL refused to give us the copy of the elusive electropherogram saying they could not do so as it 'pertains to a third party and is confidential in nature'.

'Confidential nature'? What on earth for? Finding no sense in the CFSL's response, we filed an appeal as mandated by the RTI Act. CFSL Director responded by saying that the previous reply was 'correct'. 'The information sought by you cannot be disclosed as it comes under RTI Act Rule 11(1).' The third party in this instance was the Mukherjee Commission to which the CFSL report was given. Everyone knows that the Commission wound up more than a decade ago. Its report was made public in 2006. All its records, including the CFSL report, were transferred to the National Archives in 2010 by the Ministry of Home Affairs under whose aegis the Commission functioned. This made the MHA the successor third party. So why would the MHA want to keep the main component of the Gumnami Baba DNA report secret?

Two years later, in 2019, Sayak Sen filed fresh RTI request seeking the electropherogram. This time the CFSL sent a reply that it was 'not available' with them.

This sparked off a controversy. 'The mystery shrouding the identity of Gumnami Baba, who many claimed was Netaji Subhas Chandra Bose in hiding, has deepened further with CFSL, Kolkata, saying the electropherogram of the reclusive sadhu's teeth was not available with it,' read a story in *The Indian Express*.

CENTRAL FORENSIC SCIENCE LABORATORY
DIRECTORATE OF FORENSIC SCIENCE SERVICES
MINISTRY OF HOME AFFAIRS, GOVT. OF INDIA
30, GORACHAND ROAD
KOLKATA – 700 014

No. CFSL(K)/19-20/II/RTI-55/SS/475 Date: 04.02.2020

To
Mr. Sayak Sen,

Nabagram,
PIN- 712246
West Bengal.

Sub: Information under RTI Act., 2005.

Sir,

Please refer to your online RTI application vide Registration No. DIRFS/R/E/20/00002 dated 05.01.2020 and the required information is furnished below:

1. The Electropherogram Report of this case is not available at CFSL, Kolkata.

The most incisive television debate on the development was hosted by *CNN-IBN* executive editor Anand Narasimhan. Sayak Sen, Bose family spokesperson Chandra Kumar Bose, BJP spokesperson, the authors and others participated.

The point of debate was: Was the DNA report fudged? The opening comments were made by Prof. Gyaneshwer Chaubey of Banaras Hindu University, a leading expert in the fields of DNA Sequencing, Genetics, Genetic Analysis, etc. Prof Chaubey stated that he had gone through the CFSL report supplied by the authors and was 'shocked' by it. 'I never expected to see this sort of report…most of things are really incorrect…I am really sorry, being a scientist I am reading this sort of report.' Prof Chaubey gave a thorough elaboration as he answered questions put by Narasimhan.

Rather than being intrigued by the revelation, the Bose family spokesperson flared up and began shooting the messenger that had brought the 'bad' news. 'I am not sure whether you have the complete report,' he roared. Chandrachur Ghose answered that the complete report was accessed using RTI from the Home Ministry.

'You are making a serious allegation against a government agency,' the spokesperson said in accusatory tone.

Answering in affirmative, we asked him whether he was part of the government or represented CFSL.

The family spokesperson lost his cool and accused the *CNN-IBN* editor of 'distorting' facts and 'misguiding' people. He said the authors should go to jail, and threatened to leave the show.

'Repeated attempts were made by the channel to obtain comments from CFSL, but they refused to come on record,' Narasimhan said.

Through all this, the BJP spokesperson kept silent. When pointedly asked whether his government would look into the DNA fudging charge, he parroted the findings of the Sahai Commission.

The incumbent CFSL director must have been watching it all unfold. After the controversy broke, he told Hindi daily *Dainik Jagran* that the electropherogram was not with them as it 'must have been sent to the Mukherjee Commission' back in 2004. The newspaper reporter then called us and we told him that we had the complete CFSL report sent to the Commission, containing all the annexures, and there was no electropherogram among them or even a reference to it. Not having an electropherogram with a DNA report is a serious matter. The FIR filed by the CBI as it arrested former deputy director of FSL, Delhi for fudging DNA tests in 2019 had accused him of not preserving the electropherogram.

Then a strange thing happened. The CFSL issued a new response to Sayak Sen—quite a rare occurrence. They now claimed that the electropherogram was available with them, but could not be given as it was third party information. 'CFSL has changed its stance obviously after the issue has been highlighted in the national media,' Sen was quoted as saying in the *Hindustan Times*.

hindustantimes

CFSL's flip-flop raises more questions about Gumnami Baba

Umesh Raghuvanshi
uraghuvanshi@hindustantimes.com

LUCKNOW: The Central Forensic Science Laboratory (CFSL)-Kolkata has changed its stance on having the electropherogram of the DNA analysis that CFSL conducted on the 'supposed' teeth of Gumnami Baba alias Bhagwanji, whom many believed was Netaji Subhas Chandra Bose.

After earlier informing an RTI activist that the electropherogram report of the case was not available, CFSL Kolkata has admitted the electropherogram report has been found.

In a letter dated February 24, 2020 and sent to RTI activist Sayak Sen, who had sought the information, BP Mishra, CPIO of CFSL-Kolkata said, "In continuation of your online RTI application vide Registration No DIRFS/R/E/20/00002 dated 05.01.20 and our earlier reply letter number CFSL(K)/19-20/20/II/RTI-55/SS/475 dated 04.02.2020, the required information is furnished below: 1. Some additional records related to the RTI appli-

Gumnami Baba. FILEPHOTO

has raised questions and brings into focus the DNA report, thereby further deepening the mystery over the identity of Gumnami Baba alias Bhagwanji who lived in Ram Bhawan in Civil Lines area of Faizabad (now Ayodhya) before his death on September 16, 1985.

"CFSL has changed its stance obviously after the issue has been highlighted in the national media," said Sayak Sen.

Earlier, the Justice Vishnu Sahai commission, which was set up to ascertain the identity of

state assembly in December last year.

The then CFSL director and DNA expert Dr VK Kashyap, on the basis of the examination conducted on three of the five teeth in 2004, had submitted a detailed report, concluding that the teeth belonged to an old man (Gumnami Baba) and did not match the DNA samples of the family of the mother and father of Netaji Subhas Chandra Bose and thus he (Gumnami Baba) cannot be Netaji. "The DNA evidence demolishes the claims of those who strongly say he (Gumnami Baba) was Netaji Subhas Chandra Bose," the commission observed.

Noted DNA expert Professor Gyaneshwar Chobey of Banaras Hindu University, who has studied CFSL's report, said he was disappointed to see the analysis. He said, "There are many problems with the analysis as the software used to analyse samples (bioedit) is not meant for electropherogram analysis. Only four of 20 markers could not be used to infer anything about parental lineage." He further observed

The clever officers at the Home Ministry and the CFSL must have figured out that to challenge CFSL's position we would need to go to Central Information Commission and then to the High Court, which would take years. So it was safe for them to give out this new response to stave off the debate and let it die. In the past, we had faced a similar situation when both Central Information Commission and the Delhi High Court ruled in our favour as Chandrachur Ghose sought from the Ministry of Defence a 1950s study about the Indian National Army. The defence ministry put up fresh legal hurdles to avoid providing Ghose the manuscript of the study.

Be that as it may, even as we were planning our next course of action, Covid-19 pandemic gripped the entire world. While we were confined to our homes, we requested Prof Gyaneshwer Chaubey to make a detailed study of the CDFD and CFSL reports. This was undertaken by Prof Chaubey and Asst Prof Pankaj Shrivastava, who is working with DNA Fingerprinting Unit, State Forensic Science Laboratory, Madhya Pradesh.

[Prof Gyaneshwer Chaubey and Prof Pankaj Shrivastava]

Upon studying the CDFD report, the professors found that only 'four markers (vWA, D5S818, D8S1179, D3S1358) out of nine were reported in the table'. It is likely, they stated, that because of low signal intensity the marker vWA might not have been reported. At the same time, they could not verify it independently as signal intensity was not shown for any of the electropherograms attached to the report. 'This is crucial as low signal peaks might represent artefact which one can't detect with the supplied data.'.

They astonishingly found that 'each of the loci derived from all the four markers of Gumnami Baba has a perfect match with the maternal and paternal relatives of Subhas Bose'. In other words, the data based on autosomal markers 'suggest a likely case that Gumnami Baba was probably Bose'. But since only four loci were available out of nine, as claimed by CDFD, one could not establish the biological relationship of Gumnami Baba with Bose. 'The report does not explain why the remaining teeth were not utilised,' they noted.

The 'conclusive' CFSL report was found to contain not one but 'several inconsistencies'. CFSL used different set of markers (uniparental) than CDFD to establish the biological identity—HVS-I and HVS-II markers to establish maternal identity as well as 20-YTR loci to match paternal identity of the suspect. The problem areas, according to the professors, were too many. 'The lab has reported that the suspected person was of "medium height" based on the teeth morphology. It is important to note that without any other phenotypic information, it is nearly impossible to estimate the stature of a person by studying the teeth morphology.'

'For sequence alignment, BIOEDIT software 15 was used which doesn't compare *vis-à-vis* to nucleotides with the electropherograms. Thus, it increases the chance of reporting a phantom mutation.'

'The HVS-I and HVS-II sequences from teeth samples and from the maternal relatives were reported to be different. The HVS-I haplotypes reported for teeth samples were 16223-16254. Nucleotide position 16254 is a stable mutation and has been independently hit by few times. At the phylotree 9 this mutation was reported four times, in four different haplogroup backgrounds (African specific L5b and L3a; East Asian specific M7b1c1 and West Asian specific haplogroup X2a2). It is unlikely that the Gumnami Baba will be of African or West Asian origin. The M7b1c1 is also ruled out because of absence of its defining mutation at nt. 16192. With this information, it is impossible to trace the maternal ancestry of the reported haplotype.'

The conclusion was that the CFSL report was not at all trustworthy on multiple grounds. The missing electropherogram was not the only problem area. 'With the analysis of available evidence, it is impossible to establish the biological identity of the Gumnami Baba,' the professors wrote. 'The trace files of electropherograms are not available to us for reanalysis. A fresh DNA test is required to establish the biological relationship of Gumnami Baba with Bose.'

FIVE

IDENTIFYING THE WRITTEN WORDS

IN THEIR ONE-PAGE letter to the Sahai Commission, members of the Bose family stated that 'although one handwriting expert was of the firm opinion that the sample of writings from Gumnami Baba…were of Netaji but three other equally eminent handwriting experts delivered a contrary opinion' to the Mukherjee Commission. Agreeing with the family stand, Justice Sahai wrote in his report that they were 'justified in concluding that the evidence of handwriting experts does not show that Gumnami Baba was Netaji Subhash Chandra Bose'.

As in the case of DNA tests discussed in the previous chapter, the truth about the handwriting tests lies in its details—and you won't find them in either the Sahai Commission report or any statement issued by the Bose kin.

The first proper analysis of Gumnami Baba's writing was

carried out in 2002 for *Hindustan Times* by B Lal Kapoor, a former Additional Director of the National Institute of Criminology and Forensic Sciences, Ministry of Home Affairs. Anuj Dhar had approached Lal on behalf of the newspaper, which was conducting an inquiry, after he gathered that Lal was India's topmost handwriting expert.

During his service years, which included a long stint as Government Examiner of Questioned Documents at GEQD, Shimla, B Lal had honed his skills in several forensic labs in the US, the UK, Germany and Switzerland. Post-retirement, he was taken on the panels of several government departments and banks, such as the State Bank of India and Citibank. He continued to receive cases from the police. He also delivered lectures to security officials and even judges on the aspects of handwriting testing. At the 87th Indian Science Congress in 2000, he was awarded the lifetime achievement award in forensic sciences.

[Times Now screengrab showing B Lal]

B Lal gave a positive report to *Hindustan Times*—which had no axe to grind over the Subhas Bose disappearance matter. Following the publication of a news story in *HT* based on Lal's positive report, the Mukherjee Commission approached B Lal. Later, working on different sets of

English and Bengali samples provided by the Commission, B Lal produced two definitive reports stating that Gumnami Baba and Bose were one and the same person.

Applying the fundamentals of the forensic testing of questioned documents as enumerated by Albert S Osborn (father of the science of questioned document examination) and Wildon R Harrison (another noted American expert), B Lal concluded that English writings of Gumnami Baba (questioned documents) were 'written by the same person' who wrote the admitted handwritings of Subhas Bose.

Regarding the Bangla handwritings, his assessment was that despite the time gap, the relevant questioned Bengali writings and relevant admitted Bengali writings showed characteristic similarities with natural variations and the collective occurrence of such similarities may not be found in the writings of two different persons as a matter of chance. 'The collective occurrence of significant similarities can only be explained by the fact that both the writings belong to one and the same person.'

B Lal highlighted that both Baba and Bose were in the 'habit of giving a peculiar sign when making insertion of certain words'. This peculiar caret was described by him as having a 'very high identifying value'. The following combo image illustrates the point. First is a specimen of Netaji's writing in 1936, and below it is a portion from a letter Baba wrote in the 1970s:

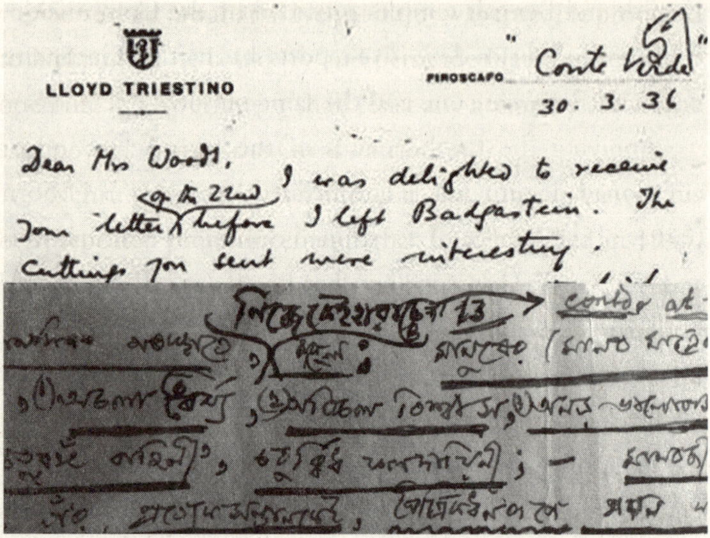
LLOYD TRIESTINO

PIROSCAFO "Conte Verde"

30. 3. 36

Dear Mrs Woods, I was delighted to receive your letter of the 22nd before I left Badgastein. The cuttings you sent were interesting.

Lal's conclusion did not match that of government experts. They concluded that Baba and Bose were two different persons. One report came from Dr SK Mandal, senior scientific officer at the Forensic Science Laboratory, Kolkata. While giving a report, a handwriting expert is supposed to state reasons for drawing the conclusions. But Mandal's report simply stated that the writings were of two different persons. His report ran into a mere two pages.

The second some what more detailed report came from Amar Singh, Government Examiner of Questioned Documents, and ML Sharma, Deputy Government Examiner of Questioned Documents. 'We have carefully and thoroughly examined the original documents of this case in all aspects of handwriting identification and detection of forgery, with the scientific aids in the Government of India Laboratory at Shimla,' they stated while explaining the reason for their opinion.

This central government report admitted that Gumnami Baba's writings 'do not show any sign of imitation or forgery in them'. This was the only common ground between them and B Lal. In his report to *Hindustan Times*, Lal had noted that Baba tried to conceal his identity by overwriting the strokes and writing in the capitals, but failed. It is not possible for a writer to change his writing habits completely, Lal explained. 'Even in an effort to hide his identity, the writer is not able to leave his individual characteristics and other peculiarities found in his handwriting. There is such a faithful reproduction of some peculiarities that even a gap of time to the extent of decades cannot hide them.'

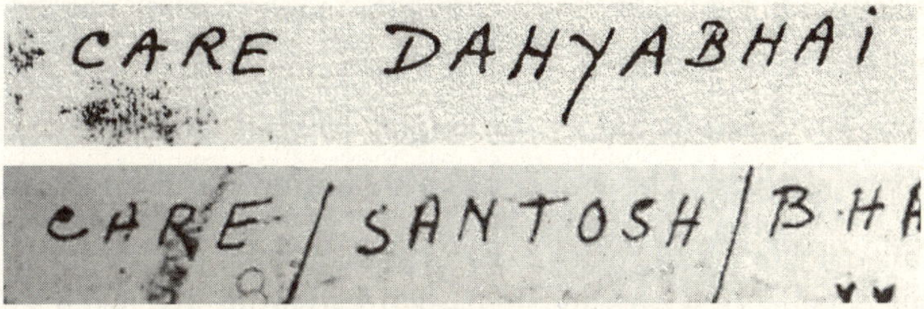

[Subhas Bose (above) and Gumnami Baba (below)]

B Lal's conclusion on this point was that he found no evidence that 'the questioned writing has been made by a writer other than Shri Subhas Chandra Bose by imitating/

copying the writing of Shri Subhas Chandra Bose'. The government report on the other hand stated that while 'both the handwritings in their pictorial appearance appear to bear a marked resemblance to each other at the first instance', an 'analysis of the structures of the letters, the study of the "master pattern" of the letters, in words as well as range of variations on close observation shows that the two writings are quite distinctive and different in their origin and are written by two different authors'.

The central government report showcased this point through a small 'juxtaposition chart' highlighting 24 instances of differences between the two handwritings.

Was that impressive? No! B Lal's report was supported by 460 large-size photographs accounting for each and every alphabetical letter appearing in the handwriting samples given to him. His report came in boxes before the commission. He also dwelt at length on the issue of 'natural variation' in handwriting. 'Every genuine writing has got natural variation since the human hand is not an exact reproducing machine and it is very important to consider this natural variation for a correct conclusion regarding authorship of a writing. If natural variations are taken as differences then there would be error in the identification.' His finding was that Gumnami Baba's handwriting showed 'natural variations which are additional symptoms of genuineness and there exists significant similarities'.

That the sarkari experts from Shimla were not confident of their report became clear when they chose to ignore the Commission's summons to appear before it in New Delhi. This was on the same day when B Lal was also to be examined. They lost their nerve, probably at the prospect of being questioned in the presence of their former boss—a legend in the field. Amar Singh, in fact, never turned up before the Commission. After skipping the Delhi hearing, ML Sharma went all the way to Kolkata to make the government's case. As the FSL Kolkata expert Mandal was being examined, Sharma, flouting the rules, sneaked into the venue and made a note of the questions Mandal was being asked by Justicc Mukherjee.

Both the experts made contradictory statements during their examination. Mandal was asked by Justice Mukherjee: 'Do you agree that to study the writing habits of the author of a document the shape of punctuation marks, their position and frequency, the choice of a peculiar punctuation sign, the mark of a caret, underscoring and bracketing need to be considered?' He answered, 'Yes.' Then he was asked: 'Did you consider all those factors before arriving at your conclusion and have those factors been reflected in your report?' Mandal responded: 'I considered all the above factors but none of those factors have been reflected in my report.'

ML Sharma too was asked by a deponent: 'Do you agree that a mature writer can have a habit of using a peculiar or unique sign or insertion in a line, which is rare?' He replied:

'Yes, it may have.' Later he was asked: 'Do you agree that such a sign has a very high identifying value in examining a writing?' Knowing the repercussions of answering in the affirmative, Sharma now said: 'I do not agree.' At the end of the examination, he could not conceal the truth. 'Do you agree that such a sign falls within the category of individual characteristics?' He said: 'Yes.' He was asked: 'Do you agree that individual characteristics of a handwriting are the most important factors to determine the authorship of a document?' Answer: 'Yes.'

Justice Mukherjee was very much annoyed with Dr Mandal in particular, but powerless to take any action as he was heading a commission of inquiry, not a court. In our view, it was a grave lapse on his part not to mention in his report that the sarkari experts gave shoddy reports—which is what he feels today.

Despite such an intriguing background and requests by those who appeared before him, Justice Sahai refused to get a fresh handwriting test done. He wrote in his report that, in his view, 'this exercise of DNA profiling and comparison of handwriting cannot be endlessly kept going on'.

Our own thought was that there was a dire need for a relook at DNA and handwriting specimens as the sarkari experts were not being truthful. DNA test was beyond us as the samples were in the custody of UP government. They would neither do anything themselves, nor allow anyone to do it. But we had Gumnami Baba's handwriting samples. After B Lal, we did not want to approach any ordinary expert. We began thinking of getting someone of international repute. This became possible when Indian Americans Deepak Nijhawan, a businessman in Kentucky and Abhishek Bose, a management consultant based out of Maryland, offered to locate a top independent expert in America. Like many other Indians and PIOs, they were eager to know the truth.

[Deepak Nijhawan and Abhishek Bose]

Deepak and Abhishek shortlisted a few experts and eventually hired the services of Curt Baggett, a leading, independent handwriting expert in the US with over forty years of experience. A skilled authority in document examination, Texas-based Baggett has completed over 5,000 cases.

He has examined documents and/or testified in court cases as a handwriting expert in all fifty states in the US, Washington, Canada, England, Ireland, the Netherlands, New Zealand and other countries. Baggett has been a consultant as a forensic document examiner for the Number 1 rated television show 'CSI: Crime Scene Investigation', and has appeared as a handwriting expert on *CNN, CNBC, Inside Edition, CBS, NBC, Fox* and shows 'Judge Alex' and 'Texas Justice'.

[Curt Baggett]

Baggett's education and training in document examination and psychology include the following: US Army, Military Police Officer's School, BA and MEd from McNeese State University, Lake Charles, Louisiana, and postgraduate studies at the University of Houston.

On our part, for the test, we selected two specimens of the letters Gumnami Baba's had written in English to Pabitra Mohan Roy after their meeting in late 1962.

These were made available to us by Roy's son Ranendra Mohan Roy, along with several other letters. Justice Sahai, on the other hand, made no attempt to reach out to Ranendra, whose father was the closest follower of the holy man whose identity Sahai was expected to find out. He made his deduction about Pabitra Roy's view about Gumnami Baba's identity on the basis of the claim made by journalist Sheetla Singh who met Pabitra once for a few minutes back in 1985.

Copies of Subhas Bose's handwriting came from different sources, including letters supplied to the Mukherjee Commission by the Netaji Research Bureau of Kolkata.

All these samples were then forwarded to Curt Baggett by Deepak Nijhawan. We did not figure in the picture as we did not want the expert to know what the test was all about.

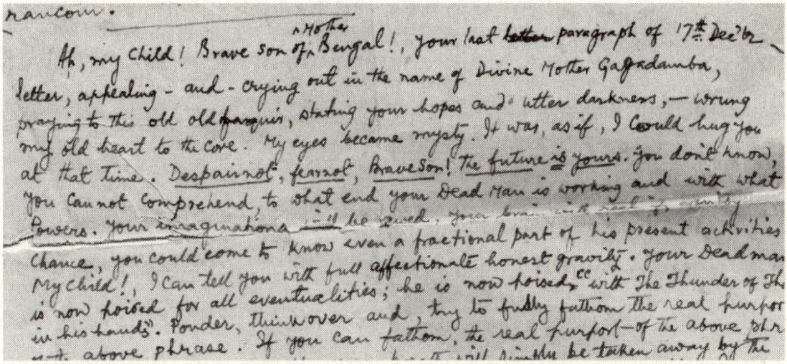
rancour.

Ah, my child! Brave son of Mother Bengal!, your last paragraph of 17th Dec'62 letter, appealing - and - crying out in the name of Divine Mother Jagadamba, praying to this old old fakir, stating your hopes and utter darkness, — wrung my old heart to the core. My eyes became misty. It was, as if, I could hug you at that time. Despair not, fear not, Brave Son! The future is yours. You don't know, You cannot comprehend, to what end your Dead Man is working and with what Powers. Your imagination [illegible] Chance, you could come to know even a fractional part of his present activities My child!, I can tell you with full affectionate honest gravity. Your Dead man is now poised for all eventualities; he is now poised with The Thunder of Th[illegible] in his hands". Ponder, think over and, try to fully fathom the real purpor[illegible] above phrase. If you can fathom, the real purport of the above phr[illegible] [illegible] be taken away by the [illegible]

[Gumnami Baba's letter to Pabitra Mohan Roy]

We ensured complete caution so that Baggett had no way of knowing that these samples were related to Subhas Chandra Bose. Nijhawan did not tell him either, nor did Baggett ask. 'This forensic document examiner was asked to conduct an examination of questioned handwriting of an Anonymous Author/Person to determine authenticity of the questioned handwriting by comparing the questioned handwriting to known,' he wrote in his report. That Baggett did not know whose handwriting he was examining placed him in a different league than experts in India who examined the Gumnami Baba samples knowing that the matter was about Subhas Bose. So, his professionalism notwithstanding, there was absolutely no chance of Baggett entertaining any preconceived notion or prejudice. As such, his opinion was going to be of greater value than anyone else's.

The brief for Baggett read: 'The questioned writings were written in 1963 by a man in his mid or late sixties. He was living in isolation, constrained by lack of access to basic comforts of life, practically living a life of an ascetic. He had very limited financial capability, would have been full of anxiety, troubled by physical illnesses such as severe arthritis in his knees and piles. He lived a secretive life, interacting with only a handful of people—very few of them literate and even fewer who could read or write proper English.... The admitted writings are formal and carefully written as the writer knew they would be preserved; whereas the questioned writings formed letters written confidentially to someone who was not supposed to share them with anyone. On the contrary, these documents were supposed to be destroyed after being read.'

Baggett provided us his expert opinion through a fifty-nine-page report. 'I am willing to testify to facts herein stated in a court of law and I will provide to the Court exhibits to show that my testimony is based on sufficient facts or data and that my opinion is correct,' he affirmed in a sworn statement before a Notary Public in the State of Texas.

Baggett employed a methodology said to be used by the FBI. In addition to this, Baggett had a second independent examination done by a qualified handwriting expert. His report reads:

The scientific methodology used in this examination consists of the "ACE" method, which means 'Analyze, Compare, and Evaluate'. The FBI, US Treasury Department, and the US

Postal Services reportedly use this reliable method in their questioned document laboratories.

Baggett confirmed that the samples (Gumnami Baba's writings) provided to him were genuine pieces of natural, free-flowing writing: 'No indications of forgery were noted on the questioned handwriting….' The process of handwriting identification was explained in Baggett's report in these words:

Handwriting is not only handwriting, but also 'brain' writing. Handwriting is formed by repeated habits of writing by the author, which are created by neuron-pathways established in the brain. These neuron-pathways control muscular and nerve movement for writing, whether the writing done is by the hand, foot, or mouth. An examination of handwriting includes establishing patterns of writing habits to help identify the author.

The handwriting on the Q [questioned] *documents were enlarged and examined scientifically in a side-by-side comparison to the known samples, under a microscope and on a light table. Measurements of letter height, lateral expansion, angles, slant and line quality were examined under a microscope. Significant similarities of the handwriting characteristics displayed in the questioned handwriting were revealed when compared to the known handwriting. The questioned handwriting, when compared to the known handwriting, displayed similar and regular line quality, flow, size, shape, slants, positions of letters, stops and starts, end and beginning strokes.*

Baggett added that his 'examination revealed significant similarities, not likely seen by an untrained or poorly skilled examiner'. In substantiation, the report listed similarities between the two sets of handwritings. These thirty-four instances were supported by enlarged exhibits.

Before drawing his conclusion, Baggett emphasised that 'the leading forefathers of document examination in the USA agree that one significant difference in the fundamental structure of a writing compared to another is enough to preclude common authorship'. Against this backdrop, Baggett wrote that questioned [Gumnami Baba's] handwritings did not 'display many distinguishable differences' when compared to the known handwritings [of Subhas Chandra Bose]. 'Normal variations exist in all handwriting,' he clarified, adding that no 'unexplainable significant differences' were noted by him in the questioned handwritings. Baggett's final conclusion was:

Based on a significant number of similarities of identifiable handwriting characteristics among the questioned handwriting, it is my professional expert opinion that the same person authored the handwritings of the Anonymous Author/Person on the Q documents.

Even though as Baggett's report was more than sufficient to settle the case, it could still be argued by the naysayers that there were two negative official government reports and

Based on a significant number of similarities of identifiable handwriting characteristics among the questioned handwriting, it is my professional expert opinion that the same person authored the handwritings of the Anonymous Author/Person on the Q documents.

I have applied the generally accepted Questioned Document Examiner principles and methods reliable to the facts in this case.

I am willing to testify to facts herein stated in a court of law and I will provide to the Court exhibits to show that my testimony is based on sufficient facts or data and that my opinion is correct. My Affidavit and Curriculum Vitae are attached and incorporated herein by reference.

Respectfully Submitted,

Curt Baggett

Curt Baggett

Forensic Document Examiner

State of Texas)

County of Dallas)

The above Letter of Opinion was sworn and subscribed before me this 21st day of February 2017.

Patricia J. Hale

Notary Public – State of Texas

PATRICIA J. HALE
Notary Public, State of Texas
Comm. Expires 02-05-2020
Notary ID 130525886

---

two positive independent reports by Baggett and B Lal—and as such the expert opinion was equally divided. Therefore we decided to consult yet another expert. We zeroed in on Delhi-based Ashok Kashyap, one of India's most reputed independent handwriting experts. Kashyap's family was synonymous with forensic handwriting tests since 1930s, when his father opened the first forgery detection firm in Delhi. All of Kashyap's older brothers were handwriting experts; he grew up among experts and honed his skills in various institutions, including Police Department Training Bureau in Miami, US.

In his five-decade-long career, Kashyap handled over 7,000 cases. He routinely made appearances in courts in and outside India. He was cited in several cases settled by the Supreme Court of India. He appeared in numerous departmental inquiries conducted by several banks, government undertakings and also given evidence before Central Vigilance Commission, TADA courts and special CBI courts.

Kashyap worked on the same Netaji and Gumnami Baba handwriting samples as did Baggett, but with the knowledge that the matter pertained to Subhas Chandra Bose. His conclusion was the same: Both were the same person.

Like Lal and Baggett, Kashyap furnished a detailed report, containing three large, laboriously created (much more elaborate than what Shimla experts did) juxtaposition charts demonstrating 50 similarities in the writings of Bose and Baba. Kashyap commented that the disputed handwritings (of Gumnami Baba) were 'written carelessly, freely & speedily in normal course of business by an above average writer without any signs of disguise & who is capable of writing gracefully and aesthetically'. He noted 'natural variation in the formation of the letters in these writings' because of 'the executions of these writings at different points in time'. He found that in both sets of handwritings reflected 'a combination of finger and wrist movements' and there were 'reasonable similarities in common letters and words' between them.

Kashyap's opinion was that 'the disputed bodywritings [of Gumnami Baba] are found to have been written by the author of standard/admitted writings...pertaining to Netaji Subhas Chandra Bose'.

In other words, the anonymous disputed writings...and the standard writings...all are the works of Netaji Subhas Chandra Bose.

Natural variations available in greater abundance in the disputed writings, Kashyap wrote, evidenced their genuineness, because 'handwriting is not a mechanical process in as much as it is not produced either by any computer or by any known means of printing process'. Handwriting is produced by the muscular coordination taking command from brain. Towards the end of his report, Kashyap, like B Lal, Curt Baggett and central government experts, forcefully ruled out forgery. Therefore, it is nobody's case that Gumnami Baba's writings were faked by anyone.

Baggett and Kashyap went on to appear on *CNN-IBN* prime time discussions, hosted by executive editor Anand Narasimhan, where they explained their conclusions to a worldwide audience with candour and ease. Justice Sahai also made a short appearance. When asked to comment about

Curt's report, he wriggled out by saying that the matter was not before him when he was inquiring into the matter. With all the mandate, authority and public resources available to him, he couldn't get the tests done despite being requested to do so by many.

Early morning from his Texas office on 13 June 2019, Baggett joined *CNN-IBN's* show being aired live in India, evening time. Narasimhan asked him if he was aware that one of the handwriting samples sent to him belonged to Subhas Bose. 'I did not know anything about the handwriting,' Baggett's crisp voice resonated via Skype.

To the question, 'Do you beyond doubt claim that the handwritings were the same?' he said, 'Yes.'

I have three opinions. 'Yes', 'No' or 'I don't know'. If I form an opinion that I feel like I can go to court and prove it, which is what I do most of the time...and so my opinion is same person wrote these [two different set of writings].

Baggett spent several minutes explaining why he formed that opinion. Narasimhan further asked him, 'Doesn't our handwriting change over a period of time? Some people would ask, this is somebody who's written a letter in 1962 and you are comparing it with his handwriting in 1936 or 1940s? So about 20-25 years later can the same person have similarities in their handwritings, even if they are trying to write differently, or if they start writing differently?.

Curt answered in the affirmative, saying that there was

little change in the handwriting of his own mother who died when she was more than 97 years old.

Another panelist on the show who was watching Curt speak offered his comment later. He was former UP Director General of Police Dr Vikram Singh, one of the most respected voices in the country today.

Curt is not an interested person. He does not have to lean on any side. He was unaware of what he was doing, and to come out with such great similarities, if there is incontrovertible clinching evidence, it is the handwriting expert's, and more so when he is prepared to testify in a court of law. What more evidence do you want?

Ashok Kashyap calmly walked into the plush *CNN-IBN* studio in Noida Film City on 16 August and took the viewers through his findings step by step on live TV. With the camera zooming in on his juxtaposition charts, Kashyap demonstrated how both samples were written by one and the same person.

Narasimhan asked him: 'Are you willing to stand in a court of law and say I believe these are the same people?'

Kashyap answered: 'Definitely, without any shadow of doubt. I can firmly say these writings are written by one and the same person.'

Narasimhan showed Kashyap the two-page report by Dr SK Mandal stating that the handwritings did not match without giving any explanation whatsoever.

'Will you write a report like this? About somebody who you know matters so much in our history,' he asked.

'No', Kashyap said, with a flicker of smile.

[CNN-IBN screengrab showing Ashok Kashyap]

Attempts by *CNN-IBN* to seek comments from Dr Mandal, who retired as director of FSL, Kolkata, met with no success. Despite his name taken publicly on a national channel in an unflattering way, Mandal was apparently scared to give his side of the story. Ashok Kashyap outlined his findings to senior journalist Sourav Sanyal's show on *India Ahead*, and on India's most watched show 'The Debate with Arnab Goswami' on *Republic TV*. There was no reaction from the government's side, and the BJP spokespersons on the show merely beat about the bush.

As the Covid-19 pandemic brought our work to a halt, we requested Kashyap to go through both Mandal's and

[Republic screengrab showing Ashok Kashyap]

central government experts' reports and give his opinion on them. To our utter shock and dismay, Ashok Kashyap passed away all of a sudden following a heart attack in December 2020. By this time, Kashyap had enumerated to us several reasons government reports were not credible. In some other case, government experts would be in deep trouble for taking part in a veritable conspiracy to mislead the people of India.

So, all this boils down to the following logical sequence: Inquiry by Justice Mukherjee, who was unbiased and sincere in his approach, concluded that there was credible eyewitness evidence backed by documentary evidence to show that Gumnami Baba was Netaji. But he could not conclude it as such in his report in view of negative DNA/handwriting reports. From that time, all the opponents of the Gumnami Baba-Netaji theory tom-tommed the negative findings of sarkari forensic experts as the gold standard of proof, the final and immutable word on the case. Justice Sahai was implored to probe the claims that the forensic tests carried out in sarkari labs were fudged, but he did not. He chose to rely on the same negative DNA/handwriting reports, citing the Mukherjee Commission report, even though a fresh inquiry by its nature is a *de novo* exercise. An inquirer is supposed to look a matter afresh, not resort to cut and paste. On the other hand, two individual of very modest means (the authors) had fresh handwriting tests done in India and America, and had the DNA test reports reviewed by independent experts. The results amply establish that a forensic fraud occurred.

Therefore the argument that Gumanmi Baba couldn't have been Netaji because DNA and handwriting tests performed by government experts were negative has been turned on its head. Even though the DNA experts consulted by us favour a fresh DNA test, it is our considered view that the act of fudging by itself proves that the conclusion of the test was positive. Otherwise, there was no point in fudging them, much less planting advance information of the fakery in *Anandabazar Patrika* to influence public opinion. 'Operation Abhigyan' was a planned subterfuge which now stands exposed.

What other conclusion would any right-thinking unbiased person draw then from all this? We hereby stick our small necks out and assert on the basis of facts sincerely

OPERATION - ABHIGYAN

DNA PROFILING TEST ON TEETH :
GENETIC IDENTITY OF ALLEGED SOURCE -
GUMNAMI BABA

NATIONAL DNA ANALYSIS CENTRE
CENTRAL FORENSIC SCIENCE LABORATORY
MINISTRY OF HOME AFFAIRS, GOVT. OF INDIA
DIRECTORATE OF FORENSIC SCIENCE
30 GORACHAND ROAD, KOLKATA

collated and presented by us that the so-called Gumnami Baba was Netaji Subhas Chandra Bose. On the basis of what we have seen and observed over the years, it is our mortification to state that our own government is resorting to skullduggery to keep the people of India in the dark.

SIX

THE BEGINNING

HAVING ARRIVED AT the bewildering conclusion that the so-called Gumnami Baba was Subhas Chandra Bose, we obviously need to know when and how he returned to India, what was he doing for all these years, who all knew about him and why he chose to live that way, never coming out to assert his real identity. For the rest of the book, we shall go into these aspects.

Leaving aside rare occasions when he called himself Subhas Bose, Gumnami Baba used several pseudonyms for himself, such as 'Dead Man'. People who were granted audience by him (it was never easy) usually addressed him by the honorific 'Bhagwanji'. 'Gumnami Baba' was a post-1985 media coinage that has become the official name of sorts for him. It's just as well then to call him Bhagwanji or Gumnami Baba while discussing his life after 1945. For all previous references, it is Netaji and Subhas Bose always.

Bhagwanji's presence in India can be traced back to the early 1950s. Surendra Singh Chaudhary, an aristocrat from Etawah, met him for the first time in 1953 in the small town of Mainpuri where he was living at the house of a Deputy Superintendent of Police as a monk. Chaudhary was accompanied by Pandit Jyoti Shankar Dikshit, who was the secretary of the provincial Congress committee of UP in the mid-1920s and later an activist of the Hindu Mahasabha. Chaudhary had never seen Subhas Bose, but Dikshit had. He had no doubts about who he had met at Mainpuri. Chaudhary found striking similarity between Swami Vivekananda and the clean-shaven Bhagwanji in ochre robes and turban.

While no mention of Dikshit is found again in the narrative, Chaudhary remained in close contact for the next six to seven years. If Chaudhary's extant account is to be believed, the starting point of the Bhagwanji story was 1950/1951. No information, however, is available from this source on how and exactly when Bhagwanji reached India.

By 1955, Bhagwanji was in Lucknow where Chaudhary had rented the house of a Sikh gentleman for him at Singar Nagar. The house still stands, though the area around it has undergone massive development in recent decades. The current owner is still intrigued by the stories of the strange tenant his grandfather had.

[Authors and filmmaker Srijit Mukherjee at the Sringar Nagar home with Inder Mohan Singh, whose grandfather had rented it to Gumnami Baba]

As Rajkumar Shukla, the son of Bhagwanji's caretaker Saraswati Devi, recollected before the Mukherjee Commission and to us, around 1956 he moved into this very house with his widowed mother. Her father Mahadev Prasad Mishra was already on the service of Bhagwanji. A Sanskrit teacher, Mahadev is said to have helped Bhagwanji enter India from Nepal in an unspecified year. Bhagwanji himself narrated to someone who became his confidante subsequently that he re-entered India from Nepalgunge in Nepal. Before that he was located in Mansarovar area Tibet.

Subhas Bose was familiar with Lucknow. He was given a public reception here when he was the Congress president and again later when he toured the country to consolidate

[Mahadev Prasad Mishra with daughter Saraswati Devi]

his Forward Bloc. Among those who had organised his reception, one became the state chief minister in 1954 and a few others would go on to occupy the same position in the coming years.

A year or so before Bhagwanji set foot in the city, Chief Minister Govind Ballabh Pant, Subhas Bose's bête noire, had been moved to New Delhi as the Union Home Minister. Pant was replaced by the scholarly Dr Sampurnanand. It is not known how and when he and Bhagwanji got in touch. By all available accounts, Sampurnanand was the person who consistently made necessary arrangements for Bhagwanji, whose real identity he knew.

Dr Sampurnanand and Subhas Bose had entered the freedom movement around the same time and both joined the camp of Chittaranjan Das, Subhas's political guru. The Sampurnanand papers kept at the National Archives in New Delhi testify to the Congress stalwart's long and close association with Subhas Bose and a deep interest in the paranormal, a pet subject for Bhagwanji.

In his book *Memories and Reflections*, which he finished writing in 1961 when he was no longer the UP chief minister, Dr Sampurnanand devoted an unusually laudatory chapter to Netaji. He described him 'one of the greatest fighters for freedom this country has known', much abler than Nehru. Sampurnanand stated that he had voted for Bose in his contest for Congress presidency in 1939 against Gandhi's nominee and hosted him in Lucknow when Bose came to mobilise support for his Forward Bloc. He made sarcastic comments about the Congress leadership's attitude towards him and his INA. Curiously enough, when the official line of his party and the central government was that Subhas Bose was dead, Sampurnanand had his doubts. 'There are some who believe that he is still alive and will someday come to India to lead the country to greater glory and prosperity.'

Most likely, it was through Sampurnanand that another person who became aware of Bhagwanji's presence in

Lucknow was renowned Sanskrit scholar, philosopher and tantra expert Gopinath Kaviraj.

[Gopinath Kaviraj stamp, 1988]

One day—so reads the diary of a follower—Sampurnanand asked Bhagwanji: 'Do you know Tripathi?' Bhagwanji replied that he had heard his name. Sampurnanand then said: 'Tripathi's guru Gopinath Kaviraj has told him about you.' The reference was to the then home minister of the state and would-be Central minister Kamalapati Tripathi, another believer in tantric rituals, who is said to have been a great influence in Indira Gandhi's quest for spirituality.

One can only conjecture as to what made Sampurnanand broach the question of Subhas Bose's fate with Clement Attlee when the former British Prime Minister halted at Lucknow in October 1956 on his way to Calcutta. We know this because in 1982 a sensational claim was made by retired IB official Dharmendra Gaur that Attlee, who was PM from 1945 to 1951, told an inquisitive UP Chief Minister that Bose had escaped to the USSR under the cover of fake news of an air crash. Gaur further claimed the conversation was bugged and the tape sent to the IB head office in New Delhi. We cannot prove Gaur's account, but there's no doubt that Attlee displayed extraordinary candour during his 1956 India visit.

One of the letters discovered from Bhagwanji's belongings (inventorised as per the High Court's order) gives a clue about the extent of his contact with the political establishment in Lucknow. In a short letter dated 15 July 1957, Babu Banarasi Das tried to convince him of the necessity of a security perimeter, assuring that such cover would be provided. At that time, Das was a parliamentary secretary in the UP government, and clearly not in a position to make such an arrangement on his own. He must have had the approval of one of his seniors who took him into confidence. Was it CM Sampurnanand himself or state home minister Kamalapati Tripathi? Or was it Sampurnanand's opponent in the Congress party Chandra Bhan Gupta, whose parliamentary secretary at that time was Banarasi Das? It is not for any ordinary person that the high and mighty of a government offers to set up a security perimeter in such secrecy.

Both Das and Tripathi went on to become chief ministers of UP. Chandra Bhan Gupta (better known as CB Gupta) was one of the organisers of Subhas Bose's reception in Lucknow on 20 November 1938. Gupta went on to serve thrice as UP Chief Minister between 1960 and 1970. Reporting on the birth centenary celebrations planned for Gupta in Lucknow in 2001, *The Times of India* saw it fit to describe him as 'an ardent follower' of Netaji.

Besides these four chief ministers, another piece of

evidence indicating Bhagwanji's connection with a fifth one was found among the material recovered from Ram Bhawan. This innocuous-looking piece of paper wasn't a letter and at first glance one could mistake it for details of a five-year deposit scheme calculations which were scribbled on one side. On the other side, however, was a rough sketch drawn by hand of the then Chief Minister's house at the city's posh residential area of Mall Road. The name of the politician wasn't written on the note, but the only chief minister to have been living in that area was Chaudhury Charan Singh, who headed the government twice—first from April 1967 to February 1968 and from February to October 1970—before going on to become the Deputy Prime Minister and then, for a few months, the country's fifth Prime Minister in 1979.

Many Bhagwanji followers have publicly claimed since 1985 that Charan Singh did visit him a number of times. Thus, five chief ministers could have been in contact with Bhagwanji. The remarkable thing about these connections was that Bhagwanji in no way seemed to have benefitted from the politicians—very unusual in a country where relationships between holy men or women and politicians have rarely been devoid of mega deals.

The story of political connections is not over yet. Another name that features a few times in the Bhagwanji narrative is that of Raj Narain—freedom fighter, socialist and also the Leader of the Opposition in the UP Assembly. Narain later shot to national fame by winning the case of electoral malpractice against Prime Minister Indira Gandhi and later in 1977, by defeating her in the general elections. As the local newspapers started discussing the identity of Bhagwanji in October 1985, journalist Ashok Tandon, who had broken the story, had a surprise visitor one evening. Raj Narain questioned him for two hours on the details of his findings.

In what seems inexplicable, the Foreign Broadcast Information Service (PBIS), an arm of the CIA, found it important enough to pick up a news item published in the *Patriot* newspaper of Delhi to include in its foreign news compilation of March 1986. The published news had reported on 13 February 1986 that Raj Narain 'firmly believes that one Gumnami Baba who died at Faizabad [now renamed Ayodhya] was none other than Netaji Subhas Chandra Bose'. The news of his death caused so much shock to him that 'he had to be hospitalised'.

Nothing more happened on this front. Raj Narain was dead by the end of the year.

When in Lucknow, Bhagwanji faced the risk of his identity being exposed. Needing a new pair of glasses, he walked into BN Baijal Opticals—a famous optician's shop in Lucknow's Ameena Bagh that in the past had for a client Mahatma Gandhi himself. While trying out a round-rimmed one, Bhagwanji, clean-shaven like a Buddhist monk, removed his headgear and looked in the mirror. In an instant, his shaved bald pate and familiar-looking visage stunned another customer. 'Netaji!' he whispered. Suddenly, two young men threw themselves at his feet. Bhagwanji had to make a hasty retreat. 'This is why I now keep this moustache and beard,' he explained to a follower a few years later.

After spending about two years in Lucknow, Bhagwanji left for Naimisharanya (Neemsar, located in Sitapur district) during the Navaratri of 1958. He moved to an old Shiv temple very close to the famous *chakra teertha*. Before long, locals started talking about the holy man purportedly with great powers who remained confined to his room. When the area sub-inspector failed to go beyond a fierce Saraswati Devi who wouldn't let him go anywhere close to Bhagwanji, he returned the next day with the station officer and a team of constables. What followed was a repeat of a situation that had occurred before and would happen again. Bhagwanji called the station officer inside and spoke with him for half an hour. By the time the officer emerged from the room, he had become Bhagwanji's disciple.

A kin of the temple priest was attracted by the recital of Sanskrit hymns with flawless pronunciation in deep baritone coming from Bhagwanji's room. Srikant Sharma approached Saraswati Devi for permission to meet Bhagwanji. He was permitted to speak to him from the other side of the curtain that hung on the door.

During Subhas Bose's tour of the United Provinces in

1939, Sharma had seen and heard him at Sitapur, Sidhauli and Biswan. When he did get to talk to Bhagwanji, his curiosity was further aroused. Srikant was going to get luckier in future.

In a surreal unfolding of events, in the summer of 1962, Professor Atul Sen—a freedom fighter who had been acquainted with the top leaders of his times—fainted while touring some remote area in Naimisharanya. He was brought to the temple complex, where he got to converse with Bhagwanji. On his return to Calcutta, Sen told his friend Dr RC Majumdar, the celebrated historian, that he had spoken with Subhas Bose. Majumdar was foxed. 'Highly educated and respected gentleman really believed that the person with whom he had conversed was Netaji,' he wrote in Bengali magazine *Jayasree* in 1966.

Ignoring Bhagwanji's warning, Prof Sen wrote a letter to Prime Minister Nehru on 28 August 1962. We obtained a copy of it using the Right to Information. Prof Sen informed the PM that 'Netaji is alive and is engaged in spiritual practice somewhere in India'. What he wrote next was spine-chlling:

From the talks I had with him for months together not very long ago, I could understand that he is yet regarded as Enemy No 1 of the Allied Powers and that there is a secret protocol that binds the Government of India to deliver him to allied 'justice' if found alive.

Prof. Atul Sen
(Ex. M. L. A.)

PHONE. Resi :-46-1815 Office :-23-5882

18/22/4A, DOVER LANE,
CALCUTTA-29

(269)

Dated August 28, 1962.
Bhadra 6, 1884 Saka.

Sri Jawharlal Nehru,
Prime Minister of India,
NEW DELHI.

Dear Jawharlalji,

I take the liberty of addressing these few lines to you in the matter of the widely prevalent belief that Netaji Subhas Chandra Bose is not dead. Mine is not mere belief but actual knowledge that Netaji is alive and is engaged in spiritual practice somewhere in India. Not the Sadhu of Shoulmari, Cooch-Behar, in West Bengal about whom some Calcutta - politicians are making a fuss at this moment. I deliberately make the location a little vague because from the talks I had with him for months together not very long ago I could understand that he is yet regarded as Enemy No.1 of the Allied Powers and that there is a

Sen asked Jawaharlal Nehru if this was true. He proposed to Nehru that he could try and persuade Netaji to return to open life if 'Government shall resist any action by any of the said powers against the Great Patriot'.

Nehru's response was somewhat odd. One, in view of his own repeated pronouncements that Bose had died in 1945, he shouldn't have taken kindly to Sen's claim that Bose was alive. Two, the bit about a secret protocol was so patently absurd that it warranted a contemptuous dismissal. Since Nehru had a marvellous intellectual capacity to personally dictate cogent responses to the numerous letters he received, it can be assumed that he applied his mind while responding to Sen's seemingly nonsensical posers on so important an issue. But Nehru's 31 August reply to Sen didn't even touch upon the main issue of Bose being alive, as if he wanted to avoid any discussion on it. The PM, however, was emphatic in his denial of the alleged secret protocol. 'Even if any country asks the Government of India to hand him [Bose] over, it is not going to be agreed to.'

Sen would never meet Bhagwanji again, but the word about his meeting 'Netaji' went around a small group of people in Calcutta. They were former members of old revolutionary group Anushilan Samity, which at one point of time included in its fold even Bhagat Singh and Dr Keshav Baliram Hegdewar, who would set up the Rashtriya Swayamsevak Sangh (RSS) later. The veterans called a secret meeting and asked Dr Pabitra Mohan Roy to verify Atul Sen's claim.

Behind Roy's ordinary looking face and his unassuming persona was his daredevil past. A medical doctor by training, he had followed Subhas Bose to SE Asia for the cause of India's freedom. Riding on a Japanese submarine, Roy returned to India in 1944 as an INA secret service operative. But his mission was doomed by betrayal. A fast-track trial under the Enemy Agents Ordinance against Pabitra, fellow spy Americk Singh Gill and Haridas Mitra, who had dared to shelter them, commenced in May and by June-end their execution orders were out. The sentence was eventually commuted and Roy was released in 1946.

Pabitra managed to meet Bhagwanji in December 1962. At that time he was serving the last year of his term as a member of West Bengal Legislative Assembly. After having tested Pabitra's patience for long, Bhagwanji opened his heart and 'secrets' to him. As that familiar stentorian voice from behind the curtain addressed Roy as *my intelligence officer*, unforgotten memories of someone who had 'died' seventeen years earlier flickered in Roy's mind's eye.

The condition in which Pabitra found his leader broke his heart. 'You cannot even understand under what awful abnormal mental stress, bodily pain and circumstantial handicaps I am living here,' Bhagwanji told him. After he returned to Calcutta, Bhagwanji wrote to him: 'I am going

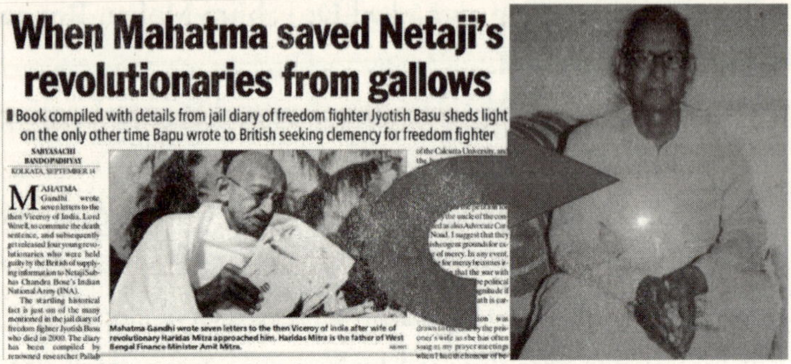

When Mahatma saved Netaji's revolutionaries from gallows

Book compiled with details from jail diary of freedom fighter Jyotish Basu sheds light on the only other time Bapu wrote to British seeking clemency for freedom fighter

SABYASACHI BANDOPADHYAY
KOLKATA, SEPTEMBER 14

MAHATMA Gandhi wrote seven letters to the then Viceroy of India, Lord Wavell, to commute the death sentence, and subsequently get released four young revolutionaries who were held guilty by the British of supplying information to Netaji Subhas Chandra Bose's Indian National Army (INA).

The startling historical fact is just one of the many mentioned in the jail diary of freedom fighter Jyotish Basu who died in 2000. The diary has been compiled by renowned researcher Pallab

Mahatma Gandhi wrote seven letters to the then Viceroy of india after wife of revolutionary Haridas Mitra approached him. Haridas Mitra is the father of West Bengal Finance Minister Amit Mitra.

[Combo image showing a September 2014 story from Indian Experess, and last picture of Roy from 1993. Gandhiji sought clemency for Haridas Mitra, Roy and others after being approached by Mitra's wife, who was Bose's niece. The British decision to free them was, however, taken for other reasons]

through all these terrible troubles and hazards of my life only for the final consummation of the mission.'

And then came his most vital order. No one was to know that he was at 'N' (Neemsar).

From this moment you must not mention me and 'N' to any one, whatsoever and whoever. When you shall meet in the future, you must not even by the slightest indication give out that you contacted me at 'N'. You shall sacrifice your head but keep your lips sealed.

Over a period of time, Pabitra was given a lowdown on Bhagwanji's pre- and post-1945 activities.

When your Dead Man was in Berlin, a great German doctor-scientist became very very friendly—affectionate and attached . . . And in the course of his talks, he said that in his lab he found that Radar beam particles do not bounce back if they strike '...', and the doctor felt astonished. That doctor could not inform any of the government agencies or other scientists. He was a bombing raid casualty…In one secret place, your Dead Man tested about the truth of that German scientist's findings, and, he found it to be 100% fact. Particles of beams, directed at a point blank range, on 'something' did not bounce back… Even now, the scientists of the Great Powers are feverishly trying to find out some means to avoid Radar detection.

Occasionally, Bhagwanji would lose himself in nostalgia, reminiscing about his childhood, parents, siblings, Beni Madhab Das, Hemanta Sarkar (Netaji's teacher and childhood friend respectively) and others. Bitter memories of the past came back very often. 'Dead Man' said he had 'no rancour for Bapu':

Your Dead Man has no rancour because Bapu at last turned a volte face and preached fighting for freedom and honour (which was your right creed); and because hearing and becoming stimulated and emboldened (he was a mere figure-head and marionette in the hands of__) by the radio exhortations of your Dead Man, he stoutly opposed partition, and during the last fateful meeting he wept like a child before them and sobbed out praying against partition (this faquir has documentary evidence) but he was overridden roughshod.

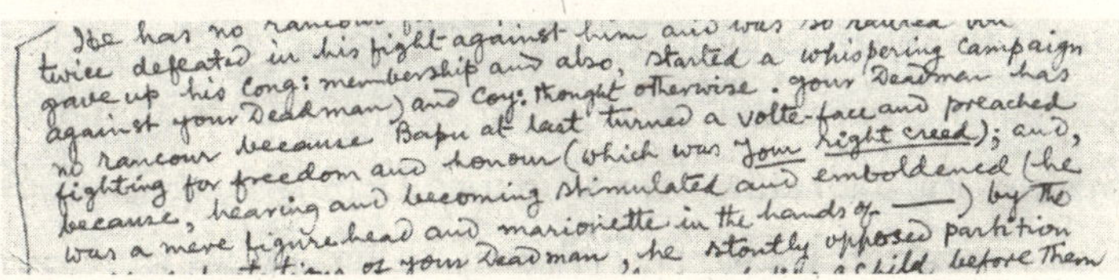
twice defeated in his fight against him and was so ...
gave up his Cong: membership and also, started a whispering campaign
against your Deadman) and Cong: thought otherwise. your Deadman has
no rancour because Bapu at last turned a volte-face and preached
fighting for freedom and honour (which was your right creed); and,
because, hearing and becoming stimulated and emboldened (he
was a mere figurehead and marionette in the hands of ___) by the
... of your Deadman, he stoutly opposed partition
... a child before them

Back to his Dum Dum residence in Kolkata from his surreptitious trip to Neemsar, Pabitra Mohan Roy was a troubled man. Bhagwanji had listed out a number of articles—strange ones at that—which he needed. Pabitra was at a loss as to how, with his modest means, he was going to arrange for them. The list included items like a 'chronometer wristwatch which must give absolutely correct time, without fluctuating a second'; a pair of binoculars which must be the 'most powerful, highest powered, longest range, utmost clarity, to be used by hands only'; a transistor, 'extremely powerful in shortwave and midwave'; cigars and a Fowler's Dictionary. The last item was to be 'packed like a presentation set'. Bhagwanji needed to gift it to a 'very learned scholar, a Siberian Deputy of the Supreme Soviet', who was of 'very great help' to him.

For a while Pabitra couldn't think of anyone trustworthy he could go to for help. Then it struck him that *Didi*, the then chairperson of the Praja Socialist Party of which he was a member, could be approached. A sisterly figure for revolutionaries, Leela Roy (nee Nag) was treated by Subhas Bose as something of an equal. Her portrait in Parliament House—unveiled in 2008 in the presence of Prime Minister Dr Manmohan Singh—evidences Roy's exalted position among the pantheon of freedom fighters. Daughter of a wealthy Rai Bahadur, who retired as Deputy Magistrate of Dhaka district, Leela excelled early in life in academics as well as sports and became the first woman to earn a Master's degree (in English) from Dhaka University. In future, Roy would become the first women detainee under Bengal Ordinance Act from the city. At the university, she met her future husband Anil Roy—who was in the process of building the underground revolutionary organisation that later came to be known as Sri Sangha—and followed him into the revolutionary fraternity. Preetilata Waddedar, a martyr of Chittagong armoury raid had been recruited by Leela Roy.

A feminist, Roy presented a paper on history of women's movement in Bengal at the Calcutta Congress session of 1928. She founded several schools for girls and started a magazine called *Jayasree*, with the blessings of Rabindra Nath Tagore. She was jailed several times between 1931-38 and 1942-46. Elected to the Constituent Assembly in 1946, Roy resigned opposing Partition of India. Thereafter, she devoted herself to rehabilitating refugees and bringing succour to victims of communal violence, for which Gandhi had praised her.

Just over three years younger than Bose, Leela Roy had known him from the 1920s. The political association between them became stronger with Roy being appointed to head the women's sub-committee of the National Planning Committee formed by Netaji as president of the Indian National Congress in 1938. Leela and Anil Roy took the responsibility of organising the Forward Bloc when Bose formed the party after resigning as Congress president in 1939. Netaji wanted her in the South East Asian theatre, but his attempts to reach out to her as the Indian National Army set foot on Indian soil also did not bear fruit. His message reached her too late. By the time she was released from jail in 1946, Subhas Chandra Bose had disappeared mysteriously.

[Leela Roy in 1946. Picture courtesy: Bijoy Nag]

On 7 January 1963, Pabitra let Leela Roy into the secret—that he had met 'Netaji' at Neemsar. Stunned, Leela Roy recorded in her personal diary that evening:

আজ দুপুরে এক অত্যাশ্চর্য সত্য উদ্ঘাটিত হোলো।অভাবনীয় তার সম্ভাবনা, অচিন্ত্যনীয় তার আনুষাঙ্গিক সবকিছুই।আমার অনুভুতিকে বিশ্লেষণ করতে বা ভাষা দিতে চেষ্টা করবো না।কেবল বলবো হে অঘটন পটিয়সী দেবতা আবার দেখলাম অকস্মাৎ কোথায় কি ঘটে—চির অসম্ভব আসে চির সম্ভবের বেশে. যাদের বল্লাম তাদের নানা বিচিত্র প্রতিক্রিয়া।

(*A bewildering truth was revealed today afternoon. Unfathomable are its possibilities; everything associated with it is unthinkable. I won't try to analyse my feelings or put words to them, but would only say: 'O God of making the impossible possible, I saw again what can happen all of a sudden, the eternally impossible appeared in the form of the possible.' Received strange and varied reactions from all those I informed.*)

Roy reached Neemsar on 23 March 1963, accompanied

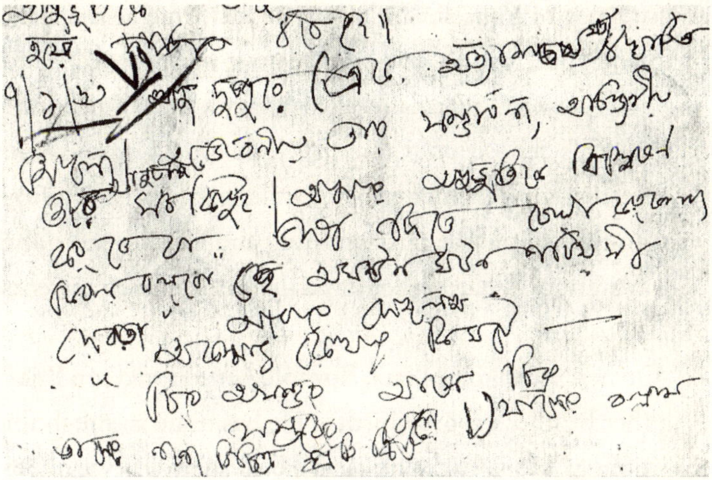

[Diary entry of Leela Roy on receiving the news of Bhagwanji from Pabitra Mohan Roy. Courtesy Bijoy Nag, Jayasree Prakashan]

by some of her followers. Anil Das had been with the INA. Samar Guha had joined the freedom movement in the mid-1930s while still in his late teens. He was to become an MP in the 1960s, and the most formidable voice for matters relating to Netaji.

The arrival of Roy turned out to be fortuitous for Srikant Sharma. He became a go-between the visitors and Bhagwanji, who now asked him to enter his room. Inside, Sharma saw an 'older Netaji', with characteristic gaps in his teeth intact. Sharma lived long enough to testify before the Mukherjee Commission.

Bhagwanji asked Sharma to convey to Roy that his coming out in public was neither in the interest of the country nor of himself. 'India was at that time at the stage of infancy and would not be able to go against UN and other big powers,' Sharma recalled Bhagwanji's words in the course of his deposition before the Mukherjee Commission.

Finally, as the much-awaited call to meet came, Roy went to the temple the next morning and from there to the railway station. Whatever followed thereafter caused torrents of tears to flow.

On her return to Kolkata, Roy told her adopted son Bijoy Nag (her brother's son by birth), 'He has done so much for the country. He is suffering even now,' she told Nag. 'Her sole aim after she returned was to ensure that Bhagwanji had the basic comforts of life,' Nag later told us.

The first thing Leela Roy did then was to dispatch alternative medicine practitioner Kamala Kanta Ghosh to Neemsar to take care of Bhagwanji's immediate medical needs. Ghosh had joined the revolutionary movement inspired by Anil Roy and was arrested in 1930 on charges of plotting the murders of the Governor of Bengal and the Viceroy. The immediate ailments of Bhagwanji that Ghosh had to treat were varicose veins and piles. Remaining holed up in a room most of times had its health hazards.

Thereafter, Roy started informing a few select people about the return of 'Netaji' to India. Topping the list was Subhas's eldest surviving brother Suresh Chandra Bose, whom Subhas used to call *Sejda*. Then came his friend

Dilip Kumar Roy. (Subhas's childhood friend Hemanta Kumar Sarkar had expired.) Also on the list were political compatriots Trailokya Nath Chakravarty, Hem Chandra Ghosh, Satya Ranjan Bakshi, Maulvi Ashrafuddin Ahmed Chaudhury, Hari Vishnu Kamath and Swami Asimananda Saraswati Maharaj. Historian RC Majumdar also figured on the list. Not everyone was going to believe Roy. She was rebuffed when she tried to reach out to the Bose family members other than Suresh Bose.

The message for Dilip Kumar Roy was conveyed through a hand-delivered letter. Born a day before Subhas, Dilip was one of his closest friends from his Presidency College days—a friendship that continued till the time Subhas was in India. He later become a famed musician (Bharat Ratna MS Subbulakshmi being his disciple) and eventually a holy man.

[The picture on left was taken at Cambridge University in the early 1920s. Dilip is sitting on the left and Subhas is standing on the right. The other picture shows Dilip around mid-1970s in Haridwar. Courtesy: Hari Krishna Mandir Trust, Pune]

Her heart in turmoil and her body wrecked by a recent stroke, Leela Roy wrote with a shaking hand…

I wanted to tell you about your friend. I am not entitled to speak much, but I can only inform you that ***'He's alive—in India.'*** *He has mentioned about your friendship with him many times. For example,* ***'It was Dilip who always wanted to make me a mystic.'*** *For this reason, this letter is important... If you trust me, then it is 100 per cent fact. No one else should know about it—this is a* ***stern injunction*** *on me.* [Translated from Bengali, except for the emphasised parts]

Reaching Trailokya Nath Chakravarty was not easy for he was in East Pakistan, later to beome Bangladesh. The revered 'Maharaj' of revolutionaries had troubled the British during the freedom struggle so much that they had kept him locked up for thirty unimaginable years in all—more than ten of which were in the notorious prison hell in Port Blair. Recent media reports and books, including one written by Congress stalwart Mani Shankar Aiyar, have cited Trailokya's grit in an attempt to try and minimise Veer Savarkar's sufferings in the Cellular Jail—where both were lodged at the same time once.

Leela Roy asked former revolutionary Sailendra Roy to sneak into East Pakistan and deliver her top secret message to Trailokya. It was a high-risk mission. Passport and visa were arranged hurriedly for Sailendra—who took the help of his old contacts in Dhaka to reach Maharaj. Chakravarty had been put under continuous police surveillance by the then East Pakistan government, and any stranger visiting him was a suspect, especially an Indian. Sailendra faced the possibility of being incarcerated or even hanged as an enemy agent, if he was caught. He reached his destination under the guise of a servant to the family who escorted him. It was a brief but dramatic meeting. On hearing who had sent him and the purpose of his visit, Maharaj asked Sailendra not to speak but to write down whatever he had to say, lest anyone overhear their conversation and report it to the police. As Sailendra wrote each page, Maharaj read and burnt it.

The formidable revolutionary was completely shaken up after he was briefed. The following letter of his was located among Bhagwanji's belongings:

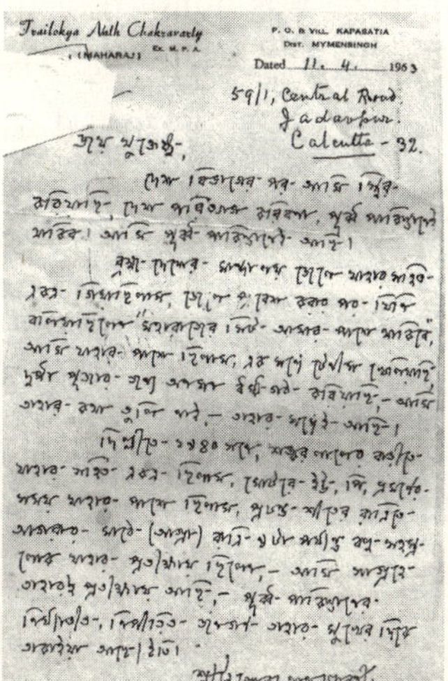

Trailokya Nath Chakravarty
(MAHARAJ) Ex. M.P.A.

P. O. & Vill. KAPASATIA
Dist. MYMENSINGH

Dated 11. 4. 1963

59/1, Central Road.
Jadavpur.
Calcutta - 32.

[Exhibit 151, Mukherjee Commission. This particular copy courtesy Ashok Tandon]

'The person with whom I was lodged in Mandalay Jail, played tennis and participated in Durga Puja—I have not forgotten him. I'm still with him,' he began. He recalled older days: 'In Delhi, in the year 1940, at Shankar Lal's residence I was accompanying him.' Shankar Lal was Forward Bloc general secretary. 'I was by his side while we toured United Province. On a chilling winter night in the Agra ground, hundreds of people were waiting for him till nine at night.' Then, a dash of emotion, a yearning to see 'him' again: 'I am eagerly waiting for the same person. The oppressed and tortured people of East Pakistan are waiting for him.'

Without writing *Subhas* even once, Trailokya made it clear who he had in mind. It was at Shankar Lal's Delhi residence in 1940 that Trailokya had last met Subhas. He was also with Subhas when he was bundled off to the dreaded Mandalay Jail in the 1920s.

Maharaj visited New Delhi in 1970 and was on 8 August felicitated at a reception attended by Prime Minister Indira Gandhi, Lok Sabha Speaker GS Dhillon and several MPs. In the wee hours of 9 August, Chakravarty passed away. The Prime Minister, who out of respect for the 83-year old Anushilan stalwart had personally served him sweets, was shocked. 'Meeting him was a moving experience,' she said.

[Trailokya Nath Chakravarty with Prime Minister Indira Gandhi a day before he passed away. Courtesy: Ananda Mukherjee]

SEVEN

FINDING THE LOST LEADER

AMONG THOSE WHO were sent to Bhagwanji by Leela Roy was someone Subhas Chandra Bose had known in the INA days: Anil Chandra Das, formerly of INA secret service. Declassified in 1997, and now available at New Delhi's National Archives is an intelligence report which reads that on his last night in Bangkok in August 1945, Subhas Bose talked to Anil Das about the underground work after the Japanese surrender (see next page). Another report speaks of the officials' eagerness to nab him, as Das had gone missing after Bose's reported death.

Yet another record shows Bose writing to Hikari Kikan—the Japanese military organisation liaising with Azad Hind Government—to hand over to Das fifty revolvers, some wireless sets and some British currency for post-war work. None of these documents were in the public domain so long

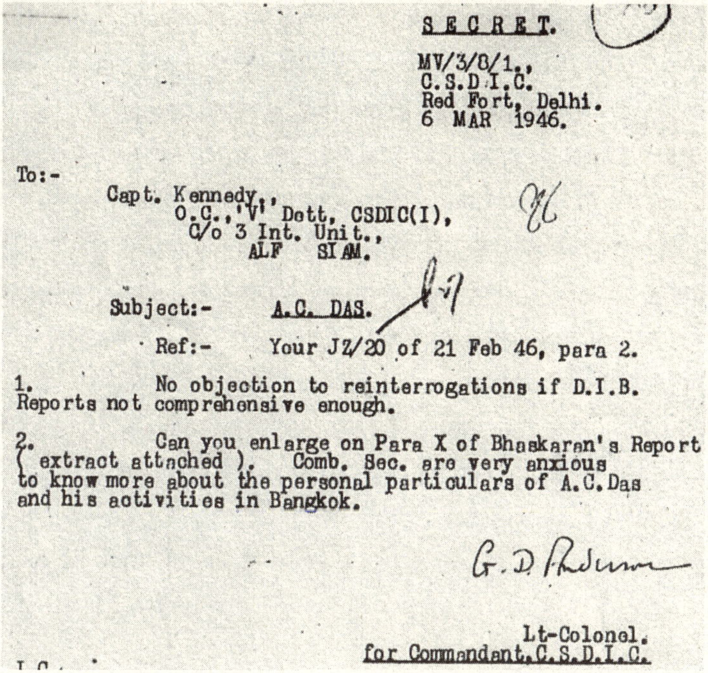

SECRET.

MV/3/8/1.,
C.S.D.I.C.
Red Fort, Delhi.
6 MAR 1946.

To:-

Capt. Kennedy.,
O.C., 'V' Dett, CSDIC(I),
C/o 3 Int. Unit.,
ALF SIAM.

Subject:- A.C. DAS.

Ref:- Your JZ/20 of 21 Feb 46, para 2.

1. No objection to reinterrogations if D.I.B. Reports not comprehensive enough.

2. Can you enlarge on Para X of Bhaskaran's Report (extract attached). Comb. Sec. are very anxious to know more about the personal particulars of A.C. Das and his activities in Bangkok.

G. D. Anderson

Lt-Colonel.
for Commandant, C.S.D.I.C.

as Das and Bhagwanji lived. And yet, recovered from Ram Bhawan was a Bengali letter Das had written to Bhagwanji in 1964. It was an *aide-memoire*, vetted and approved by Leela Roy. Das had recapitulated his role in the freedom struggle, beginning in the 1930s and lasting beyond 1945. 'On the night before he left Bangkok, Netaji took individual interviews of a number of people. I was one of them. When Netaji called me, it was half past 2 am. He told me about the post-war work and cautioned me against getting arrested. He gave me a letter addressed to Hikari Kikan,' he wrote in Bengali.

Netaji said that wherever he may go, he would remain in contact with us via wireless.... When I heard the news of the crash of Netaji's plane, I knew such a news would come and it would not be true. I waited for over a decade and in 1956 I visited India and told everything to auntie [Leela Roy]. *In 1961 I left Bangkok for good and last year auntie sent me to Naimisharanya and thereafter whatever small or big news I wanted to know I came to know from her. Now I am waiting for your orders.*

After perusing this letter, Bhagwanji specifically asked Das about what had really happened after 16 August 1945 and what statements were given by the captured INA personnel. Das elaborated in another letter that he had 'received two wireless sets and a few revolvers, pistols and stenguns from Hikari Kikan'.

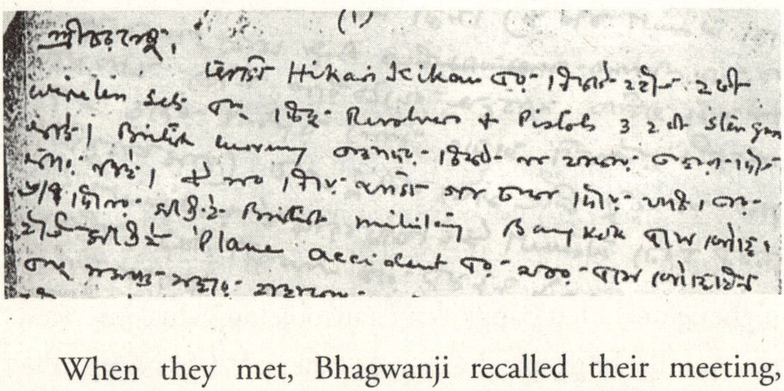

When they met, Bhagwanji recalled their meeting, correcting him on a point. 'No one other than Netaji is supposed to know about this interview,' Das later reported to Roy. He couldn't see Bhagwanji but heard his voice. 'It was exactly as during the days of the INA.'

Through Leela Roy only, her foremost aide Sunil Das was to become one of many eyes and ears of Bhagwanji. Several of Sunil Das' letters to him read like intelligence reports. Everything and anything concerning Subhas Bose was digested and sent for the information of Bhagwanji. In January 1964, for instance, Sunil Das wrote to Bhagwanji about his 'chance meeting' with a lawmaker from Delhi at Bengal Chief Minister's office. Surendra Mohan Ghose was once a close revolutionary associate of Subhas Bose who had fallen out with him later, switching loyalty to the Congress high command. Describing Ghose as 'an agent of Sri Jawaharlal Nehru,' Das wrote:

Then he [Ghose] *went on to say the Allied Powers (this is Govt's opinion) have by common consent struck off the name of Netaji from the list of war criminals because they have officially concluded that Netaji was dead. Now, if Netaji reappeared he would immediately be declared an 'imposter' by the Allied Powers!*

Bright enough in his student days to have his paper published in *The American Journal of Physical Chemistry*, Das chose to be a freedom fighter like his siblings, all three of whom died for the nation, unsung. His elder brother was beaten to death while in police custody in 1932. Das himself was first put in jail in 1931 on charges of attempting to assassinate the District Magistrate of Dhaka. He was arrested again in 1933 on the charges of conspiring to murder the

District Magistrate of Midnapore. This time he was detained in several prisons without trial till 1938. He was back in jail in 1942 and was not released till 1946. Post-independence, he was elected to the Bengal Assembly. He would go on to resist the Emergency and edit the Bengali volumes of collected works of Subhas Bose as editor of *Jayasree* publication. So long as he lived, Sunil Das kept his mouth completely shut about his Bhagwanji connection, even though he was active in intellectual circles in Calcutta and elsewhere.

The closest Das came to discussing the Bhagwanji matter was in 1972 when he was being examined before the Khosla Commission. Watching him was Niharendu Dutt Majumdar, former law minister of Bengal and the lawyer for the Bose family. Amar Prasad Chakraborty, the counsel for Forward Bloc and a would-be Member of Parliament, tried to get Das' secrets out:

The point that I want to ask from you is that you knew Netaji intimately so as not to mistake his identity?

His identity? So far as I am concerned, good heavens, never. How can I mistake his identity?

Do you think that if Netaji is really alive, there is something really insurmountable which would prevent him from coming into the arena when the country is in utter confusion and chaos?

Your question has two parts. Regarding the first part of the question my reply is, I believe that Netaji is alive. Regarding the second part I have no competence to go into it...

...Did Didi* [Leela Roy] *ever write regarding the disappearance of Netaji?

There were occasions when this subject cropped up in editorials [in her magazine *Jayasree*] *after 1963. I should say, we noticed a change in her—within herself. Although I happened to be her closest colleague and in many matters she shared counsel with me, as you know, we had been trained in the crucibles of secret revolutionary politics, and we have developed a code and we maintain the code in this way. Unless I am specifically told, if somebody in the hierarchy wants to keep something within himself or herself, we do not try to get it. That has been our training. Up till now I carry that thing with me.*

[Right to left: Sunil Das, Sunil Krishna Gupta, Amar Prasad Chakrovarty in suit, and Bose family lawyer N D Mazumdar. Das was unwell and so the commission examined him at his residence. Source: Jayasree Prakashan]

The list of such persons of impressive background who were convinced Bhagwanji was Subhas Bose contained many more names as several people secretly met him over the years. Around forty people of Leela Roy's group in Kolkata were aware of his existence. Not everyone, of course, got to meet him or even exchange letters. One of the older revolutionaries who was part of the team that decided to send Pabitra to Neemsar was Ashutosh Kali, an Anushilan Samiti veteran who went on to become one of the trusted associates of Rash Behari Bose, and recruited Rajen Lahiri of Kakori Conspiracy fame. Like Maharaj, Kali too had been prevented by long years in prison from playing a bigger role in the freedom struggle. His arrest in 1940 came after he threw in his lot with Subhas Bose's organisational work for consolidating the radicals.

Before he died in a tragic accident in 1965, Kali visited Bhagwanji in May 1963. This is what he wrote to him:

Ever since we got news of you, all of us, the entire Anushilan group, have been yearning to gain from your guidance and work under your instructions...I have crossed the age of seventy (but) the idealism that I imbibed from the valiant revolutionaries, the courage with which I fought everything is still burning bright within me...If you give the clarion call, even at this point of life, I will not hesitate to join the movement. I wanted to inform you that Basanti Devi is desperate to receive news of you. She has requested us to let her know about your whereabouts.

The reference to Basanti Devi in Kali's letter was to Subhas Bose's mentor Chittaranjan Das' wife, a motherly figure to him, who lived to a ripe old age.

After being tipped off by Leela Roy, Suresh Bose sent his confidant Sunil Krishna Gupta to Bhagwanji.

[Suresh Bose paying respects to Leela Roy who died in 1970. Courtesy: Bijoy Nag]

Suresh Bose subsequently made public statements that his brother was alive. Actually, he asserted as much before the Khosla Commission on oath in 1972:

Q:23-Did you make a statement on 20.2.66 xx that Netaji was alive and that he would come in 1966 in the Amrita Bazar Patrika and Hundusthan Standard dated 7.3.66 ?

A: I have no knowledge about it but I have already been convinced that Netaji did not die as alleged and is alive even kdm today.

[From Khosla Commission oral proceeding records. Accessed under Right to Information]

Asked to 'take this Commission into confidence and to say what are the reasons for believing this,' Suresh Bose curtly said, 'There is no reason why I should take this Commission into confidence.' Whatever the Bose family wanted to say, it did through its lawyer.

GD Khosla wrote in his report that Niharendu Dutt Majumdar 'on behalf of the family of Bose, argued with considerable vehemence and persistence that the government of India has deliberately suppressed or destroyed evidence which would have proved that Bose's name was included in the list of war criminals'.

This was Bhagwanji's allegation, and this was the Bose family's stand as well. The family told Justice Khosla that the charge that Netaji was still a war criminal was the 'most important, if not the only reason, for his remaining incognito' in the early 1970s.

If Netaji had been killed in either Taipei or Siberia, there was no question of his being treated as a war criminal decades later. So there was the Bose family lawyer, amplifying Bhagwanji's private utterances. The holy man bristled when he heard in January 1971 that India had agreed to a UN treaty stating that persons responsible for war crimes during World War II would not escape prosecution merely because no legal case is brought against them within a specified period. Before Justice Khosla, Niharendu Dutt Majumdar made a point-blank query:

limitations for prosecution of War Criminals. I am wondering what was the special urgency or occasion for India at this time to make such a ratification and what was India's special interest in this matter, unless India has somebody in view or may be for reasons not known to me. Now the question therefore arises that whether in the fitness of things, this Hon'ble Commission should not have a copy of such a Convention placed before it by the Government of India.

[Khosla Commission record obtained under the Right to Information]

In spite of this background of the Bose family believing that Netaji was alive in the early 1970s, the family members of today are engaged in opposite posturing. They go ballistic when others suggest what their own family elders had brought on record before the Khosla Commission. Why? While he allowed locals in UP, old revolutionaries and their kin from Bengal into his secret circle, Bhagwanji shunned his own family members—with only one or two possible exceptions other than his brother Suresh. Rightly or wrongly, he did not trust them. In a letter written to Pabitra in 1973, Bhagwanji alleged that Congress government had spent a few crores to have the family members under their control.

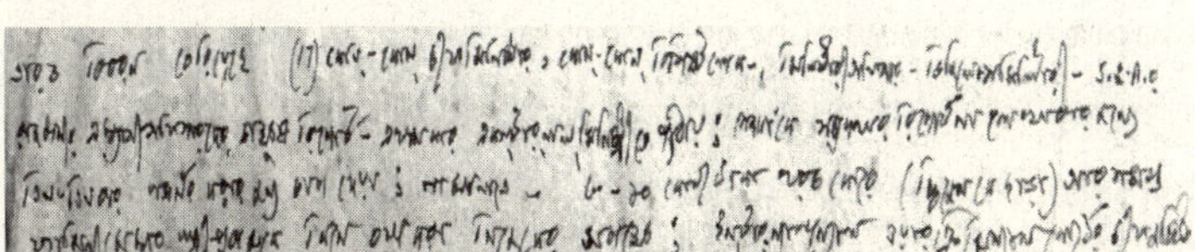

So it falls into place. The kin oppose the Gumnami Baba angle because, if proven, it would not show them in favourable light. Egotism and pomposity can make even most reasonable people unreasonable and mean.

The man despatched by Suresh Bose to meet Bhagwanji lived up to 2010 to tell his incredible tale of being in touch with 'Netaji' secretly. 'I gave all my love and affection to Sukrit [Sunil Krishna Gupta] after *Sejda* sent him with his long letter,' Bhagwanji would write to Pabitra. The brothers exchanged letters till one month before Suresh Bose's demise in 1972. When Santosh Bhattacharya brought the bad news, Bhagwanji wept like a child. Certain personality traits do not change with time. As recouted by a Japanese general, Netaji had cried inconsolably when he heard the news of his mother's passing away.

Bhagwanji told Suresh Bose to destroy all his correspondence. 'Fortunately, he was able to destroy all those letters in time. It was only one letter that he didn't want to destroy; his heart didn't permit. He returned it to me after Tripti [Santosh Bhattacharya] explained the risks to him.'

Sunil Gupta was deputed by Bhagwanji to keep an eye on Khosla's inquiry. 'I used to apprise him of the proceedings,' Gupta told the Mukherjee Commission.

All of Gupta's siblings were freedom fighters, with nephew Dinesh Gupta (elder to him in age) being one of the legendary Benoy–Badal–Dinesh trio. In a heroic tale not too well-known outside Bengal, the three teenagers in 1930 made a daring entrance into the Writers' Building and shot dead a top cop for he had mistreated Subhas Bose and others.

In the 1990s, Sunil Gupta was the moving force behind Rudra Jyoti Bhattacharjee's PIL leading to the formation of the Mukherjee Commission in 1999. An article in *Time* magazine described Sunil Gupta as someone who 'demands no recognition and even refuses to be named'. If you took Gupta's name before the Bose family members of today, they would feign ignorance. Luckily, in one of the files declassified by the Narendra Modi government, there is an interesting exchange from the late 1950s. Intelligence Bureau Deputy Director S Balakrishna Shetty—the officer in charge of matters relating to Subhas Bose—ratted Sunil Gupta to the Home Ministry. Gupta was accused of possessing some classified records relating to Netaji. The Home Ministry sounded off the Bengal government. Following an investigation, Bengal Chief Secretary found out:

Sunil Krishna Gupta...is well educated, possesses considerable cultural attainments and is intimately known to the Bose family. All the members of Sunil's family, including his two grown up sisters, were associated with the political movement in the Far East sponsored by the late Subhas Chandra Bose.

Sunil Gupta was not the only member of his family devoted to Bhagwanji. His elder brother Atul kept in touch and so did their nephews Jagatjit and Surajit Dasgupta.

More names were added to the list of people sent to Bhagwanji by Leela Roy and Pabitra Mohan Roy over the years. There was Kumar Bishwanath Roy, a former legislator who had the financial means to provide for Bhagwanji's many requirements. For Kumar, there was no beating around the bush—he was as direct as one could be regarding Bhagwanji's identity. 'I was a boy of twelve years when you had come along with Deshbandhu to campaign for Bidhan Roy in 1923 at the field adjacent to my house; attracted to your personality, I had resolved to become someone like Subhas Chandra when I grow up,' he wrote to Bhagwanji.

In 1965, Leela Roy sent another of her ardent followers, Dulal Nandy, for whom Bhagwanji took a great liking. Nandy visited Bhagwanji every year from 1965 to 1985 (except 1973) but claimed never to have seen his face. His compatriot Santosh Bhattacharya, who had served Bose as young party worker in the late 1930s, was luckier. It was a letter from Bhattacharya's daughter that Vishnu Sahai cited as evidence of Bhagwanji not being Netaji.

[Bijoy Nag, Madhusudan Pal, Dulal Nandy, Anuj Dhar, Prof Nandalal Chakravarty and Surajit Dasgupta in Kolkata a few years ago. Surajit and his friends Chakravarty & Pal were most active deponents before the Mukherjee Commission]

Of Bhagwanji's five main followers from Bengal, three were alive to depose before the Mukherjee Commission: Sunil Gupta, Dulal Nandy and Bijoy Nag. Since then, the first two have departed from this world. But the man whose testimony carried more legal weight was 94-year old Apurba Chandra Ghose. A Leela Roy loyalist, he had met Subhas Bose many times. One such time was back in 1939 at Manikganj, Dhaka. Ghose was in charge of Bose's lodging at *kutcharibari* [office building] of a zamindar. When Ghose met Bhagwanji, he was asked where he was from…

I replied that I hailed from Manikganj…He then asked me whether I was the man who had offered him a hair comb when he came out of the bathroom in that kutcharibari after having his bath. I replied in the affirmative. He then asked me whether I could remember that he smiled when I offered him the comb. When I replied that I had noticed him smiling, he told me that he smiled because I made a silly mistake while offering him the comb. He told me that I should have offered the comb on a plate or dish instead of offering it with my bare hands.

With the old faithfuls coming in contact with Bhagwanji at Neemsar and the volume of letters written by him increased, his handwriting became his first point of attention. Although, by his own admission, he was writing in Bengali after nearly two decades, he received feedback that his writing style and usage of phrases were very much identifiable. Even his diction. 'The vocabulary you use, you cannot change and the vocabulary would lead to your identification. No Bengali uses the words, idioms etc. that you do,' Leela Roy cautioned him. Bhagwanji replied:

Sometime back three people came to meet me, one after another. I don't know how they got my contact information. Among them was one who was introduced by Deshbandhu [CR Das] *himself in his drawing room when the 'dead' returned from England after becoming an ICS... They told me, 'You have survived...only because you are living in these conditions in UP. Had you been in Bengal it would have been 100% impossible to avoid being found out, even if you lived in a house protected by seven layers of walls. Your way of talking hasn't changed a bit... the way you speak Bengali with a lisp, prolonging the utterances, has remained exactly as before.' I nearly stopped breathing on hearing this...*

Today you are also saying the same. Le style, C'est L'hommemême (The style is the man himself)—this French dictum is true. Therefore a change is absolutely essential. No chance, no risk, no failure. Please do something to help your 'dead'—please write down along with your comments a number of long, long passages which are diametrically opposite to my manner of writing, use of language and talking. I will start thinking, talking and writing accordingly. (Bengali parts of this paragraph translated into English)

It cannot be said with certainty, but most probably Roy did follow up on Bhagwanji's request. One of the items recovered from Ram Bhawan was a notebook which had twenty-four different types of writing styles and handwriting patterns. While examining Bhagwanji's handwriting, B Lal observed that he tried to conceal his identity by trying to change his handwriting. He failed.

There is no way to make a full accounting of who all kept in touch with Bhagwanji believing he was Subhas Bose. All those who met him were sworn to secrecy, and Bhagwanji would destroy much of his correspondence. Dwijendra Nath Bose, freedom fighter nephew of Netaji, was also sounded out, but exact details were not divulged. Dwijen asserted before the Khosla Commission on oath in 1972 that his uncle Subhas was alive but refused to elaborate. All he would say was:

If I give a clue in this committee, that would be made public and the Government will know of it and that is dangerous to Netaji. It is for him (Netaji) to decide when that should be made public or when he should return to India.

However, people from Kolkata or Uttar Pradesh formed only a part of Bhagwanji's network. In total secrecy, many were getting in touch with him from different corners of the country. One of those names would give goose bumps to the RSS–BJP rank and file: Madhav Golwalkar. The Guruji of the entire current top brass of the Sangh Parivar—former Deputy PM Advani, former HRD Minister Dr Murli Manohar Joshi, RSS chief Mohan Bhagwat and, above all, Prime Minister Narendra Modi.

A letter written in late 1972 by Golwalkar to Bhagwanji testifies that he held the latter in the highest esteem. Golwalkar started his letter with the salutation: 'I bow before you a hundred times.' The contents of this letter, coupled with Bhagwanji's utterances, make it clear that Golwalkar, who ran India's biggest social organisation, was taking instructions and words of advice from a seemingly non-descript, mostly-unseen holy man. Dr Joshi was good enough to identify Golwalkar's handwriting. Bhagwanji scribbled 'Dr Hedgewar' at the top of the letter. On its backside, he appeared to have made some astrological calculations about Golwalkar, who was rather unwell at that time.

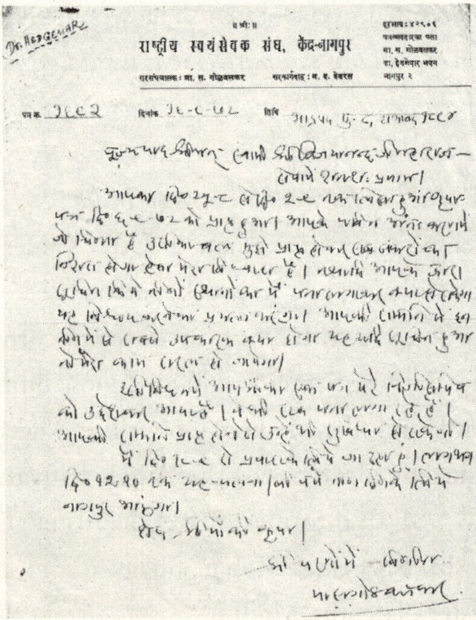

Dr. HEDGEWAR

॥ श्री: ॥

राष्ट्रीय स्वयंसेवक संघ, केंद्र-नागपुर

Golwalkar would be alive for only nine more months. Following his death, Bhagwanji lamented, 'No one will ever know or understand what a loss this has been for me.'

The salutation used by Golwalkar for Bhagwanji was not that used for a politician or senior statesman, but one that shows almost devotional genuflection. We have no information when this contact was established and how it developed over the years, during and after the tenure of Golwalkar. The unambiguous public proclamations by KS Sudarshan, the fifth head of RSS, in April 2005, however, show that the highest leadership of the organisation has been well aware of his existence. The only question that remains unanswered is just how much did they know and what was their role? Interestingly, as early as 1948, RSS was rumoured to be linked to Netaji, as recorded in a CIA information report. 'Some people believe that Bose is alive. According to their theory, Bose is at present active in the underground RSS movement,' the report dated 10 January 1949 reads.

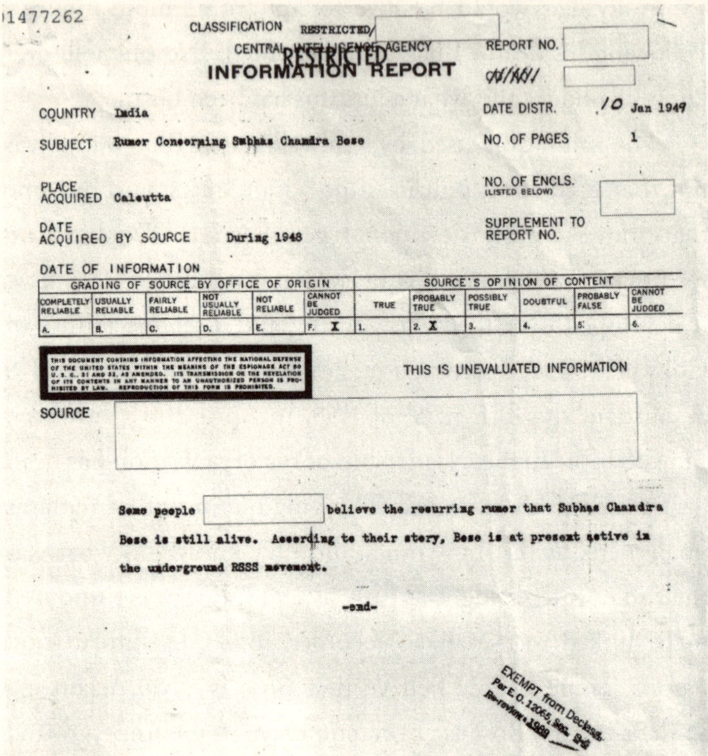

1477262

CLASSIFICATION RESTRICTED/

RESTRICTED

CENTRAL INTELLIGENCE AGENCY

INFORMATION REPORT

REPORT NO.

COUNTRY India

DATE DISTR. 10 Jan 1949

SUBJECT Rumor Concerning Subhas Chandra Bose

NO. OF PAGES 1

PLACE ACQUIRED Calcutta

NO. OF ENCLS. (LISTED BELOW)

DATE ACQUIRED BY SOURCE During 1948

SUPPLEMENT TO REPORT NO.

DATE OF INFORMATION

GRADING OF SOURCE BY OFFICE OF ORIGIN						SOURCE'S OPINION OF CONTENT					
COMPLETELY RELIABLE	USUALLY RELIABLE	FAIRLY RELIABLE	NOT USUALLY RELIABLE	NOT RELIABLE	CANNOT BE JUDGED	TRUE	PROBABLY TRUE	POSSIBLY TRUE	DOUBTFUL	PROBABLY FALSE	CANNOT BE JUDGED
A.	B.	C.	D.	E.	F. X	1.	2. X	3.	4.	5.	6.

THIS DOCUMENT CONTAINS INFORMATION AFFECTING THE NATIONAL DEFENSE OF THE UNITED STATES WITHIN THE MEANING OF THE ESPIONAGE ACT 50 U. S. C., 31 AND 32, AS AMENDED. ITS TRANSMISSION OR THE REVELATION OF ITS CONTENTS IN ANY MANNER TO AN UNAUTHORIZED PERSON IS PROHIBITED BY LAW. REPRODUCTION OF THIS FORM IS PROHIBITED.

THIS IS UNEVALUATED INFORMATION

SOURCE

Some people believe the recurring rumor that Subhas Chandra Bose is still alive. According to their story, Bose is at present active in the underground RSSS movement.

-end-

EXEMPT from Declass. Per E.O. 12065, Sec. 3-3 Re-review 1989

[Document accessed under US Freedom of Information Act]

EIGHT

A JOURNEY THROUGH TWO DECADES

BY AUGUST 1963, Bhagwanji had made up his mind to move out of Neemsar. Finding a new location wasn't easy. Eventually, Anil Das, Kamalakanta Ghosh and Santosh Bhattacharya executed the stealthy shift, which was the first of a series of frequent moves in the coming years. Bhagwanji traversed the distance of over 200 km from Neemsar to Darshan Nagar village, about 6 km to the east of Faizabad in Ayodhya district, crouching on the floor between the two rows of seats in a car, while Saraswati Devi and Rajkumar remained on the backseat.

The new residence—Shankar Niwas in Darshan Nagar village—was soon found to be unsuitable for living, being damp and swamped with insects, but more importantly with only one route for entry and exit, which went against Bhagwanji's security plan in choosing accommodation. And one day, it all went awry. Intrigued by the arrival of a strange personality, some villagers climbed the high trees around Shankar Niwas to catch a glimpse of him. Suddenly appeared a man with a gun, threatening to shoot the intruders. They all fled.

Early in August 1964, the support team from Calcutta settled Bhagwanji at Lal Kothi in Ayodhya's Baksaryia Tola, owned by Vishnu Narain, Lucknow entrepreneur and proprietor of Speed Motors. Narain would later tell Allahabad-based daily *Northern India Patrika,* 'Swamiji never appeared before anybody and always remained within the cloistered quarters of his room. The behaviour of the inmates did lead me to believe that he was a mysterious man indeed'. Soon, word reached Jitendra Bahadur Singh, the inspector in charge of Ayodhya kotwali. So he did what cops do: swoop down on Lal Kothi in the dead of night with his posse. All they found were empty rooms.

'Dead Man' arrived next in Basti, 70-90 km east of Ayodhya, in 1965. The first accommodation was much too small. So, he was shifted by Dulal Nandy and others to Sharista Kothi at Raja Maidan in Purani Basti—property of the royal family of Basti. It now lies in ruins. Here, Bhagwanji spent the longest time among all the places that he lived—over ten years.

The key new person to make an entry into Bhagwanji's circle of trust at Basti was local lawyer Durga Prasad Pandey.

As in other places, rumours started flying thick and fast in Basti about the real identity of the sadhu in hiding. Groups of unknown Bengalis visiting him, the postman delivering letters and magazines like *The Illustrated Weekly of India* and *Time* (American) in big piles in a back-of-beyond town had the local rumour mill spinning. Mohammed Mobin, the beat constable at Basti, watched men with an air of importance about them emerging from their cars and under cover of darkness walking towards Sharista Kothi.

After many unsuccessful attempts to get an audience with Bhagawanji, Pandey wrote a letter to him in fairly good English for someone living in this part of the country in 1967. 'Here at Basti, I have been constantly keeping my watch while your honour had been residing in Sri Roop Kishore Vakil's house and now shifted to Raja Basti ka Hata,' Pandey wrote. 'The letters, the telegrams, the purchases in the market and buying standard English magazines and periodicals are another side of the coin to dazzle and puzzle the mind of the beholders about your mystery'.

Then he broke the secret source of his information: 'An old and very religious ex-Revenue officer, late Sri Jwala Prasad Misra, told me as to your honour's identity while breathing his last.' Without mentioning the recipient's name, Pandey didn't leave any scope for doubt that he knew who he was writing to: 'You had been an ex-ICS of profound scholarship…January 23rd was celebrated as your birthday here, the most auspicious day of the country, when the immortal words "Jai Hind" resounded through and through all the flora and fauna on the Indian soil…I pledge to keep this secret as long as I am in this world.'

Pandey's imploring met with this evasive response from Bhagwanji:

I am a bonafide dashnami sanyasi and you will know that a man under the holy orders incurs death according to the civil laws and a sanyasi is dead to his former life.

As an afterthought, he added:

In passing, you shall find cogent answers to all your hypotheses, queries, thoughts…both as expressed in your letter, and which remain unexpressed in your heart. Peruse with your heart calmly, quietly, lovingly. Every word, phrase, sentence and their constructions are pointers for you; they are pregnant with possibilities. Seek and thou shall find.

Pandey's persistence would pay off. He was gradually allowed the access only a few had. He saw the man. About three decades later, an eighty-four-year-old Pandey told the Mukherjee Commission that Bhagwanji was the same person he had seen from a very close distance making a two-hour-long speech in 1940 at the Ganga Prasad Memorial Hall in Lucknow: Subhas Chandra Bose. 'I noticed considerable hair fall from his head and long beard on his face. That apart, I found that his abdomen was swollen.'

While Bhagwanji lived in Basti, momentous political

events were taking place that went a long way in changing the political identity of India. India emerged victorious in the 1965 Indo-Pak war; by January 1966 Prime Minister Lal Bahadur Shastri had died immediately after signing the Tashkent Pact, initiating the era of Indira Gandhi. The year 1971 saw the next Indo-Pak war and ascendancy of Mujibur Rahman as the leader of the new nation of Bangladesh. Alongside these developments, people noticed unusual things happening around the mysterious guest.

As the local investigation by the team of *Northern India Patrika* journalists in 1985-86 found, 'Strange events transpired only in darkness…heavily curtained cars of all makes, Indian and foreign, city sahibs in three-piece suits' would appear all of a sudden and vanish equally suddenly.

When time came to move on from Basti, the responsibility for securing a new place for Bhagwanji fell on Pandey. He selected Prahlad Dharmashala in Ayodhya, owned by Panda Ram Kishore Mishra. On the day of Dhanteras in 1974, he took Bhagwanji to Ayodhya by car. An initially reluctant Mishra had agreed to rent out his accommodation when Pandey pleaded that his aged Guruji was having difficulty in finding a place to stay and agreed to pay the rent for the two months that he would live there in advance.

Mishra went to meet his tenant, who he had been told was a '*Sant Mahatma*'. He had already been told that he did not meet anyone face-to-face and therefore wasn't surprised when he had to speak with his tenant across a closed door. When Mishra visited again after a couple of days with his wife, Bhagwanji established a connect with them which both would fiercely protect till the end of their lives. 'You are my Nanda baba and she is my Yashomati Maiya. Now that I am in your shelter, it is up to you to protect me from any disturbance to my sadhana.'

The discussion left the couple convinced that they had come across a person of very high calibre. From his Hindi pronunciation, it was clear to Mishra, who hosted people from all regions of the country, that the *Sant* was a Bengali. At the same time, the frequent use of Urdu words intrigued him.

In time, things began to get curious and curious. On a wintry night in Ayodhya, suddenly realising that the septuagenarian holy man must be cold, Kishore offered him the brazier he was using, only to be told, 'This body has lived in Siberia. It does not require warmth.'

Bhagwanji left Prahlad Dharmashala after two months. The next few years—January 1975 to May 1978—when he lived at Ramkot Ward, Gurudwara Brahmakund, were troublesome. Landlord Gurubaksh Singh Sodhi spoke of his befuddlement to *NIP*: 'He was always in hiding, being called upon by strange people at night in cars of all sizes and shapes, with an extraordinary voice and sources of income which were unknown. Yes, some people said he was none other than Netaji Subhas Chandra Bose.'

Current chief priest of Gurudwara Brahmakund Sahib, Gyani Gurjeet Singh Khalsa, accidently caught sight of Bhagwanji's face when he was 17 years old. 'The radiance on his face was astounding. It cannot be explained in words,' he told *The Times of India* in 2015.

As in the previous towns, gossip started flowing thick and fast. Sodhi wanted his tenant out. He tipped off Virendra Kumar Mishra, a journalist representing *Current*, a weekly published from Bombay. Mishra carried out his inquiry and thought it serious enough to be reported to Superintendent of Police Gyaneshwar Jha through a *gopniya* (secret) letter. Mishra wrote that there was 'something suspicious about Gurudev Swami' [Bhagwanji]. 'Some people say Babaji is a CIA agent. He has a transmitter and he sends messages' he wrote, adding that others are of the view that 'Babaji is Subhas Chandra Bose and wants to remain in hiding'.

Taken aback by this claim, Jha took some men along drove to Bhagwanji's place. He stomped inside with the usual cop-like swagger. When he emerged after a while, he looked panicky and was on the verge of breaking down. Quietly he gestured his men to pull out. The next day his transfer orders were on his table—Mishra told us. If only Justice Sahai had tried to find out the truth, for Jha lives and the letter is there on the official file. This is no rocket science we are dealing with.

Another journalist who had a fascinating experience was

VN Arora. Now a retired principal of Saket Postgraduate College of Ayodhya, Arora got wind about Bhagwanji's existence in 1978. Desirous of meeting the holy man, he left a message with Saraswati Devi, who asked him to come the next day at 4 pm. Arora would forfeit that chance. He was visited by one NP Tiwari, an IB officer of the rank of deputy superintendent of police who, Arora told us, 'seized my time from 2 pm to 6.30 pm and persuaded me not to disturb a saint who is practising meditation for self-realisation far from the public eye'. The significance of IB man's mind altering persuasion dawned upon Arora in late 1985 as he started inquiring into the matter as part of the *NIP* team.

If Bhagwanji's stay at Brahmakund was marked by unwanted attention drawn to him by external troublemakers, it also saw the entry of a few people who would stay with him till the end. Among these were Dr TC Banerjee, a well-known homeopath, Dr Raghunath Prasad Mishra, the district surgeon, Dr B Rai, an anaesthesiologist, and Krishna Gopal Srivastava, an art teacher at the Rajkaran Vaidik Pathshala Inter College, Faizabad. Also getting access to Bhagwanji was Dr Dashrath Prasad Tomar, another Ayodhya-based homeopath. Tomar, a graduate from the Calcutta Homeopathic Medical College and Hospital who speaks fluent Bengali, touched a chord in Bhagwanji's heart when he told him that his teacher in Calcutta was Bijoy Kumar Bose, a revolutionary-turned-physician.

Dr TC Banerjee's case was most unusual. According to the account related by his son Dr Priyabrata Banerjee, one afternoon in 1975, Saraswati Devi came to their clinic and begged his father to visit a seriously ailing Bhagwanji. The father returned after hours looking flabbergasted. He had been walking on the roads aimlessly unable to make sense what had happened to him that day. In his first visit to Gumnami Baba, he managed what others could not even after years of devoutness. The doctor had to see his patient. He saw Bhagwanji and his spine froze. Flashback 1939, Lucknow: A young TC Banerjee standing attentively, beholding the Congress president.

Some time later, Dr Banerjee unburdened his emotions in front of Ram Kishore Mishra. Once, when Mishra reached Gurudwara Brahmakund, he found Dr Banerjee standing outside. After the usual discussion about Bhagwanji's health, Mishra recalled, Dr Banerjee couldn't restrain himself anymore. '*Aap dhanya hain jo ke Subhas babu ki seva mein kuch samay de paatey hain* (You are blessed to be able to spend some time in serving Subhas babu),' he blurted out. Mishra was dumbstruck for a few minutes.

Before long, Banerjee's wife Pushpa and her son and daughter-in-law Priyabrata and Rita Banerjee were allowed into the inner precincts, where they interacted with the man sitting right in front of him. One of their kin also managed access denied to most. Gorakhpur-based insurance agent

Dilip Kumar Mukherjee, a nephew of Banerjee, unexpectedly got lucky after years of persistent trying. This was in the early 1980s. He entered the room to feel Bhagwanji's penetrating glance from behind silver-rimmed glasses. Overawed by the unimaginable spectacle of seeing 'Netaji' right in front of him, Dilip burst out into tears, his body trembling. After Bhagwanji helped him regain his composure, he managed to ask him a few questions. His favourable comment on Communists invited scolding from Bhagwanji in Hindi. 'What do you know about them? I have seen them from close. I have been to Russia. I saw how a few luxuriated while the rest suffered. I went to their grand palaces. This body even endured torture in Siberia.'

Misfortune struck another blow in 1981 when Bhagwanji broke his femur from a fall in the bathroom when he was staying at Lucknow-wali Hata, Ayodhya. From then on, he needed a wheelchair. It was in this condition that he made his final move. Mishra brought Bhagwanji to Ram Bhawan in Civil Lines area in Ayodhya in 1983. He was lodged in a rented outhouse on the backside of a bungalow named Ram Bhawan. Owner Gurubasant Singh (Shakti Singh's father) never saw his tenant. He only heard him speak. 'I've never heard a voice like that in my life. The tone and tenor was more like that of an army commander's than a sadhu baba's,' he'd recall.

Ravindra Shukla, one of the close followers of Bhagwanji

in his last years, told the Sahai Commission that the day Indira Gandhi was assassinated, he heard Bhagwanji ruing that his repeated instructions to RN Kao to increase Indira's security were overlooked. 'No one should ever hurt a woman,' Bhagwanji said, bristling in anger. Unknown to most people in Ayodhya, in 1984, RN Kao was the Prime Minister's security advisor. In 1971, he was heading the Research & Analysis Wing as its first head.

It was at Ram Bhawan that Bhagwanji breathed his last. This was on 16 September 1985. He was 88 years old, having been born on 23 January 1897 at 12.15 pm. When he was living, his birthday used to be observed right at this moment.

For two days after he was gone, Bhagwanji's body remained under the constant guard of the family of Dr Mishra, the man in charge. Mishra told the rest of the local disciples that the wait was for the Bengali followers of Bhagwanji who had been notified of his death. When no one showed up for inexplicable reasons, Dr Mishra manoeuvred the crowd by announcing that the body was being taken to Ayodhya for cremation. After aimlessly driving around for a while, a Matador van carrying the body was swiftly re-routed to Faizabad cantonment, to a secluded place on the banks of the River Sarayu near Guptar Ghat—where Lord Ram had taken *jal samadhi*—on the evening of 19 September.

A funeral pyre was erected within minutes. Present

at the cremation site were thirteen disciples including Dr Mishra, Dr Rai, Ravindra Shukla, Dr Priyabrat Banerjee, Panda Ram Kishore Mishra and Rajkumar Shukla, son of Saraswati Devi. As the flames wrapped the mortal remains, the disciples were consumed by emotional turmoil. They had all given their word to Bhagwanji to keep his identity secret. Now the man was gone. Panda Ram Kishore was the first to bewail: 'We are only thirteen here to see him off on his last journey. There should have been thirteen lakhs.'

The matter would have died out there and then had it not been for an intrepid journalist. Ashok Tandon, editor of local Hindi daily *Naye Log*, mustered courage to report it. His news sense aroused, Tandon asked reporters Chandresh Srivastava and Ramteerth Vikal to make inquiries. The result was the breaking news on 28 October 1985.

The *Naye Log* story sent ripples across the town. Tandon heard about the systematic attempts to suppress the circulation of the newspaper, but the news was too big to be contained. As the state machinery adopted a wishy-washy attitude, more and more journalists started connecting the dots.

The commotion then attracted the attention of Tushar Kanti Ghosh—one of the most prominent names in Indian journalism, a Padma Bhushan awardee and editor of *Amrita Bazar Patrika, Jugantar* and *Northern India Patrika*. After reviewing the developments, Ghosh approved an investigative series to be published in the now defunct *NIP*.

A team of Nirmal Nibedon, Vishwambhar Nath Arora and Sayed Kausar Husain, the news editor, ran the investigative series that started on 20 December 1985 and continued in seventeen parts, culminating on 23 January, Subhas Bose's birth anniversary, next year.

The *NIP* reports on 'the man of mystery' pushed the people of Faizabad into a vortex of emotions. But the instant reaction of the state government was to float a conspiracy theory that the Janata Party and the BJP were behind the public outcry. The truth was that the public discontent was spontaneous, with every section of society, including local Congress leaders, pitching in. The man who had in a sense let the cat out of the bag—Panda Ram Kishore—was in fact a well-known Congress party leader of Ayodhya.

NINE

DEAD MAN'S TALES

OF ALL THE claims that have been made about Subhas Bose's presence in Soviet Russia after his reported death, the closest to direct evidence was rendered by a former chief engineer with the Heavy Engineering Corporation (HEC Ltd). A postgraduate in mechanical engineering from the UK, Ardhendu Sarkar, for good measure, testified on oath before the Mukherjee Commission.

Later, in his plush, high-rise apartment home in Kolkata, he would unassumingly recall his experience to one of us. This had happened in the early 1960s at Gorlovka machine building plant, near Donetesk in Ukraine, then part of Soviet Russia. Sarkar's superior officer at the plant, BA Zerovin, became friendly with him after he learned that he hailed from Bengal. In a moment of camaraderie, the Russian let it slip that Zerovin was not his real name. He was actually a German Jew who had been brought to the USSR after World War II, sent to a Siberian gulag for indoctrination, given a new identity and was married to a Russian.

Then, to Sarkar's shock, he said that he had met Subhas Bose in Berlin during the war, and 'again in 1948' in a gulag somewhere beyond the end of Trans-Siberian Railways in the vicinity of the Ural Mountains. He said that Bose was apparently being treated fine, given a car and was moving around with two guards. In their short exchange, Bose told Zerovin that he expected to go back to India soon.

Soviet Russia, Siberia, gulags and Russian leaders figured heavily in Bhagwanji's talks with his close followers and in his letters and their notes about their conversations with him. He said he spent quite some time in a gulag in south central Siberia, somewhere in the vicinity of Lake Baikal and the Ural Mountains. 'Stalin did not treat me like an enemy, my own people did,' he said during a conversation with Sunil Gupta.

The escape to Russia was planned much in advance, long before the 'plane crash', in a secret visit to Russia in late 1944.

The official position is that in the last few months before the war ended, Subhas Chandra Bose visited only Tokyo. The Shah Nawaz Committee report reads that 'in October 1944 Netaji visited Japan for the third and last time'. However, declassified intelligence records now available now at Delhi's National Archives throw up another scenario. SACSEA

Commission No. 1 report of 6 November 1945 states that Bose visited Tokyo in December 1944 to discuss with the Japanese government a possible rapprochement with China and Russia.

But why would Netaji want to go to Russia? Japanese interpreter Kinji Watanabe in the course of his interrogation by Intelligence Bureau recalled Bose's words:

I earnestly request Tokyo to act as 'go-between' and let me approach Soviet Russia. Once I have been given an interview with the Russian ambassador, I have perfect confidence in my success in persuading Russia to help our independence movement and at the same time I am sure that I can do something to improve the relations between Japan and Russia, and it might serve to decrease the menace Japan is feeling on the Manchurian side.

In the late 1980s, after the fall of the USSR, Russian researcher Victor Touradjev located in the KGB archives in Moscow a letter that Bose had written in October 1944 to Yakov Malik, the Soviet Ambassador in Tokyo. The letter bore a comment from the Commissiar of State Security (NKGB) to the chief of the fifth division of the first command of NKVD—the forerunner of the KGB. Bose had written to Malik that he wanted 'to pay a visit to Your Excellency and find the way through which your Government can help us for success of our struggle for freedom'.

Yet another declassified record at the National Archives in New Delhi speaks of a rumour about Bose's secret visit to Russia.

In November 1944 there was a general rumour...that SC Bose was preparing to leave for Moscow in order to place all information about the Indian freedom movement before the leaders of the USSR. ...In December 1944, Lt Sadhu Singh of HQ, 1 Div, INA, was acting as QM of the YE-U rest Camp, informed B 766 that SC Bose had left for Moscow and was soon expected back in Tokyo.

For reasons we can now appreciate in hindsight, Suresh Bose made a similar claim before the Khosla Commission. A *Times of India* report dated 6 November 1970 quoted him saying that Bose's plan to go to Russia 'was drawn up in early 1944 and it was accepted by the Japanese government'. In pursuance of this plan, what Subhas did next according to Suresh was reported by *Hindustan Times*:

In December 1944, when the Azad Hind Government was functioning and the INA was engaged in the battlefields, Netaji was absent from there for about a fortnight. During this period, Netaji had been to Russia and had probably met Marshal Stalin.

According to Bhagwanji, he was not only present in the erstwhile USSR after 1945, but his presence was coveted by their top leadership. Soon, he was put in touch with the Chinese by the Russians. Moreover, he claimed to have operating bases somewhere in the Central Asian region he frequently travelled to. The initial days, he indicated, were not easy. But before long, he was 'absolutely and entirely free and independent' in his sphere of activities over 'far-flung regions (territories) the major portion of which do not come either in Russia or China'. This area, he claimed, 'has been notified as prohibited region under international laws'. There was an 'extremely important & vital secret base there,' which even Russian 'aircrafts do not fly over'.

Interestingly, Bhagwanji indicated how the story of his imprisonment in Siberia gained currency in India. He was part of a secret mega-project undertaken by Russia in a huge uninhabited area in Siberia, along with other 'experts'. Large-scale machinery was set up for the project and the area was declared out of bounds for even government officials. Arrangements were made for accommodation of the heads of the several divisions of the project, and for him too. Bhagwanji claimed that he was accompanied by several men from the Azad Hind government. This news somehow reached the Indian ambassador Vijaya Lakshmi Pandit, India's first ambassador to Russia, Nehru's talented younger sister.

Bhagwanji also mentioned that Foreign Secretary KPS Menon too heard about him and asked the Soviets for permission to visit the area, but probably was denied permission. Bhagwanji explained that as news of his presence in the Siberian project leaked out and spread through rumours, people assumed because of the place's notoriety for hard labour camps that if he was in Siberia, he must have been a prisoner. But he was a guest of the Soviet government.

While no reference about Bose's presence in Siberia is to be found in the Nehru era files declassified by the Modi government, a CIA report accessed by the authors under the Freedom of Information Act does show that as late as 1950, rumours that Bose was in Siberia and waiting to make a comeback were floating in New Delhi circles. Indian intelligence files, provided they were not destroyed like some other Bose-related papers, are likely to contain far more information but have been kept out of the purview of the declassification drive undertaken by the Modi government. '*Satyamev Jayate*' may be a good ideal, but the good old Official Secrets Act of 1923 reigns supreme in the land of truth and ahimsa.

To his followers, Bhagwanji described in detail the layout of the Siberian prison camps which indicate his intimate knowledge of the area. This was before Alexander Solzhenitsyn's classic *The Gulag Archipelago* provided a ringside view for the first time.

Concentration camps of central Siberia contain male and female labourers, farmers, craftsmen, authors, scientists and teachers—from 5 thousand to 25 thousand in each. Not one or two, there are almost 49 concentration camps. They are manufacturing ultra-modern goods for daily use. These are transported to the retail outlets in the main cities. Those who buy those products do not know that they may have been manufactured by their parents, brothers, sisters or other kin.

If you came to know what goes on there you would run for your life. Driven by hunger, people have gone to the extent of eating their own flesh. A new camp was being constructed; so the soldiers took 10,000 prisoners with them. But there was no hut there. Their duty was to install pillars by digging 12 feet holes in the ice to surround themselves. 'Keep your back hot by heavy work'—anyone who does not follow this will freeze and die. [Translated from Bengali]

Decoding Bhagwanji's coded letters to his closest followers, especially Pabitra, a hazy storyline of how he gained influence in the Soviet land emerges. From Stalin's days, Russia had been trying to do something in that area in absolute secrecy against China, in a way that no one would suspect its involvement, but had failed repeatedly despite its power and resources. Thereafter, when Bhagwanji arrived, he took it over and helped the Russians succeed. This helped Bhagwanji establish himself in high places in Moscow; it led to the Russians holding him in high esteem, which gradually turned into 'affectionate love'. Russia was extremely grateful to him for the things he had done for them, he claimed. However, the more he saw of Russia, the more Bhagwanji came to despise Communism.

When he left Soviet Russia around 1949 at the close of the war crimes trials, Bhagwanji did not have an immediate plan to return to India, because he felt—or was given this impression—that India was still not a free country. That under some secret pact the colonial rulers had with the Indian leaders at the time of the Transfer of Power in 1947, he was to be tried and handed over to the Anglo-Americans as a 'war criminal'. For such a sordid state of affairs, he blamed Nehru, chiefly. 'He shall always rave, spew and curse the English for hours and hours—but shall always act just the opposite.'

In one of his early letters to Pabitra, he made a flurry of allegations:

You must understand once for all that JN is a confirmed communist—in disguise...He knows very well the gullibility of the Indian masses, who are mostly illiterate kisan-labourers etc—it is on their cheated votes that he is in the chair. And he is a past master in guiles. It is solely for him that the Communists are flourishing. In order to usher in Communism, he has been juggling with words and phrases all these years to whitewash communism with the brush of socialism, welfare. And he has tricked India in such a sinister-satanic web that, it may well require God's own intelligence to rescue Mother India from this diabolic plot...All his near and dear and other relatives have got huge fortune: all of them have been extremely well and highly placed. About a crore is being spent on his own self. He has but a few years to live. So, what does he care, what happens of India or the world after his death. He does not believe in God. He is a Godless man. So, why shall he feel the qualms of consciousness?

These charges are as revolting as they are disturbing.

From Bhagwanji's point of view, Nehru frittered away India's interests by making her part of the British Commonwealth of Nations after independence. Worse, he implied that India's long-term strategic interests were made subservient to those of the world powers, and that if it were not for what he [Bhagwanji] did post-1947, India would turn into a battleground for the Cold War. He wrote this in 1962:

JN has played his treacherous game (of Mir Jafar, Jaychand, Vibhishan) with the people of India in such a manner and has manipulated the whole thing in such a way that any miscalculated step by them might make simple and innocent India and her people victims of the most horrible and undesirably hellish (game of) war!

Bhagwanji even claimed that as and when all the documents concerning the Transfer of Power in 1947 are made public, Indians would know why he had to go into hiding. While most Transfer of Power records are now in public domain and they do throw some light on Subhas's fate—that he might have not perished in Taiwan and was probably in Soviet Russia—there are some more records that are still being held classified by the British government. In May 2013, the Ministry of External Affairs in New Delhi revealed in response to a Right to Information request filed by well-known RTI activist SC Agrawal that the historic records relating to India's joining the Commonwealth of Nations in 1949 were, quite unbelievably, untraceable.

Some valuable insight is nevertheless available. Legendary TN Kaul, former Ambassador to the USSR, the US and Foreign Secretary, wrote in his memoirs that even after independence, Russians 'still looked upon India as a colony of Britain' and 'could not understand why we still wanted to remain in the Commonwealth [group of former colonies of the British Empire], when we had suffered so much at the hands of British imperialism'. Strong words from a man *India Today* described in the review of his book *Reminiscences, Discreet and Indiscreet* as 'a self-confessed unrepentant Nehruphile'.

In January 1950, Joseph Stalin granted an audidence to Indian ambassador Sarvepalli Radhakrishnan, the would—be President. 'Stalin asked several questions regarding India's position in the Commonwealth and seemed anxious to know if she was more or less independent than, say, Canada,' reads the MEA record of the meeting, kept at Nehru Memorial Museum and Library.

When it had come to the crunch in 1947, all vows of attaining *Purna Swaraj* (complete independence) were discarded by the Indian leadership of the day. They settled for dominion status. Mahatma Gandhi favoured it, but Subhas Bose always opposed it. He would have never liked India to be a part of the Commonwealth.

'Free' India remained a no-go area for 'Dead Man'. The chiefs of the Indian Air Force and the Navy were still British, and many of their Indian subordinates were more British

OGDENSBURG JOURNAL THURSDAY, MAY

Gandhi's Successor May Be Man Who'll Seek Full Independence From Britain

Chandra Bose Clinches His Hold on Indian Congress

By MILTON BRONNER

London—After Mahatma Gandhi—who?

That is a question asked not only by the massed millions of India, but by the British government which must face the future desires of over 350,000,000 people in that great sub-continent.

Pandit Nehru

Time was when it looked as if the man who would be the favorite leader of the masses would be Pandit Jawahar Lal Nehru. But now Gandhi's successor is expected to be Subhas Chandra Bose.

The two last in past times have been Gandhi's bright young men. Both at times went far beyond his desires. Nehru broke away, but now stands more with Gandhi again. Bose has brgken away entirely.

Mahatma Gandhi

Both have been president of the Indian National Congress, that powerful political party which has 5,000,000 dues-paying members and which controls the government in nine out of the 11 provinces of British India.

Subhas Chandra Bose

Officer of the big city of Calcutta and later, in 1930, was elected Mayor. In 14 years, he was arrested 10 times and jailed for a total of eight years, often without any trial. At one time, as Mayor, he conducted his office in jail. Several times the British had to release him lest he die of tuberculosis.

Last year he mocked Chamberlain, asking why, if he was so concerned about self-determination for the Sudeten Germans, he did not grant the same right to nationalists in the British Empire.

He scorns the constitution the Brisith parliafent voted to India. His objective is complete Indian independence, with the Indians making their own constitution.

"Then," he says, "we will determine our future relations with Britain through a voluntary treaty in which we will meet as equals."

N. BARNES, WIFE ARE GUESTS AT NORFOLK

Norfolk — Mr. and Mrs. Nelson Barnes of Brookdale spent Sunday

[Ogdensburg Journal on 11 May 1939]

than them. Indians did not head the Indian Army, Air Force and Navy until 1949, 1955 and 1958. Such was the state of affairs that India's national security structure did not undergo any change after the British left. 'The framework Lord Ismay formulated and Lord Mountbatten recommended was accepted by a national leadership unfamiliar with the intricacies of national security management. There has been very little change over the past 52 years,' the Kargil Review Committee report of 1999 flatly accepted.

In the wake of the disastrous war with China in 1962, India was compelled to overhaul her military. Consequently, Mountbatten and top British commanders visited India in May 1963 at Nehru's invitation. In the intelligence arena, British suzerainty continued till the late 1960s, if not beyond.

MI5 itself made it known to the entire world a few years ago, even as the nation which propagates the ideals of truth and ahimsa to the world continues to resort to great secrecy. The British intelligence agency's official website informs us: **'The government of Jawaharlal Nehru agreed to the stationing of an MI5 Security Liaison Officer (SLO) in New Delhi after the end of British rule.** ...In other newly independent Commonwealth countries, as in India**, the continued presence of an SLO became a significant, though usually undisclosed, part of the transfer of power.'** [Emphasis by authors]

These startling details also appeared in the authorised history of MI5 by Prof Christopher Andrew, which revealed on the basis of official records that in March 1947 deputy head of MI5 Guy Liddell obtained the agreement of the Nehru government for the stationing of the SLO. The first SLO was Lieutenant Colonel Kenneth Bourne, through whom MI5 was supplied with information pertaining to Bose by the Intelligence Bureau.

If all this could have been kept secret for so long (India is officially completely silent till date), what if there is more to it? What if there were other secret, unwritten, undisclosed agreements as power was transferred to those Indians who were amenable to the British proposals?

His disapproval of the state of affairs in India in post-1947 period prolonged Bhagwanji's self-imposed exile.

MAIL TODAY
SUNDAY
YOU COULD DIE AT A PETROL STATION
GUNG-HO
PARRIKAR SAYS RAFALE DEAL IS LIKE OXYGEN TO IAF
'Bourne paper' from National Archives shows how British-era surveillance on Netaji's family continued after Independence
IB RATTED ON BOSE'S KIN TO BRITISH INTEL
EXCLUSIVE
MAIL TODAY & INDIA TODAY
AS MORE damaging revelations tumble out of the snooping on Netaji Subhas Chandra Bose's family by the Jawaharlal Nehru government, a declassified document from National Archives shows the Intelligence Bureau (IB) informed British internal secret service MI5 about its discoveries.
Turn to Page 2

[Mail Today, 10 April 2015]

Instead of returning home, he went from Siberia to China on a covert mission to help his Soviet benefactors in return for their generosity in giving him shelter. He always felt indebted towards Russia and China. He blurted out in an angry moment years later: 'Russia and China have given me everything. They have put everything at stake to keep me alive…Should I be theirs or India's who has abandoned me?'

Despite his apparent support to Russia and China, he had no illusion about their ambitions. 'Don't think I am with all that China is doing,' he told Bijoy Nag in 1973. His debt of gratitude didn't cloud his vision, or his intent. At the end of the day he was, in his own words, 'a fanatic of his only God, his motherland'.

In 1949, rumours began to do the rounds in India and elsewhere that Subhas Bose was in China. A bombshell was then dropped by Sarat Chandra Bose, Subhas' (and Suresh's) elder brother, the person closest to him. No one disputes that if Bose were alive, and in a position to communicate after 1945, the one person he would have reached out to was his *mejda*. Sarat made a public declaration, fitting well with the narrative Bhagwanji would outline later. On 7 October 1949, Sarat's paper *The Nation*, ran this frontpage story:

The Nation

Chairman, Editorial Board: SARAT CHANDRA BOSE

CALCUTTA, FRIDAY, OCTOBER 7, 1949. ASWIN 20, 1356 B.S. TOWN EDITION TWO ANNAS

LEUCODERMA (WHITE SPOTS)

LEPROSY

NETAJI IN RED CHINA

SARAT BOSE ASSERTS GOVT. POSSESS INFORMATION

Why Truman Invites Nehru

Greater Betrayal In Offing

(By The Nation's Staff Reporter)

Mr. Sarat Chandra Bose said here yesterday (Thursday) that the Government of India were in possession of definite information that Netaji Subhas

It goes without saying that a person of Sarat's standing and intelligence would not have published this in such a manner, without being sure about it. When asked why his brother was 'not coming to India', Sarat Bose replied, 'I don't think the time is ripe for his coming back home.' In 1956 came another shocker. Close Subhas Bose associate Muthuramalingam Thevar, whose statue now stands in the Parliament House precincts in New Delhi as a tribute to his eminence, told newspapers such as *Hindustan Standard*, that he had secretly visited China on Sarat Bose's instruction.

Wednesday, April 4, 1956

STORY OF MEETING NETAJI LAST FEBRUARY

REPORTED STAY NOW IN CHINA

From Our Delhi Office

APRIL 3.—Sri Muthuramalinga Thevar, member of the Madras Legislative Assembly and a Forward Bloc leader, told a Press conference in New Delhi on Tuesday that he would furnish conclusive proof that Netaji Subhas Chandra Bose was alive if the Inquiry Committee appointed by the Government of India to go into this question was reconstituted.

HE said that he was prepared to tell the Committee as much as it was possible in the circumstances, provided he was convinced that the Committee would be able to resist outside influence.

His suggestion was that Dr. Radhabinod Pal, the eminent Jurist, be appointed Chairman of the Committee.

Sri Thevar who claims to have been a member of the 5-man War Council formed by Netaji before his mysterious disappearance from India said that he might tell the Prime Minister also about Netaji if he was sympathetic.

war criminals in Tokyo should be invited to function as the Chairman.

Apart from this, it is necessary on the part of the Govt. to make it known categorically to the public whether Netaji's name is still in the list of war criminals and if not, when it was removed and how? Subhas Babu

25th March, 1946 said that Mr. Nair (who was Engineering-in-Charge of Municipal Works of Singapore at the time of its fall to Japanese, said "I do not believe the story of Netaji's death, because the plane in which he was travelling and which is alleged to have crashed was seen in Hongkong the next day without any damage or repair—on March 12th, 1946.

Gandhiji while talking to Messrs. Shah Nawaz and Seihgal, the I. N. A. heroes, said "whatever you may tell me to the contrary, I still believe in my heart of hearts that Netaji Subhas Bose is alive."

Subhas Babu was taken to Manchuria by the Japanese because it is due to Subhas Babu that the neutrality pact between Russia and Japan was kept in tact in spite of Japan remaining in the Axis Block and Russia declaring war against Japan before one week of surrender. The surrender of Japan was an arranged affair, to avoid Anglo-American entry into Manchuria. The military might of Japan land, navy and air to a very great extent had been transferred to Manchuria long before the surrender. War ended in September, 1945. An Asiatic Liberation Army was formed by Netaji and the Japanese, Chinese (under the leadership of Mao Se Tung), Burmese Indo-Chinese, Malays, Indonesians, Phillipines, Siamese had all joined this army with the assistance of the Russian Govt. The army started fighting in January, 1946, in China. This was reported as a Communist revolt. The so called revolt was able to drive Chiang-kai-Shek out of China because the Chinese military men had understood the co-operation of China, Japan, India and all the South-East Asian countries. Then they came to the conclusion that Chiang-kai-Shek was a show-boy of America. So the

Between his anecdotes and commentaries on Russia and China, Bhagwanji would often regale his followers with tales of his travels in the mysterious and mountainous terrain in Tibet, Roof of the World, in the 1950s. While much of his association with Tibet appear to have been spiritual in nature, he made an astounding claim about the milestone event that has defined relations between India and Tibet, with long-term implications for Indo–China ties. He guided the Dalai Lama out of the land increasingly coming under Chinese occupation into India, he said. Not only that. Bhagwanji said that he trained in guerilla tactics the local warrior tribes that rose in revolt against Communist rule and facilitated the Dalai Lama's escape. The year was 1959. Three years later, India stood on the verge of a war with China.

With the knowledge of an insider, Bhagwanji described some of the instances of betrayal that helped bring on the Chinese onslaught. 'A son of Bengal had sent an expert report to JN on measures that needed to be taken at key positions to prevent incursions by enemies across the Himalayas, but JN was not allowed to receive the report,' Bhagwanji wrote in a letter in the mid-1960s. In a scandalous allegation, he claimed that the report was smuggled out of the Defence Ministry to Pakistan and from there to China. China used exactly the same routes marked in the report. In a recent book, Ashali Varma, daughter of Lt Gen PS Bhagat, the co-author of the Henderson Brooks-Bhagat report on the 1962 debacle, stated something strikingly similar.

According to Bhagwanji, China had no intention of grabbing Indian territory initially. It was Prime Minister Nehru who made China aggressive by his bravado. 'It is suicidally foolish and sheer meanness to underestimate and make fun of one's adversary.'

The exchanges Bhagwanji had with Pabitra Mohan Roy soon after the war make interesting reading:

Whether war should be brutal, cathartic or a human

business is besides the point. Everyone knows that no war can be conducted and fought with kid gloves. Modern war, especially, takes an appalling toll both of human life and property. No civilised nation risks it lightly, but when it is forced on it, it has to be waged in a manner that makes the opponent wince. This is done not in any vindictive spirit but in a cold, calculated manner to break the opponents' morale so that he is forced to sue for peace. Abstract principles have nothing to do with the waging of war.

The central strategy of warfare, according to him, was the sequence of 'concentration-dispersion-distribution', which he explained to Pabitra. 'The whole principle of war is condensed in this one single word "concentration".'

Basically, the approach is simple: The enemy must be made to disperse his forces under pressure and should be kept in the dark about the point or points where a concentrated attack will be made to bring about disorganisation. To ensure success, two major problems must be solved—disorganisation and exploitation. One precedes and one follows the actual blow. You must somehow wrest the initiative from the invader and aim at bringing about disorganisation of his forces in some vital sector in the frontline as well as on his home front. The more you make it clear that you shall fight only at the places of his choosing and disperse your forces at his dictation, the more you shall place yourselves at a disadvantage. You have to parry the enemy on all fronts including the home front. The so-called wise men of the world say, and hope,

'War will have no future.' But experience suggests that war has some purpose that is beyond the ambit of human reason, despite its palpable unreasonableness as a way of settling human issues. That purpose may be as a corrective to greater evil, as a cleansing of the spirit of a people and age from corruption and sins.

The Chinese, he said, were following to the letter the elementary rules of strategy laid down by 'experts in warfare'. 'JN and his henchmen', he added, should be made aware of it. Bhagwanji's Do's and Don'ts for strategists and tacticians were:

Dos

- *Adjust your ends to your means…It is folly to bite off more than you can chew, and the beginning of military wisdom is to know what can't be done. So, learn to face facts while still preserving faith.*
- *Keep your object always in mind while adapting your plan to circumstances.*
- *Choose the line (or course) of least expectation.*
- *Exploit the line of least resistance.*
- *Take a line of operation which offers alternative objectives. For you will then put your opponent on the horns of a dilemma, which goes far to assure the chance of gaining one objective at least—whichever he guards least—and may enable you to gain one after the other.*
- *Ensure that both plans and dispositions are elastic or adaptable.*

Don'ts

- *Don't lunge whilst your opponent can parry. The experience of history shows that no effective stroke is possible until the enemy's power of resistance or evasion is paralysed.*
- *Don't renew an attack along the same line or form.*

Bhagwanji's self-proclaimed first major direct involvement in India's national affairs came during the Chinese invasion of 1962. There are divergent views as to why on 21 November 1962, China unexpectedly declared a unilateral ceasefire on the Sino-Indian border. 'Dead Man' told Pabitra, as the latter noted in his journal, that it was his intervention which made the Chinese back off. Atul Sen had informed Nehru about Bhagwanji in August 1962. Pabitra landed in Neemsar soon, but had to wait for a while before he could contact Bhagwanji sometime in November. The reason for the prolonged wait was Bhagwanji's absence from Neemsar.

'This old faquir had to go out twice, while here. Once for about 5 ½ weeks before Nov, and once for about 7 weeks (a month before that),' Bhagwanji wrote to Pabitra in one of his earliest letters, written in December 1962. He went out, he claimed, to manoeuvre his way through the Chinese leadership in order to ensure the withdrawal of the PLA. *It is not for nothing that an old man, in the course of the recent months went out of India twice, braving all the fatal hazards to his life and frail body. The result is before you. As I have told you, war is not an emotional business. It is a cold calculated affair.*

To Leela Roy, he mentioned that the unilateral ceasefire was announced within fifteen days of his return. Then, in another Bengali letter to her in 1964, he hinted that Indian government was tracking his movements, and thought that he was in China (whereas he was in India). *Someone dead is not on this side of the Himalayas. Do you understand? That is to say that officially Mritabhoot is not on this side.*

The 'intelligence' shared by Bhagwanji on the post-war period was even more sensational. He indicated that he had prevailed upon the Chinese to make a top secret conciliatory offer to Nehru—an offer that China agreed to make only out of deference to him, even at the cost of losing some standing in the global Communist order. Along with the proposal went a message from him to Nehru, 'I want to come back.' But there was no response. The message was sent a second time through a mutually known and respected foreigner, and then again for a third time through an Indian. Each time the message was met with silence. Bhagwanji mentioned that after Nehru's death, Lal Bahadur Shastri too remained silent about his desire to 'return' to India.

It is impossible to determine the veracity of these claims till all intelligence files have been released by the government. However, stray references suggest that the rumours about Bose and China peaked during the 1962 war and were noted by the Intelligence Bureau. As a matter of fact, former Delhi Congress chief Jagdish Kodesia told something startling to the Khosla Commission. He testified that during the 1962 war, he overheard at Home Minister Lal Bahadur Shastri's house that 'information during Chinese aggression did come that Netaji was living'.

One declassified Top Secret IB record we accessed under RTI is dated November 1963 and is signed by BN Mullik.

> to exploit Netaji's name. They have been propagatin
> since the last 14 years that the Netaji would return
> A propaganda was even started when the Chinese invad
> our country last year that Netaji was coming with
> the invading army. This group, whose leadership

As the undisputed czar of the Indian intelligence apparatus for an incredible fourteen years, Mullik met Prime Minister Nehru virtually each day and was one of his closest confidants.

As any junior-level intelligence officer can tell, the IB Director's personally signed notes such as this one are distilled from heaps of material. So, for this one document, there must be several reports detailing each and every aspect mentioned in it. The IB must have several reports regarding the 'propaganda' during the Chinese attack that 'Netaji was coming with the invading army'.

How we wish Justice Sahai Commission had made an attempt to extract information from the intelligence agencies! In our affidavit before it, we had specifically requested for 'a full accounting of Intelligence Bureau's insight concerning

Netaji mystery, including Gumnami Baba angle'. If the commission had gone along this line, we would have advised it to start with consulting retired intelligence officers—because only they know the system well enough to get things out of it.

Till such time, all we have is Dead Man's tales. Piled up one on another, each more incredible than the previous one. Some leave us flabbergasted. In the 1970s, Bhagwanji claimed to have visited a whole city in the deep underground with all modern amenities in China, which, he claimed, could not be destroyed by ten atom bombs. Dixia Cheng, a massive bomb shelter beneath Beijing, remained unknown to the world till it was opened to tourists in 2000. How could he have known about it back then?

Though he approved of Soviet and Chinese leaders at personal levels, Bhagwanji repeatedly predicted the demise of Communism. It would die in the land of its birth, he wrote to Leela Roy in early 1963, and eventually it shall disappear as a political force 'on both sides'—probably a reference to the Soviet Union and China: 'Diabolical Godless Communism shall be buried 1,000 fathoms deep, never to rise.'

Bhagwanji's insights were way above ordinary at times:

China is dreaming that it has to re-establish the Central Celestial State that it once was. Communism is a fencing for the outer world…China is a huge race which was asleep or was under the spell of addiction for a very long time. It was under the domination of foreign races. A sleeping race like this cannot be reawakened to do something big by imposing a democratic framework. [Translated from Bengali]

Speaking at Halifax International Security Forum in November 2020, top US diplomat Kenneth Braithwaite made these remarks: 'The Chinese are looking to their history. They know that at one point in time, they were the Middle Kingdom where most advances in mankind came out of. They know that they have the opportunity to do that again.'

To Pabitra, Bhagwanji gave a detailed account of what he claimed to have seen in Russia:

Communism, as was understood by dogmatists, is no more in 'R'! Yes. It is a fact. 'R' has got, now, five distinct social classes or strata: (1) The very uppermost class (2) The upper or elite (3) The privileged Bureaucracy-cum-Party cadre (4) The middle class and (5) The common people (just like here). Now the 'Govt & Party' is vigorously encouraging and inviting women of 'R' to look more sleek and thin and cultivate and have figures like the sophisticated West! ...'R' is now being governed by oligarchy....

The war of 1965 with Pakistan and the subsequent developments left Bhagwanji disappointed with the Indian leadership. Yet again, speaking on the subject like someone who had top level intelligence inputs from several sources, Bhagwanji claimed that Pakistan plunged into the incursion with tacit encouragement from the UK. The Pakistan army decided to go for the jugular, Bhagwanji wrote to Leela Roy, at a time when the prestige of the Indian Army had taken a beating after the 1962 China onslaught.

He referred to a conversation between Ayub Khan and Lal Bahadur Shastri in London where the former apparently told the latter 'I can walk over to Delhi, any hour I want to, you know?' leaving Shastri speechless. He went on to claim that Ayub spoke in similar vein many times in Pakistan, showing great contempt towards Hindus. 'These *dhotiwala* Hindus, what do they know of fighting? They know only to lose and run away from the battlefield. They only know how to be good slaves.' As it came to be known much later, Ayub Khan did send his army chief General Mohammad Musa a Top Secret order (Annexure G to GHQ letter no 4050/5/MO-1 dated 29 August 1965): 'As a general rule, Hindu morale would not stand for more than a couple of hard blows delivered at the right time and the right place. Such opportunities should therefore be sought and exploited.'

Taking a dig at India's political leaders, Bhagwanji retorted, 'Whatever the Pakistanis thought and said is the bitter truth—but those truths are applicable only to the politicians, not to the Indian Army.' Bhagwanji gave strong hints of not only sending messages to a few unspecified persons in the military establishment 'through some roundabout/convoluted channels', but also claimed to have crossed over to Pakistan, which would be impossible without the help of the Indian Army. However, he was disappointed with the end result. His cues, he rued, were 'not used to the hilt'. He wrote to Leela Roy:

Pak military were fleeing Lahore like squirrels. It was a matter of punching—taking...Sialkot, Muzaffarabad and 1/3rd *of Kashmir were a matter of one week. 'Someone' was there himself. Someone crossed and re-crossed Ichogil. Thrice had been in Shalimar! Hell of Hells, that thumbnail area of Chamb could be literally turned into a veritable inferno and not a soul to call Allah! Dash it all! They behaved (both sides—India, Pakistan) just like copybook puppet soldiers. Both sides stuck to the set pattern of Sandhurst* [British military academy] *manoeuvres. The generals of each side could anticipate the next move of the other side. Yet something more would have happened (in seven more days the Kashmir problem wouldn't be there, Lahore would have been yours) if LB* [Lal Bahadur Shastri] *didn't wilt at the scolding of the 'others'. I couldn't imagine that Jayantababu* [Army chief Jayanto Nath Chaudhuri] *would get entangled in politics.* [Translated]

Writing to Leela Roy in a letter shortly after the Tashkent declaration, Bhagwanji made an astonishing prediction. In East Pakistan, the agitation over the 'six point formula' demanding provincial autonomy had commenced in June 1966, led by Sheikh Mujibur Rahman. There was, however, no indication yet of the magnitude of the political eruption that would shape up in the next few years, tearing the eastern part of Pakistan away to form a new country. There was nothing in the air to indicate the extent of military suppression that East Pakistan would be subjected to. It was at this time that Bhagwanji wrote to Roy:

A terrible situation is being created in East and West Pakistan because of which Ayub will have to become Nadir Shah in order to trample down East Pakistan. If Ayub cannot fully become Nadir Shah for fulfilling the goal only then there shall be found another one, to take his place, to become full Nadir Shah....India Govt's security shall stand jeopardised, but adequate arrangements have been made to ensure that other powers are not able to join in. [Translated]

All these were spoken and written by Bhagwanji much before the conflagration in East Pakistan took secessionist form. In his evidence before the Khosla Commission on 6 September 1972, Sunil Das recalled that in 1965, Leela Roy had warned her close associates that 'something was likely to happen in the Indo-Pakistan border—between India and East Pakistan' which would result in the influx of about 50-60 lakh refugees. Roy, along with her colleagues, spent hours travelling along the border. 'In March 1971, Indo-Pak conflict came about...when one crore crossed the border from East Pakistan to India....Whether this was a hint sent to her or whether it was a divine disclosure, I do not know,' said Das, without mentioning Bhagwanji.

As the Indian Army started training the Mukti Bahini, Bhagwanji wrote to Pabitra in July 1971, 'Match carefully all that I explained to you in Naimisharanya [with the current developments]....This is the beginning of the fulfilment of the last two phases of my divine promise.'

When Bijoy Nag reached Basti in September 1971 to spend the days of Durga Puja, Bhagwanji was more specific, 'It will be a line written in history that this area was known for a short time as Pakistan.' All of a sudden, he started talking about the strategic importance of Jessore. 'Have you seen the Jessore fort? I know its layout,' he asked: 'On the top at the *agnikon* (south east) is the barrack of the Baluch Regiment—a huge armoury beneath that; towards east from there are the officers' place; in the *ishankon* (north east) the Pathan Regiment—there is a huge oil reservoir underground, like a lake—at the middle there is a huge pillar; on the north west—a huge runway. This could have been captured during the days of the heavy monsoon. The fort can be taken in three days.'

Confined to a decrepit room of a dilapidated building in north India, a man in the garb of a *sanyasi* was talking casually about the military importance of a town in another country, whose importance would be known to the country more than two months later.

On 7 December 1971, Jessore became the first city of East Pakistan to be cleared of Pakistani forces by the Indian

Army, without any resistance. As reported in *The New York Times*, just after Jessore had fallen, General Sam Manekshaw issued a message for Pakistani troops: 'Your fate is sealed.'

Bhagwanji indicated several times that he had been travelling in and out of the country, both before and after the war. Of the many letters from Bhagwanji written during this period, the most astounding was one written to Pabitra on 11 November 1971 embossed with the official emblem of the Indian government. 'Today I am somewhere else,' he wrote, with the 'responsibility of many keys and levers in these hands'.

Around the same time, Bhagwanji informed Pabitra that he had returned to Basti after undertaking a few missions abroad, and that until the specified tasks are accomplished, he will have to remain in the background. The aim of the mission was to 'disintegrate P[akistan] and to ensure that India stands to gain from its military intervention 'if no mistake is committed out of fear, as [General J N] Chaudhuri did'. The letter also refers to some of the identities by which he was known to different involved parties.

Going by the followers' recollections of what Bhagwanji had told them, Sam Manekshaw was aware of Bhagwanji's existence. It started before Manekshaw was elevated as Army Chief. When he was GOC-in-C of the Eastern Command, Manekshaw would secretly confabulate with Bhagwanji's emissary, goes one of the claims. Sometimes, in the dead of night, like a scene from an espionage thriller, Manekshaw would join Bhagwanji in a secret place to take stock of the war. It is further claimed that bombing of the Governor House in Dhaka one day before Pakistan eventually surrendered was at Bhagwanji's instance. While he did not approve of Indira Gandhi, Bhagwanji nonetheless admired her courage and held that she had a better sense of national security than her father Jawaharlal Nehru and Lal Bahadur Shastri.

The flip side of the story is that there is no published material or declassified record to show any role of any mysterious figure in the 1971 war. To the best of our knowledge, only one reference to Subhas Bose appears in declassified US records. A derisive, stray comment was made in a State Department telegram originating from the US Embassy in Dhaka on 3 January 1975. Referring to the reported shooting of a political leader, the embassy telegram said that unless his body was displayed, 'there will soon grow up stories that he still lives, *a la* Subhas Chandra Bose'. This meant that the rumour that Bose was still alive was current in Bangladesh too in that period.

There is no doubt that Bose's memories were summoned during the Bangladesh liberation war period. Going by Yatindra Bhatnagar's book *Bangla Desh: Birth of a Nation,* Bose's classmate at Cambridge and later ICS officer CC Desai, who used to be India's envoy to different countries including Pakistan before becoming an MP, saw shades of his friend in Rahman's tactics. Mujib's 'directives immediately before Yahya troops struck, may be well compared with Netaji's thesis of anti-imperialist struggle and Samveda [Samyavad] propounded by him in 1933'. Mukti Vahini's war cry '*Joi Bangla*' was inspired by '*Jai Hind*'.

Surely, we are not qualified to authenticate Bhagwanji's boast that he orchestrated what happened in East Pakistan. But we are perplexed to note that invaluable records pertaining to the 1971 war were destroyed, as reported in *The Times of India* on 9 May 2010.

Bangladesh war files destroyed by Army

True Story Of 1971 Is Lost Forever

Josy Joseph | TNN

New Delhi: The history of the 1971 India-Pakistan war will never be fully written. Most official records of the war that led to the liberation of Bangladesh have been destroyed. The destroyed files include those on the creation of the Mukti Bahini — the Bangladesh freedom fighters — all appreciation and assessments made by the army during the war period, the orders issued to fighting formations, and other sensitive operational details.

Authoritative army sources said all records of the period, held at the Eastern Command in Kolkata, were destroyed immediately after the 1971 war. This has remained secret until now.

According to at least two former chiefs of the Eastern Command and other senior army officers TOI spoke to, the destruction may have been deliberate.

They say the destruction may have happened when Lt General Jagjit Singh Aurora, the Indian army's commanding officer on the east-

General A A K Niazi (centre) signs the surrender documents in Dhaka on December 16, 1971. Lt General Aurora is on the left

The Missing Files

- Include those on the creation of the Mukti Bahini and sensitive operational details
- The files were probably shredded when Lt General Jagjit Singh Aurora, hero of the war, was heading the Eastern Command
- Army headquarters may have some records but the picture can never be complete

were part of the operations

er in August 1974 I asked to

The story was filed by award-winning journalist Josy Joseph. The destroyed files include those on the creation of the Mukti Bahini, all appreciation and assessments made by the Army during the war period, the orders issued to fighting formations, and other sensitive operational details. The Indira government had resorted to burying deep in the ground time capsules with a view to perpetuating myths favouring the Nehru-Gandhis, so this destruction of 1970 war records must be viewed with suspicion.

We are further intrigued by the fact Bhagwanji had a connect with Sitaram Omkarnath Thakur, a highly revered Bengali saint who had known Subhas Bose prior to 1945, and many other leading personalities of that era too. Omkarnath's leading disciples were IB Director BN Mullik and Major General Sujan Singh Uban.

[Sitaram Omkarnath Thakur and BN Mullik. Source: Reflections of an eternal being: Photographic kaleidoscope of Sri Sitaramdas Omkarnath]

Uban was the first head of India's secret force named Special Frontier Force. SFF was created after the 1962 war by the Intelligence Bureau. Later, SFF operated under the operational command of R&AW. In 1971, SFF carried out highly successful operations in East Pakistan that are the stuff of legends. SFF is hardly discussed in India. One rare instance was in September 2020, when it came to light that SFF was involved in the operation to occupy previously unoccupied heights in Ladakh as China and India had a face-off.

Here is a detail guaranteed to send a chill down your spine. In his book *The Gurus of India*, Major General Sujan Singh Uban disclosed that in December 1970, when 'there were no signs of war anywhere', Omkarnath took him to a temple. Standing before an idol of Durga, he said, 'Ma, this is Sujan. He will be going to war…Make him a powerful instrument to bring victory to the country.'

What actually happened in the war cannot be described here but it proved to me and my command that a force of immeasurable magnitude was working for us, destroying the enemy's will to fight and protecting us like an impenetrable shield.

Apart from the roles he played in the three major armed conflicts in the subcontinent, Bhagwanji claimed his involvement in other global affairs too. For this, he claimed to have travelled frequently.

Oh, you simply cannot understand how terribly floating the

[Maj. Gen. Uban with Omkarnath. Source unknown to authors. Will be credited once known]

Ghost of the Dead shall have to be! The Ghost of the Dead shall have to float in and out…shall have to float here and there and 'other places', like a 'spectre'…Prince Lucifer somewhere, in some Erebus, and somewhere as Gabriel.

We cannot comprehend how Bhagwanji was able to allude to the explosion of Chinese H bomb in 1964, Arab-Israel talks—inside information on highest level diplomatic negotiations between Russia and Egypt—when these were either within the realm of state secrecy or far away in the future.

A follower told us that Bhagwanji possessed more than one fake passport. In March 1963, during the initial days of contact with his followers and just after the Indo-China war, he wrote, 'After crossing over to this side, I have made 25 trips including the last two journeys. Try to understand, how much stress can this old body take.' One of the reasons he chose to be in UP was that it was close to the porous Nepal border. 'I know the Himalayan region like my palm.'

He further claimed that he had set up five doubles, who could function as him in his absence. He wrote that he himself was training them, telling them all the details of his life which were known to none other or to a very few.

The picture of himself painted by Bhagwanji was no less than a superman in the shadows moving across the world, engaging different powers, all with the same purpose: to bring glory to India. All his sacrifices, hardships, travels, negotiations and interventions had this specific outcome.

This old faquir of yours gives his most solemn word of honour in the inviolable and most divine name of Mother Jagadamba Durga Bhavani Chandi that Bengal, India shall rise again in her full glory.

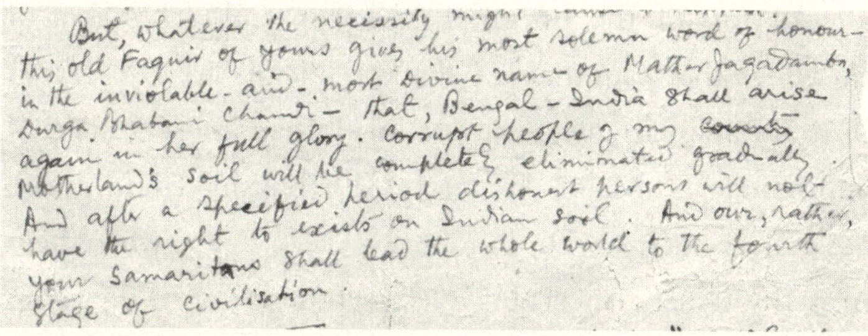

But, whatever the necessity might [illegible]
this old Faquir of yours gives his most solemn word of honour –
in the inviolable – and – most divine name – of Mother Jagadamba,
Durga Bhabani Chandi – that, Bengal – India shall arise
again in her full glory. Corrupt people of my country
Motherland's soil will be completely eliminated gradually.
And after a specified period dishonest persons will not
have the right to exists on Indian soil. And our, rather,
your Samaritans shall lead the whole world to the fourth
stage of civilisation.

TEN

IMPOSTOR BABA?

STICKING TO THEIR core argument that it was not possible for Netaji to become some Gumnami Baba, a number of people continue to claim that he was an impostor. To them, all the evidence put forward means nothing. All they do is to shake their heads and say, 'I don't believe it.'

On top of the list of disbelievers and debunkers of the belief that Gumnami Baba was Netaji are BJP leader Dr Subramanian Swamy, one of India's most respected commentators Major General GD Bakshi (Retd), and researchers such as Dr Purabi Roy. We agree with them on many issues concerning Netaji, but not their views on Gumnami Baba.

It was not our critics, but we only who furnished to Justice Vishnu Sahai Commission the details of different theories of Gumnami Baba's identity for whatever they are worth. The commission used our information selectively, picking up those parts that suited its approach to discount the Gumnami Baba-Netaji link beforehand.

All the same, different claims about Gumnami Baba's identity are that he was:

- One Krishna Dutt Upadhyay, a murderer in hiding
- An Anand Margi
- A CIA agent
- A Subhas Bose impostor, set up by the Intelligence Bureau

The theory that Bhagwanji was actually one Krishna Dutt Upadhyay was floated by Hindi newspaper *Janmorcha* on 3 November 1985. It was reconstructed and expanded thirty years later through a series of four articles in online news portal *Scroll.in* by Dhirendra K Jha, a political journalist. The man responsible for the original story in *Janmorcha* (who appears to have inspired the *Scroll.in* investigation) is Ayodhya-based veteran journalist Sheetla Singh, the paper's editor. *Scroll.in* culminated with the presentation of 'facts' that 'hint at' Gumnami Baba being Krishna Dutta Upadhyay or Kaptan Baba.

The grounds on which this claim is made are essentially the following:

1. A team led by Sheetla Singh visited Kolkata back in 1985 and interviewed Pabitra Mohan Roy, who stated

'with certainty' that Gumnami Baba was not Netaji. *Janmorcha*'s original frontpage story ran with the headline 'Close associates of Netaji say that he was not Netaji.'

2. *Janmorcha* received an anonymous letter on 2 November claiming that Gumnami Baba was indeed Upadhyay who had fled Ayodhya after committing a murder and after some time started living in Basti. The newspaper published the claim made in the letter the next day.
3. The Lucknow edition of daily *Amrit Prabhat* reported on 8 November 1985 that the police were investigating whether the man of mystery was Upadhyay in hiding.
4. Indu Kumar Pandey, former district magistrate of Faizabad (now Ayodhya) told *Scroll.in* that there were rumours that Gumnami Baba 'had killed somebody and was in hiding'. But the investigation into Gumnami Baba's identity was closed after the Allahabad High Court ordered preservation of Baba's belongings.
5. Brother of man murdered by Krishna Dutta Upadhyay claimed that one of the closest aides of Upadhyay was Seth Ishwardas Beni Prasad. *Scroll.in* claims Gumnami Baba's close follower Dr RP Mishra's wife told him that her husband used to meet Prasad often at Varanasi at the behest of Gumnami Baba.

In addition to the above, *Scroll.in* tried to blame the

Sangh Parivar, especially Shakti Singh of Ram Bhawan, for propagating the conspiracy theory that Gumnami Baba was Netaji.

Our responses to these arguments are:

'Statement' of Pabitra Mohan Roy: The police inquiry report of 1985, whose copy we possess, reads different from what *Janmorcha* reported: 'A police party was sent to Calcutta to talk to Dr Pabitra Mohan Roy and other associates of "Netaji" but 'none of them were able to give any information about this matter and, in fact, they appeared to be reticent about providing any information to the police.'

The same Pabitra Mohan Roy around that time told a Bhagwanji follower, 'Nation would burn, if he opened his mouth'. A mere claim in a newspaper doesn't by itself becomes gospel truth. Assuming it does, there were reports in other papers, such as *NIP*, detailing what transpired when cops questioned Pabitra, how he was not talking straight.

What actually happened is that Roy evaded the cops and the journalists who drove with them to Kolkata. Pabitra's son Ranendra, himself a Bhagwanji follower, confirmed to us that his father dodged cops and journalists. 'My father was Netaji's solider,' is how soft-spoken Ranendra introduced his father to us at his residence in Kolkata. As stated earlier in this book, he said his father had the order from his 'general' to 'keep his lips sealed'. We recorded an interview with Ranendra Roy and put it up on You Tube for everyone to see. Pity that Justice Sahai did not take evidence from Roy, and instead drew conclusion from Sheetla Singh's claim that Pabitra denied Bhagwanji was Netaji.

Roy's family scoffs at Sheetla Singh's claim. 'Netaji' was the pivot around which Pabitra's world revolved. As his granddaughter Indrani told one of us at her home in Michigan, USA, her grandfather addressed Bhagwanji straight and simple as 'Netaji' in his final years. Therefore, the claim that Bhagwanji was not Subhas Bose because Roy said so stands flipped on its head. The handwriting samples tested by Curt Baggett and Ashok Kashyap came from Pabitra's collection kept by his son, which establishes the oral claim.

Anonymous letter of 2 November 1985: A letter from an unnamed *Janmorcha* reader was turned into a page one-story by Sheetla Singh. This is not journalism, as any claim has to be cross-checked. *Janmorcha* provided no evidence in support of this claim. How do we know that letter was not planted by someone sitting in the local intelligence office to muddy the waters?

***Amrit Prabhat* investigated Gumnami Baba-Upadhyay link:** So? What was the outcome? Did the police arrest him? Why don't we find any reference to Upadhyay in the police report about Gumnami Baba's identity? It refers to only the claim that he was Netaji. There was never any other option.

Indu Kumar Pandey's claim: Pandey, who retired as the Chief Secretary of Uttarakhand, indeed handled the Gumnami Baba matter as the District Magistrate (DM) of Faizabad in 1985-86. We have copies of the relevant files from DM's office.

First, the quote attributed to Pandey in *Scroll.in* that 'investigation was closed after the Allahabad High Court took over the matter' is factually wrong and appears to be motivated. The files establish that the local inquiry into the identity of Bhagwanji was closed long before the Allahabad High Court issued an interim order on 10 February 1986 to secure Bhagwanji's belongings. In any case, court never asked the government to stop any inquiry.

With regard to Pandey's statement to *Scroll.in* that there were 'rumours that Gumnami Baba "had killed somebody and was in hiding"' (which means he could be fugitive Upadhyay)—nowhere in the bulky files, which also contain Indu Kumar Pandey's signed notes, etc. can we find any evidence to support the 'rumour that Gumnami Baba had killed somebody and was in hiding'.

If Bhagwanji was suspected to be some fugitive murderer, the authorities would have splashed this everywhere, given their intent to vociferously dismiss the claim that he was Netaji. In fact, Lalita Bose in her PIL before the Allahabad High Court charged Indu Kumar Pandey of 'sitting tight over the matter in a very callous manner'.

As it happened, at no point in time did the DM's office offer any evidence to back this line. We don't even see a single reference to Upadhyay in the official papers accessed by us. The state government never spoke along these lines either in the UP Assembly, where lengthy discussions took place in February 1986 and in March 2013, or before the Allahabad High Court as the case dragged on for years. The detailed counter-affidavit filed by the state government in 1999 in response to Lalita Bose's 1986 petition has no reference to Upadhyay at all. All it says is that the man couldn't have been Netaji because the [sham] police inquiry found no clear evidence.

Before the Allahabad High Court, all that the UP government did was deny that Gumnami Baba was Netaji. At no point in time was a reference to Krishna Dutt Upadhyay or someone else made. From this circumstantial evidence, we can deduce that the Upadhyay theory was pushed in media and on grapevine to muddy the waters. If only Justice Sahai had sought access to all records, especially those in the intelligence files. He never wanted to find out how deep was the rabbit hole.

Summarising the outcome of the official inquiry, Indu Kumar Pandey himself commented on 2 March 1986 that 'State Government has been informed of the inquiry conducted by the police in this matter and further instructions of the Govt are awaited.' See it for yourself! You see references to Pabitra, Netaji but no Upadhyay:

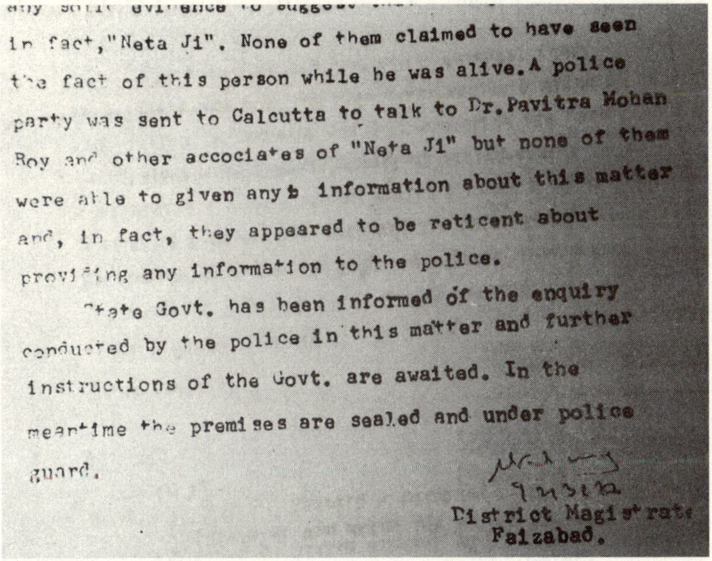

any solid evidence to suggest that ... in fact, "Neta Ji". None of them claimed to have seen the fact of this person while he was alive. A police party was sent to Calcutta to talk to Dr. Pavitra Mohan Roy and other accociates of "Neta Ji" but none of them were able to given any information about this matter and, in fact, they appeared to be reticent about providing any information to the police.

State Govt. has been informed of the enquiry conducted by the police in this matter and further instructions of the Govt. are awaited. In the meantime the premises are sealed and under police guard.

District Magistrate
Faizabad.

[DM of Faizabad sums up the case on 2 March 1986]

Claim of brother of man murdered by Krishna Dutta Upadhyay: How logical is *Scroll.in*'s attempt to link Bhagwanji with Upadhyay on the basis of a claimed connection with Seth Ishwardas Beni Prasad? Assuming that the Seth was a friend of Upadhyay and also had contact with Bhagwanji in no way proves that Bhagwanji and Upadhyay were one and the same. If 'A' is friends with 'B' and 'B' is friendly with 'C', it cannot be construed to mean that 'A' and 'C' are the same.

Secondly, not one person who knew Bhagwanji ever identified him as Upadhyay. Anyone with a surname like that would at least know Hindi properly. Given unusual structuring of sentences and preponderance of Bengali and Urdu words, Hindi was clearly not Gumnami Baba's first language.

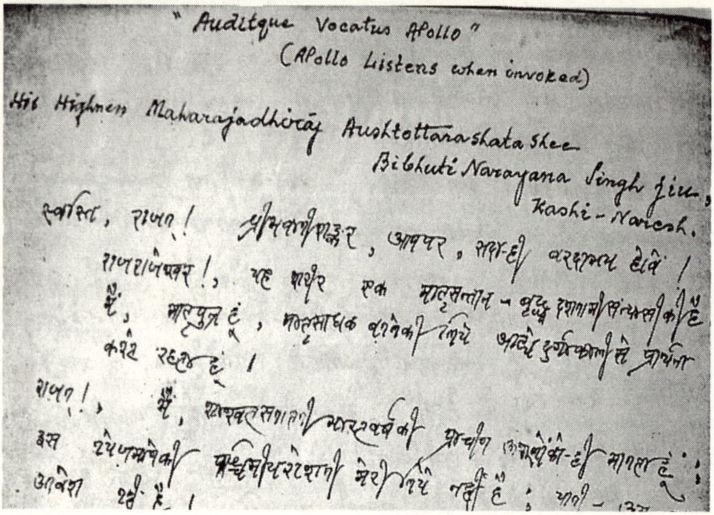
"Auditque Vocatus Apollo"
(Apollo Listens when invoked)
His Highness Maharajadhiraj Aushtottarashata Shee
Bibhuti Narayana Singh jiu,
Kashi-Naresh.

['I am a son of the motherland.' Bhagwanji writes to Dr Vibhuti Narayan Singh, former king of Kashi. Courtesy Ashok Tandon]

Thirdly, among the thousands of pages of records that we have seen, there is not a single mention of Beni Prasad anywhere. Certainly, a prominent well-wisher would find a mention somewhere? Nor do the living followers of Bhagwanji in Kolkata, who shared his secrets, remember ever hearing this name. The only Prasad who knew Bhagwanji lived in Kolkata. Shiv Prasad Nag (called 'Prasad' by Bhagwanji) was a teacher, not some businessman. His son appeared before Mukherjee Commission as witness.

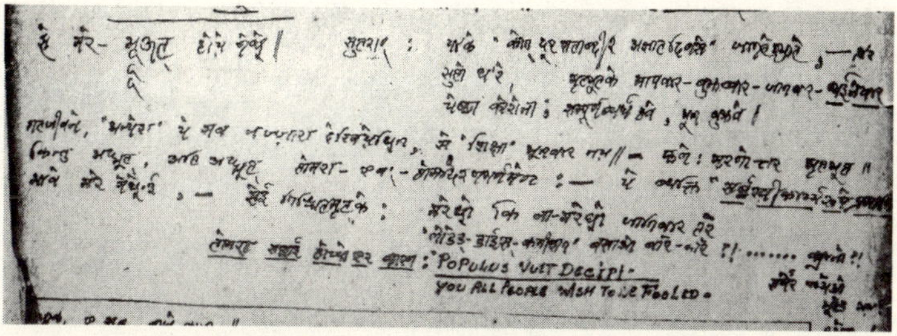
POPULUS VULT DECIPI -
YOU ALL PEOPLE WISH TO BE FOOLED.

[Bhagwanji to Prasad. Bengali written in Devnagari script: 'I have died and become a ghost. Very strange are you and your government that they constitute "loaded dice commissions" over and again just to know whether I am dead or not! You all are the reason behind this. Populus Vult Decipi - You All People Wish To Be Fooled]

Fourthly, *Scroll.in*'s source of information on Bhagwanji's alleged connection with Prasad—Dr RP Mishra's wife—is curious. Perhaps the old lady referred to Shiv Prasad Nag. The couple was usually not very forthcoming. Dr RP Mishra and his family, under whose care Bhagwanji spent his last years, consistently maintained a stony silence in public about his identity. Dr Mishra concealed the truth before the Mukherjee Commission and the Sahai Commission. Justice Sahai was constrained to write in his report that along with late Saraswati Devi, Mishra was 'the best person to shed light on the identity of Gumnami Baba…but regrettably he is not doing so. What a pity.'

Multiple interactions with the Mishra couple, now no more, convinced us that what they say for public consumption and what they hold secret are polar opposites. A little bit of true investigation would have informed *Scroll.in* of this. It is significant that although *Scroll.in* quoted

Mrs Mishra, they remained silent on her take on the identity of Bhagwanji. Did she tell them that he was Krishna Dutta Upadhyay? That is not the impression we get from them and their children. Mrs Mishra told us she never saw Bhagwanji's face, but her daughter accidentally did. Once, when she returned home after meeting Bhagwanji she exclaimed on seeing a photograph, 'This is the same man that I just met.' The photo was of Netaji.

Another piece of *Scroll.in*'s investigation that fails to stand up to scrutiny is the allegation that Bhagwanji-Netaji rumours are being spread by people aligned to the BJP-RSS. It may not be out of place here to state that Sheetla Singh's leftist orientation is a matter of public knowledge. They have picked on Shakti Singh, a known BJP leader, but made no reference to Panda Ram Kishore, Congress leader and Bhagwanji's follower whose outspokenness was the reason the news got out in September 1985. Nor has *Scroll.in* considered in their investigation the seminal *Northern India Patrika* inquiry by Sayed Kauser Hussain, Nirmal Nibedon (whose father was the bishop of Assam) and VN Arora (having no affiliation to any political party like Ashok Tandon); the PIL filed by Lalita Bose (then in Congress party) with Mohammed Haleem (associated with Raj Narain) and Vishwa Bandhav Tewari.

Neither was there any allusion to the fact that the 1986 order for securing Bhagwanji's belongings was given by

Justice Saiyed Saghir Ahmad (a would-be Supreme Court judge) and Justice GB Singh. Anuj Dhar's 2002 inquiry was under the aegis of *Hindustan Times*.

The bare fact of the matter, which the authors have been stating publicly, is that the BJP government in UP and the Centre have shown no interest in the Bhagwanji issue and they are toeing the Congress line on the Netaji issue more or less.

For the last word on the KD Upadhyay theory, we may have to refer to Justice Sahai's report. Much as he was eager to disregard the Netaji connection to Gumnami Baba, and despite giving much importance to claim made by Sheetla Singh about Pabitra Mohan Roy's belief, Justice Sahai had to dismiss his Upadhyay fancy as a mere 'suspicion'. 'I am not inclined to accept his claim that Gumnami Baba alias Bhagwanji was actually KD Upadhyay,' he wrote.

A similar fate awaited the purported Anand Marg connection which was invented by one Rakesh Kumar under the aegis of *Navbharat Times* as he did six 'investigative' articles on the Bhagwanji controversy in 1985-86. In the last installment on 7 January 1986, having rejected outright the view that Gumnami Baba was Netaji, Kumar somehow reached a conclusion that he was 'either some spy or some blind Anand Margi follower of Netaji'.

After the Bhagwanji matter was stifled in 1986, Kumar has not been heard of again. He made no attempt to make his case which, if true, would have shot him into national spotlight, either before the Allahabad High Court or Mukherjee Commission, and even local authorities. The same applies to Sheetla Singh who appeared only before Justice Sahai. If only Sahai had located him, Kumar could have been asked to furnish proper details, such as source of his information, the name of Anand Margi or the spy he had in mind when he indulged in such absurdity in the name of journalism.

A little aside: Bhagwanji disapproved of Anand Marg.

The CIA agent theory is based on local rumours. Ayodhya-based journalist Virendra Mishra brought it to the notice of Faizabad Superintendent of Police in February 1979. His letter appears in the District Magistrate's file concerning the controversy. Older and wiser, Virendra Mishra has now come around to backing the Netaji link. He told us after receiving the letter, SSP Gyaneshwar Jha personally raided Gumnami Baba's residence. The authors in their statement to the Justice Sahai Commission furnished relevant details, expecting that Jha (now retired and living in Noida) would be summoned before the Commission to state on record what action he took after receiving Mishra's letter and what was the outcome. What did they do with the alleged CIA agent, sitting in, of all places, Ayodhya? But neither did the Commission summon Jha nor asked the state or central government to throw light on this claim.

Central government did have its chance long ago, but

blew it. In 1988, it was specifically asked in Parliament who Gumnami Baba really was in view of the claims that he was Netaji or a CIA agent. They wouldn't respond. This is what happens when you are engaged in a conspiracy of silence.

For the theory that Bhagwanji was a Netaji impostor, some arguments have been marshalled by researcher Prof Purabi Roy, a former member of the Indian Council of Historical Research (ICHR).

While giving a talk at the Ahmedabad-based Indus University, Roy claimed that she has seen files containing exchanges between Nehru and IB director BN Mullik over Netaji's fate. According to her, the files show that responding to the queries of Nehru 'perturbed' about the implications of Netaji's return from Russia, Mullik asked him to set up ten dummies of Netaji. Thereafter, Indira Gandhi used one of those dummies to 'create' Gumnami Baba in 1975.

No such files exist among the declassified lot. Where Dr Roy has seen these files only she can tell and she has not told anyone that we know of. She did not write anything about these files in either her books or articles. As such, her claim must be treated as a figment of her imagination.

Roy also alleges that Bhagwanji's handwriting samples could have been faked by the authorities. This line of thinking exists among others who want to junk the evidence of handwriting experts because of their personal belief that Bhagwanji couldn't have been Netaji.

The problem with this hypothesis is that the fabrication of so many handwriting samples is an impossible feat. It was beyond the capacity of the Intelligence Bureau or any authority in India to pull through a forensic fraud of that scale. Yes, documents can be fabricated, but only on a smaller scale.

A case in point pertains to the 'Black Diaries' of Irish revolutionary Roger Casement, purportedly containing accounts of his homosexual liaisons with young men. They came into the possession of Scotland Yard after Casement's capture in 1916. They were then used to publicise Casement's 'sexual degeneracy' before he was hanged. Since the 1930s, a controversy has raged about the authenticity of the diaries. It was repeatedly claimed that the British authorities had forged the diaries in order to discredit Casement. In 2002, tests carried out by Audrey Giles, an internationally respected figure in the field of document forensics, established that the handwriting appearing in the diaries was indeed that of Casement.

Commenting on the issue in 2009 in *The Defence of the Realm: The Authorized History of MI5*, Christopher Andrew, the foremost expert on the history of intelligence service, wrote that it was never possible for any British intelligence service to fake so many handwriting specimens. 'Even the KGB, whose disinformation department Service A made far more use of forgery than any Western intelligence agency, never fabricated a handwritten document of comparable length.'

Scores of handwriting specimens, written by Bhagwanji across a span of three decades, couldn't have been fabricated even if the CIA or the KGB were to attempt such a feat in 1985 or earlier. It is scientifically impossible for a man to write in someone else's handwriting in two different languages, English and Bangla, for decades. In any case, B Lal, Curt Baggett, Ashok Kashyap and even government experts who gave negative reports did not detect any signs of forgery in Bhagwanji's handwriting samples. The handwriting is there, it's genuine, and it matches with Netaji's completely. We cannot help it if people say they don't believe it.

The non-forensic circumstantial and material evidence also brings us to the same conclusion that the handwriting analysis yielded. It's not that we did not try to explore the impostor angle. Two grounds make the proposition absurd. First, it is easy to imitate someone on specific characteristics. But as the composite character sketch makes abundantly clear, maintaining consistency for nearly three decades on the looks, mannerisms, recollections, handwriting and knowledge of the world is practically impossible. The second factor working against the hoax or impostor theory is that what was played for three decades cannot be a hoax. An impostor plays the hoax to gain something, not to sit and wait in the wings for three decades.

In the end, it's time to deal with the theory that Bhagwanji was an 'impostor' or 'dummy' planted by the

Intelligence Bureau to cover up the matter of Bose's killing in Russia by drawing a red herring that he was in India, alive.

Subramanian Swamy's case is that Netaji faked his death but Stalin put him in a jail in Siberia, where somewhere around 1953, he was hanged or suffocated to death. Swamy further holds that the Gumnami Baba myth was planted by IB in Nehru's era.

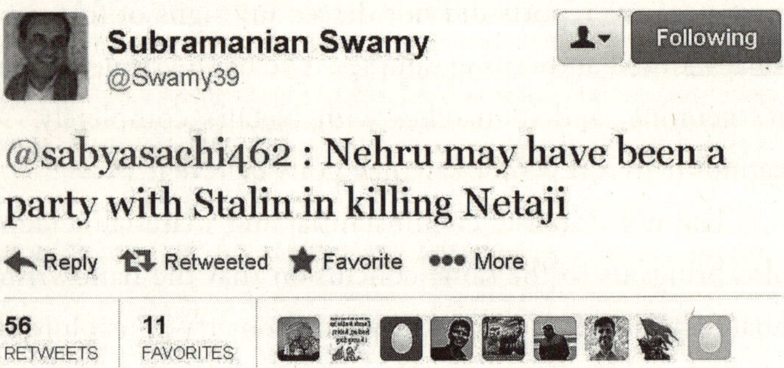

Swamy's reasoning, to cite a *Times of India* report from 2015, is that that Stalin wrote a letter to Nehru in December 1945 that Bose was in his custody and asked Nehru what he should do with him. Nehru, after receiving the letter, immediately summoned his stenographer Sham Lal Jain and dictated a letter meant for the then British PM. Jain stated these facts before the Khosla Commission. To quote *ToI*:

Swamy said as per Jain's version, Nehru had told the British PM that he had received information that Bose was in a jail in Soviet Union. 'In my opinion, soon after that British officials reached the Soviet Union and ensured Bose was put to death.'

Swamy's charge about Stalin, a ruthless dictator, liquidating Subhas Bose seems plausible but is not a fact. Stalin had no particular liking for Nehru, described by him as a 'political prostitute', according to a claim by Asiatic Society researchers in 2000 after seeing records in Moscow. Russia clearly helped Netaji in 1941 and there is much on record to show that Netaji sought asylum in Russia in 1944.

As for Jain's statement before the Khosla Commission, for what it's worth, Swamy distorts it to suits his preconceived notions. Swamy changed Jain's words 'Bose…has been allowed to enter Russian territory by Stalin' to 'Bose was in a jail in Soviet Union'. If we chose to rely upon it, Jain's testimony would only boost our side of the story. We have a copy of his full testimony, obtained under RTI. Not only did Jain not support the theory that Bose was killed in Soviet Russia, he actually believed that Netaji was alive at the time he deposed before the Khosla Commission. He claimed that he met Netaji in UP in 1967.

Swamy's line that Bhagwanji was planted by IB in the Nehruvian era is preposterous. Gumnami Baba matter came to light only in late 1985 after he was reported dead. At that time, the Congress party commanded the largest ever majority in Parliament in the history of India. So, for the IB to plant such a story at that time made no sense. Why would the Rajiv Gandhi government want to revive a long-dead issue at the peak of its popularity?

Lest we forget, it is Swamy's own party that is in power now. He can pull strings we cannot even think of. If Gumnami Baba was an IB plant, a trick played by Nehru government to cover-up something far more hideous, all that the BJP government has to do is to order IB to release its records. As things stand today, the Government has not released a single IB file, nor ever offered any explanation about snooping on Netaji kin and others.

In our statement to Justice Sahai, we requested that Swamy be summoned before the Commission so that his views can be taken on record and later be verified by seeking response from the IB. Fair and simple. But Justice Sahai wouldn't do any such things.

In his book *Bose: An Indian Samurai* (KW Publishers, Delhi, 2016), Gen Bakshi argues that Bose's personality was such that he couldn't have lived incognito for two decades plus. We are taking it up in the next chapter. Elsewhere in his book, Bakshi puts forward another hypothesis that since the British intelligence agencies had signed two agreements with the NKVD (forerunner of the KGB) during the war, it is possible that the British invoked them 'to seek to interrogate Bose in Soviet prisons and get him executed there, as it would avoid any repercussions or public outcry in India'.

Bakshi reads too much into war-time pacts between the Soviet and British intelligence agencies. Pact or no pact, handing over Bose to the British after he had sought shelter from the Russians would have done them no good. Moreover, relations between the Russians and British were not exactly cordial. They had simply been brought together for the sake of defeating a common enemy, Nazi Germany. What to speak of them, even relations between the cousins on either side of the Atlantic Ocean were not what they seemed.

In *Intelligence and the War against Japan: Britain, America and the Politics of Secret Service*—a penetrating account of the interactions of both the British and American intelligence agencies—Dr Richard J Aldrich demonstrates that from 1942, the Allies increasingly spied on each other's future ambitions, rather than the common enemy. By 1944, Aldrich writes, 'this had translated into a barely disguised "Great Game" to achieve the upper hand in clandestine pre-occupational activities across South East Asia. At times, the war against Japan appeared relegated to a sideshow'. In our era, even the CIA has been reported to be wary of sharing everything with the FBI, and this was one of the reasons the 9/11 attacks could not be averted. Here in India (General Bakshi would know better), there has been much talk of rivalry between R&AW and IB.

There are multiple reasons to discount Gen Bakshi's claims that Russia killed Netaji. On 14 October 2015, a delegation comprising the Bose family members, General Bakshi and the authors requested Prime Minister Narendra Modi and External Affairs Minister Sushma Swaraj to raise

the issue with the Russians at the highest level.

On 9 March 2017, Swaraj stated in Parliament that the Government of Russian Federation had informed that 'consequent upon receiving the fresh request of the Indian Government, a fresh search was conducted and no documents pertaining to Netaji Bose's death were found in the Russian Archives'. To break it down into comprehensible language—the Russians have consistently made it quite clear that they have no information about Netaji's death, which they would surely have if he had died in their territory. Back in 1970, the Soviet embassy had issued a terse, single statement that the Soviet authorities 'had absolutely nothing to do with the fate of Subhas Chandra Bose'.

Bhagwanji would have agreed. In an undated letter to Pabitra, written during the time when the GD Khosla Commission was running its inquiry, he wrote that it was beyond the 'fourteen generations' of the Indian government to extract the real truth about him from the Russians.

ELEVEN

WHY DIDN'T HE COME OUT?

THE QUESTION 'WHY did Bhagwanji, if he was Netaji, not come out?' is made most difficult to answer because of the warrior image of Subhas Chandra Bose etched on our minds. Why would a man who challenged Mahatma Gandhi and the entire Congress top leadership, hopped across continents raising armies and setting up a government-in-exile, charmed the biggest of the world leaders (and dictators), generated the final push that expedited the end of the British Raj, hide away in his own country for such a long time?

So overwhelming is this argument that it has taken the shape of axiomatic truth. This, in turn, has become the No. 1 counter against the Gumnami Baba theory. Most people refuse to even consider the possibility that he was Netaji because it was not possible for Netaji to live in hiding. Courage and defiance were hallmarks of Subhas Bose's character. What could he have been afraid of, how could Netaji be reduced to such state?

But then, isn't it like putting the proverbial cart before the horse? Shouldn't we first figure out whether or not there is evidence linking Bhagwanji to Netaji, and if yes, then ask the question about his non-appearance?

Now that we have robust eyewitness, documentary and forensic proofs that Bhagwanji was Netaji indeed, we can dive into this aspect.

Obviously the statements made by and attributed to Bhagwanji will guide our quest. But we have severe limitations on that front. Most of his top followers died long ago. Those we met were not as forthcoming as we expected them to be. Virtually no letter from his side is available for the period 1952-62. From late 1962, when he came in touch Bengal revolutionaries, hundreds of letters and notes were written by him. Bulk of this correspondence is lost today as Bhagwanji's followers resorted to total secrecy. While we were lucky to have accessed letters written by Bhagwanji to Pabitra Mohan Roy, the INA spy himself destroyed those containing sensitive information.

What we have is scattered pieces of information. Nonetheless, out of this we can join the dots to get a picture of why Bhagwanji did not or could not reveal himself to his country. Different reasons, interwoven with multiple strands of national and international factors, seem to have been predominant at different times, reflecting changes in the contextual reality.

Take, for example the hypothetical scenario of Subhas Bose's return to India in 1945 or thereafter and its implications. Socialist leader Ram Manohar Lohia in his book *Guilty Men of India's Partition* (BR Publishing Corporation) wrote: '[If] Netaji Subhas were ever to have returned home after his great and peerless adventure for freedom, he would have given six months of acute trouble to Mr Nehru but no more. If Mr Nehru had been able physically to survive the return of Mr Bose, he would have been on top again after six months, so that Subhas Bose, would either have to go in opposition or to become the second in command. Mr Bose did not possess Mr Nehru's cunning and refinement.'

The common thread that runs through all the 'what if' scenarios is the assumption regarding the starting point. They all start with the presumption that Netaji would return in 1946 or 1947. But the scenario would vastly change if we advance the starting point to the early 1950s—the time when Bhagwanji actually crossed over into India through the porous Indo-Nepalese border.

By this time, Sardar Patel was dead, and Pandit Nehru was firmly ensconced at the helm without any serious challenge from within the Congress or any of the opposition parties. The Congress party had captured almost the entire Lok Sabha, winning 419 of 489 seats. The principal opposition was the Communist Party, followed by the Socialist Party. While the Communist Party had nothing but bitter hatred towards Netaji, the Socialist Party's desertion when its support mattered in 1939 is something that he wouldn't forget.

Syama Prasad Mookerjee (regarding whom Bhagwanji displayed favourable feelings) had set up the Bharatiya Jana Sangh, but he was dead by 1953. In the South, Chakravarti Rajagopalachari was on his way out of Congress, but the ideological differences between him and Netaji were far too wide, and their history of confrontation since the time he joined the Congress was too deep to be forgotten. Bose's own party Forward Bloc had split into two and was on the cusp of further splits. In Bengal, Dr BC Roy, who had crossed over to the Gandhi-Nehru camp in the 1930s was the Chief Minister. The opposition in Bengal was headed by the communists, a mere reference to whom Bhagwanji could not stand.

In short, except for a few splinter groups, there was no large political party which would stand behind Bose if he returned or surfaced. Even if they gave in to prevailing popular sentiment, there was no common ground that could make such an alliance sustainable. Nor were there national political figures whom Bose could count on as loyal allies. He would have been his own man. The former revolutionaries who had stood with him didn't succeed in creating a formidable power base to challenge the Congress organisation. INA veterans and Bose's aides and supporters were not allowed to regroup in free India. And Bose's association with the Axis powers in WWII meant that most nations in the world would flatly refuse to support him in any way. In all probability, they would refuse to deal with him if he rose to a position of power. India, a poor country that had just gained independence, would stand isolated and Indians would suffer as a result.

For sure, stepping out of the shadows was very much part of Bhagwanji's plan. As late as 1980, he told Panda Ram Kishore that '*Jab hum bahar ayenge to hum hi hum honge*' (When I emerge in public, only I will prevail). At the same time, he was also worried that his emergence would lead to a confrontation between his supporters and those of his opponents, leading to a serious law and order situation. During the course of a conversation July 1977, when he was queried by Sunil Das as to why the new Janata government could not ask him to 'come back and occupy his rightful place', he replied that a 'lot of innocents will die'.

There were also times when he made comments to the effect that he is going to serve India and just fade away. He wrote the following to Pabitra soon after their meeting in 1962:

Your Dead Man took nothing from 'you' (meaning Bengal–India–and home)...He took away nothing, he kept nothing for himself, he did nothing for himself. He wanted nothing for himself or his personal aggrandizement and for power. He gave himself to India. He gave something to India and effaced himself away. He again shall be giving something to Bengal–India–Southeast Asia. And he shall again efface himself away. He is a Dead Man, he is a mystic.

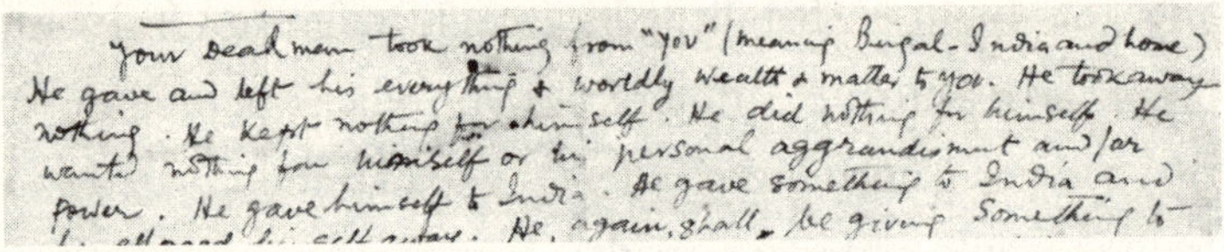
Your Dead man took nothing from "you" (meaning Bengal-India and home)
He gave and left his everything & worldly wealth & matter to you. He took away
nothing. He kept nothing for himself. He did nothing for himself. He
wanted nothing for himself or his personal aggrandisement and/or
power. He gave himself to India. He gave something to India and
He, again, shall be giving something to

In the backdrop of these varying claims, let us discuss the matrix of options. In picking the most reasonable of these, we are going to be guided by 'Occam's razor' and 'The Sagan standard'. The first is a well-established philosophical principle (razor) of reasoning and investigation used to discard improbable options in a given situation. Occam's razor holds that a simpler explanation is better than a more complex one. One of the best-known quotes of Arthur Conan Doyle is what he put in the words of Sherlock Holmes in *The Sign of the Four*: 'How often have I said to you that when you have eliminated the impossible, whatever remains, however improbable, must be the truth?' The 'Sagan standard' is an aphorism used quite often in scholarly publications. Made famous by celebrated astronomer Carl Sagan, it asserts that 'extraordinary claims require extraordinary evidence'.

For the first option, we have Bhagwanji's claim of supernatural powers. Seen from the perspective of his hardcore followers, Bhagwanji had moved on to a different plane altogether. This is a matter of common knowledge. It is not disputed that Subhas Chandra Bose was spiritually inclined. He left home in his teenage years and roamed in the Himalayan region in search of a guru. He titled his unfinished biography *An Indian Pilgrim*. He told a friend in Germany in the 1930s that certain holy men in India have the power to project themselves elsewhere.

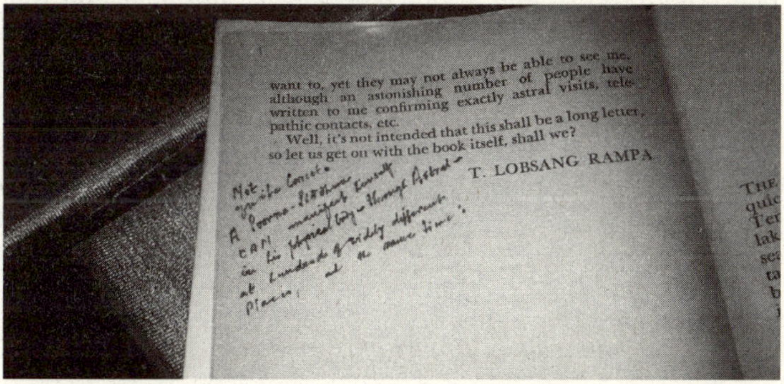

[Bhagwanji's comment: 'A Poorna Siddha can manifest himself in his physical body—through Astral—at hundreds of widely different places, at the same time.']

Bhagwanji repeatedly told his followers that he had fully embraced spiritualism in his quest for India's good after the end of WWII, when matters did not unfold the way he wanted. His letters and other accounts of his disciples also show that he had full command over the *Itihasas, Puranas, Vedas* and *Tantric* texts. He would call himself a *sadhak*, a practitioner in tantra. Being so, Bhagwanji said, was the consummation of a desire he had always had from his childhood days:

Shakti-sadhana is to awaken the kulakundalini. The Mother is called kulakundalini energy. Shakti-sadhana is to awaken and direct this power. This is also the aim of the extremely secret rajayoga. On the way of awakening the kulakundalini, a sadhak has the option to move ahead of the point where rajayoga stops. He will go on if he has the courage. Rajayogis do not know of this path. That is the main difference between a rajayogi and a tantrik—though both their aim is to awaken the kulakundalini. Those who are really tantriks will never claim to be one. Anyone who says he is a tantrik, can never be one. The way of tantriks is very hazardous. They are bound by strict laws. The network of their organisation is spread all over the world; but India is their nerve-centre. A tantrik will never divulge their secrets even if you cut them into pieces. Tantra-sadhana is the ultimate of ultimates.

Through *sadhna* he gained *siddhis* (spiritual powers described in Hindu scriptures) beyond comprehension of average humans—such as the power to move about in *sukshma sharir* (subtle body).

'Once your *sadhana* reaches a stage, the *prana sharir* (subtle body) can be taken out of this *sthula sharir* (material body). After getting used to this, one can go anywhere in his *prana sharir,'* he claimed, adding, 'At the highest level of attainment, one's movements even in space, among the planets and galaxies, become unrestricted.'

As human beings, we are, at all times radiating energy,

which is soaked and stored by items around us. Even our thoughts radiate and create an electrical field which leaves an imprint on objects in the form of energy,' wrote Bhagwanji. He cited the work of one Genady Sergeyev to claim that 'every human being leaves an energetical imprint...as well as informational imprint on objects that he touches or is close to.

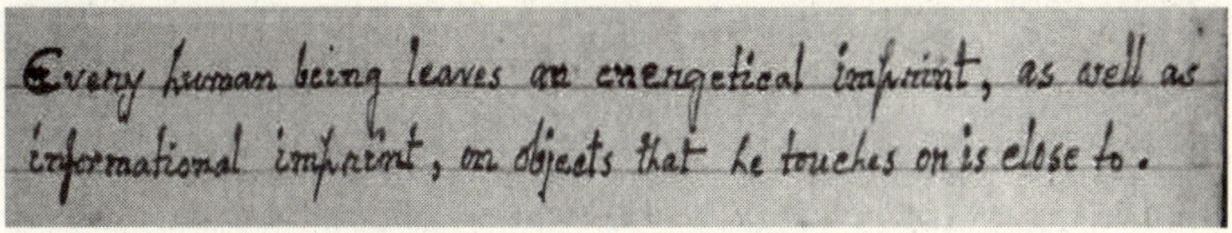
Every human being leaves an energetical imprint, as well as informational imprint, on objects that he touches or is close to.

[From a letter Bhagwanji wrote to Dr Priyabrata Banerjee of Faizabad. Courtesy Rita Banerjee]

Dr Genady Sergeyev turned out to be a prominent mathematician for the Soviet military, who devised important mathematical and statistical methods that allowed parapsychologists to follow and depict the actions of telepathy in the brain. This was stated in a 1972 Defense Intelligence Agency (DIA) report, declassified in 2004 by the Central Intelligence Agency (CIA).

The report discusses Sergeyev in the context of research in Soviet Union in the area of psychokinesis (PK) or mind over matter. He conducted intensive lab research on Nina Kulagina, a Russian lady who claimed to have psychic powers. Sergeyev registered heightened biological luminescence radiating from Kulagina's eyes during the apparent movement of objects by PK'. He postulated that the 'bio-plasma' of the human body 'must interact with the environment to produce PK'.

Bhagwanji said he used his spiritual powers for the good of the nation. 'India will become so great that it cannot be explained in words,' he told them.

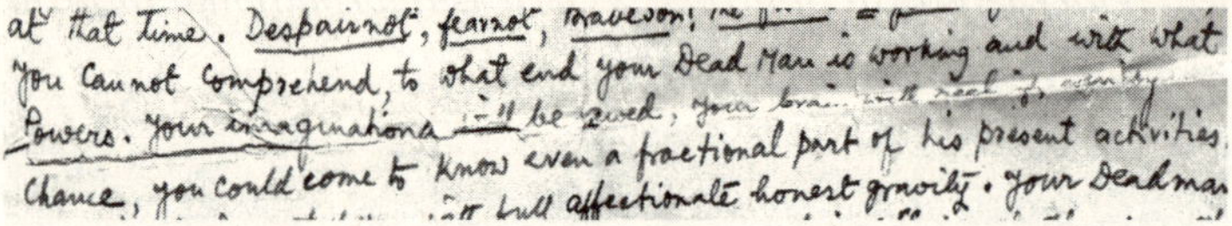
at that time. Despairnot, fearnot, braveson; ...
You cannot comprehend, to what end your Dead Man is working and with what
Powers. Your imaginations will be awed, your brain will reel if even by
Chance, you could come to know even a fractional part of his present activities.
... full affectionate honest gravity. Your Dead man

[Bhagwanji to Pabitra: 'You can not comprehend to what end your Dead Man is working and with what Powers. Your imaginations will be awed, your brain will reel if even by chance, you could come to know even a fractional part of his present activities.']

Almost all his close followers, from Pabitra Mohan Roy to Dr RP Misra, believed him when Bhagwanji said he would be alive for many more decades to come. They did not believe that Bhagwanji was dead in 1985, and waited for him to return. That was the reason they resorted to secrecy and evasion.

The first option on the matrix that Bhagwanji became a sadhak/tantric in his quest for India's good and will return is too fantastic to be considered as a valid reason for his non-appearance.

The second option relates to Bhagwanji's claims that he became involved in Soviet covert operations with the larger aim to ensure that India was not caught in bloody proxy wars between the free and Communist worlds. Because of his covert activities, unpublicised role in international events, the tag of 'war criminal' from WWII years put together,

Bhagwanji thought he was regarded as 'Enemy No. 1' by the Anglo-American bloc. In his estimate, if he emerged, people of India would have suffered as there would have been economic sanctions and other instances of arm-twisting to ensure his capture, which would have been opposed tooth-and-nail by his supporters in India. 'My coming out is not in the interest of India,' he summarised to a follower.

We have to admit that the claim that Bhagwanji was involved in covert operations and hence could not surface does not pass the 'Sagan standard'. In absence of clear-cut evidence, such as official documentation or declaration, all his claims, though not wholly devoid of substance, can only be treated as cues or interesting leads. Bhagwanji's followers have many more of his letters and notes and they might contain information which could turn these leads into evidence. But since they did not give us full access to their collection, we have no other option but to draw our conclusions on the basis of what is available to us.

The controversy about Netaji having been declared a war criminal during WWII went on for decades. It is still believed by many that his name was put on the list of war criminals. Today the lists compiled by the United Nations War Crimes Commission (UNWCC) between December 1944 and March 1948 have been declassified along with the corpus called the Central Registry of War Criminals and Security Suspects (CROWCASS). Subhas Bose's name doesn't figure in any of these lists. Bhagwanji's claim that that the US and UK were desperately hunting for him long after WWII also does not pass the test of scrutiny unless his role in global developments is established with proper evidence.

The third option is a deduction emerging from Bhagwanji's claims. As things stand today, this option offers a logical reasoning behind his non-appearance. We started considering this heartbreaking scenario after we came across a letter Bhagwanji wrote (in English) in February 1963 to Pabitra Mohan Roy, who copied its text and either returned the original or destroyed it as ordered.

In the letter, Bhagwanji made a series of incredible claims about WWII, about himself and, most importantly, about Douglas MacArthur—American five-star general and Field Marshal of the Philippine Army, who commanded the Southwest Pacific Theatre and administered post-war Japan during the Allied occupation. When war in Korea erupted, MacArthur headed the United Nations forces but was after a few months relieved of his command by President Harry Truman in what became the topmost controversy of that time in the US.

Using bombastic language, Bhagwanji claimed that MacArthur's dismissal was in reaction to his sending 'a final report' to Truman. The 'gist of the report', in Bhagwanji's words, was:

'Subhas Chandra Bose has escaped again.' Do you understand the weight and force of this report? The mighty Himalayas can be moved and proved false. But not that report of all reports of 5 Star General Mac to his S/C C-in C. Such reports are inconvertible.

This was in the context of the war in Korea, where Bhagwanji claimed he had been sent by the Russians to settle old scores with the Americans for their help in the defeat of the INA.

Even as one struggles to absorb this, Bhagwanji came up with a delusional theory—that Winston Churchill forced the hand of US President Truman to drop atom bombs on Hiroshima and Nagasaki, partially to 'get at one single man at all costs'.

There was absolutely no necessity of those two hellish A Bombs but they were dropped. You know whose strategy got Singapore, the much vaunted 'largest and biggest impregnable base in the world' as per official British quotation. Then came the three provinces of India proper, reconquered. The Allied high command (more pertinently the UK) became extremely jittery. The whole country was seething. They became panic-stricken with the certainty of 'the whole country including the forces rising in revolt the moment '__' come down to the plains. There was absolutely no time to lose. Every moment was precious and vital. Every day '__' was giving a clarion call—I am coming, I have come. We shall reach Delhi in no time once we get down to the plains. Oh, he had to be stopped—come what may. Because he shall not give any quarters to the Alien forces and nationalities. He must be stopped. It was UK which forced the hands of Truman. Nagasaki, Hiroshima were the only two ports of disembarkation; everything came to a shuddering stop….

This bears no match with anything in historical records. Subhas Bose was only of peripheral interest to Americans. It was their ally the British who wanted him out of the picture. The issue of the dropping of the atomic bombs on Japan, given its significance in history, has been a matter of considerable research for the last several decades. Reams of official documents and memoirs have been available in the public domain for some time now. No reference to Subhas Chandra Bose appears anywhere. Similarly, the removal of MacArthur in April 1951 has been a much-discussed topic over the decades given its importance in American history. All sorts of things were said and discussed, but nowhere does anything appear which could even remotely be associated with Subhas Bose.

In India, there is a clear reason for concealment and official silence over matters relating to Subhas Bose. Let us assume that the British government is also not telling much because of the legacy of the Raj—but the United States has no reason to hide something of this sort if it really happened. In America, the levels of transparency and accountability are so high that even the highest level of security classified material routinely makes its way to the public domain, either lawfully or otherwise. A case in point for the latter is of the Pentagon Papers. This was a Department of Defense Top Secret study of United States' political and military involvement in Vietnam from 1945 to 1967. The entire volume was leaked to *The New York Times* in 1971.

From this we are led to another problem area in the Bhagwanji narrative. On 24 January 1973, Bhagwanji described in an unusually long narrative, replete with use of coded language, a secret conference between the representatives of Russia, China and the US, overseen by 'a pride of nine generals and a shadow behind them', on the fate of the Vietnam War. He claimed that the 'shadow' advised the US representative to opt for a 'face-saving ceasefire' since they had already lost the war. The 'shadow' was none other than Bhagwanji himself. The conversation in Basti took place three days before the signing of the Peace Accord in Paris that set in motion the ceasefire in Vietnam and the withdrawal of the US troops.

To test the veracity of Bhagwanji's claim, we rummaged through declassified US records about the Vietnam war—there are virtually lakhs of them—and found nothing in the records we browsed. Not even a hint! Putting an official seal of approval on this finding was the Defense Intelligence Agency (DIA), the top US military spy agency, which informed us under US Freedom of Information Act (RTI) that it does not have any intelligence reports pertaining to Bose's claimed involvement in the Vietnam war.

DEFENSE INTELLIGENCE AGENCY

WASHINGTON, D.C. 20340-5100

U-12-3,827/DAN-1A (FOIA)

JAN 10 2012

Mr. Anuj Dhar

India

Dear Mr. Dhar:

This responds to your request under the Freedom of Information Act, dated September 24, 2007. Therein you requested information concerning copies of Intelligence Information Reports created in between 1962 and 1972 pertaining to Subhas Chandra Bose, specifically in the context of the war in Vietnam. I apologize for the delay in processing your request. DIA continues its efforts to eliminate the large backlog of pending FOIA requests.

Based on the information contained in your request, the Defense Intelligence Agency searched its systems of records for responsive documents. Despite a thorough search, no documents responsive to your request were found.

We even tried with the more well-known CIA, seeking from the agency relevant information from among the 'finished intelligence reports'—the high-end information used for national-level policy deliberations by the US policymakers. The Central Intelligence Agency processed the request under the provisions of the FOIA and the CIA Information Act and 'did not locate any records'—that is finished intelligence reports—on Subhas Bose created between 1960 and 1970. If what Bhagwanji claimed about himself was true, there must have been several such reports, but it turns out there are none. It must be emphasised that there are several things that Bhagwanji talked about which aren't historically correct.

Going by his own words, Bhagwanji came back to India in early 1950s with a group of people. There is no light on how these people came together. All we hear is that these people were together in the Mansarovar region as they travelled towards the Nepalese/Indian frontier. Two men were lost in the inhospitable terrain. Those who survived went in different directions. In the early 1960s, Bhagwanji 'revealed' the identity of these men to Shrikant Sharma in Naimisharanya's Shiva temple. Adolf Hitler! According to Bhagwanji, Hitler eventually died in 1965 at Kankhal, Haridwar, a place swarming with mystics from around the world. Bhagwanji warned Shrikant that if his whereabouts were disclosed, 'India will be the venue of third world war'.

The very idea of Bhagwanji returning to India along with Hitler defies imagination. And so do his self-proclaimed forays into the paranormal—out-of-body experiences, Gyanganj (a mythical abode in the Himalayas where he met yogis several centuries old) and ghosts.

Only the human body has been made in a way that if used properly, ghosts, gods and goddesses, apsaras and gandharvas become visible. Only the human body can break out free of this limiting web, with the help of Siddha Purush Shri Shri Sadgurudev. Gods can't attain liberation even if they want—for that they have to take birth in a human body, do sadhana and then attain liberation. [Translated]

We are perfectly aware that such things are believed

by a large number of people, including persons of greatest eminence world over. But we are simple researchers who must restrict themselves to what would be accepted by courts of law, academia, intellectuals, media in general. There is no way we can prove or substantiate Bhagwanji's utterances. How can we say that Bhagwanji's claim that 'Abraham Lincoln's ghost comes to the White House' is true?

But consider this: In February 1987, then US President Ronald Reagan said that he would like to meet Abraham Lincoln's ghost 'which haunts the White House'. Reagan's wish was not fulfilled—the closest he came to it was noticing that his dog would not enter the bedroom Lincoln once occupied and would just stand 'glaring as if he's seeing something and barking'. His daughter and son-in-law were convinced that they had 'really seen it'—this is according to an AFP story published in *The Indian Express*. They joined many others who are believed to have spotted a transparent person with a pinkish aura. Presidents Theodore Roosevelt, Herbert Hoover, Harry Truman, Winston Churchill...the list is long. Instances of extraordinary people believing in, or giving credence to things science can't explain are legion. In June 2007, when she was a contender for the top post, former President Pratibha Patil, publicly said that a long dead holy man had given her 'a "divine premonition" of greater responsibility coming her way'. Noted former Supreme Court judge VR Krishna Iyer claimed that he spoke with his departed wife through a medium. In his 1996 book *The Choice: How Bill Clinton Won*, Watergate star reporter and former *Washington Post* editor Bob Woodward claimed that Hillary Clinton, then US First Lady, had a session with Mahatma Gandhi's spirit. One of the most well-known claims of reincarnation (believed in by Bhagwanji) relates to a little girl in India of the 1930s. Shanti Devi's claim of having been born again was investigated by a committee of fifteen eminent people as advised by Mahatma Gandhi himself.

We consulted two specialists in the field of psychiatry. In our brief, we outlined the two personas—Netaji (A) and Bhagwanji (B) and drafted the following question: 'Assuming PERSONS A and B were the same, what could induce such a transformation? He claimed that he had undergone complete metamorphosis compared to his previous life. Can this be scientifically or psychologically explained—with and without torture scenarios?'

The first to apply his mind was Dr Arabinda Brahma, a Kolkata-based psychiatrist and assistant general secretary of Indian Psychiatric Society. Since Dr Brahma was aware that the matter referred to him was about the Gumnami Baba theory, we thought it better to consult a foreign expert as well. We reached out to one in an Australian university. This expert (who wished to remain anonymous) had no clue at that time that the matter pertained to the Gumnami Baba/Subhas Bose controversy. All she received was the questionnaire from an Indian acquaintance residing in Australia—who kept us and the background of the case out of the picture.

The responses obtained from the experts not only provided a logical explanation as to why Bhagwanji behaved the way he did and could not return to public life, it also resolved several of the anomalies in the entire Bhagwanji narrative.

Bhagwanji suffered from post-traumatic stress disorder (PTSD), which manifested in false memories, hallucinations, delusions (paranoid and grandiose). Recent research suggests a link between schizophrenia and insomnia, and Bhagwanji clearly suffered the latter.

The claims about Hitler and MacArthur clearly fall in the category of false memory. Research shows that the syndrome can affect the sense of identity and personality of an individual. In her remarkable book *The Memory Illusion*, criminal psychologist and memory expert Dr Julia Shaw offers this insight: 'Any event, no matter how important, emotional or traumatic it may seem, can be forgotten, misremembered, or even be entirely fictitious.'

These disturbing signs could not be detected by those around and close to Bhagwanji because they treated him like a God-like figure. They believed he could perform miracles, such as going out of his body, which science does not accept. Even in his decline, the man was so exalted intellectually, compared to the people around him, that the adverse signs remained invisible to them.

Bhagwanji's psychological problems are hinted at by Curt Baggett's report and observations made by Ashok Kashyap. With his main report, Curt appended a handwriting analysis in order to help determine the personality and character traits of what he thought was an 'anonymous person'. Curt found out that he turned out to be 'an enigma of personality', with 'so many strong, tremendous outstanding positive traits sprinkled with a handful of traits which did not always serve him well'.

Some of the motivational traits observed by Curt remind us of Netaji: Initiative, diplomacy, fluidity of thought, artistic and/or writing ability, dreamer, quick wit and quick sarcasm, trust issues, secretive, stubborn, defiant, physically aggressive, missing father image, strong will power, love of debates, loyal, good organisational ability, blunt, talkative, generous.

And then there are these negative traits: resentment and anger, sensitive to criticism of his ideas or person whether real or imagined, fear of success, good listener except when he did not want to hear something, had a trauma at about age 15, touch of paranoia.

We can only hazard a guess or two as to what might have brought this change in the personality of Bhagwanji/Subhas Bose. Going by his statements, he was greatly affected by the condition he was in, his inability to free India through INA's invasion because of lack of support, the treatment he was meted out as he was booted out of Congress in 1939 and then panned by intellectuals and media in Bengal. The subsequent partition of India, and the fate that befell Bengali women in the wake of his motherland's division tormented him no end.

As long as he lived, Bhagwanji would tell his followers from Bengal that had the people of his home state in particular stood like a rock behind him when the INA entered India, he would not have to suffer like this. He used to bemoan that 'Bengal has killed Him'. He often gave heart-wrenching accounts of tragedies in East Pakistan and cried for the women who suffered. This might explain his extreme hatred for Jawaharlal Nehru, whom he held responsible for the ravages of Partition.

Can we rule out that Bhagwanji suffered physical torture at some point in time? Is there a possibility that the horrifying scenario thought of by Dr Subramanian Swamy and Major General GD Bakshi (Retd) actually happened? They have suggested openly that Netaji was tortured to death.

Even though he made claims of having been treated like a VIP by the Russians, Bhagwanji made certain disturbing comments in his notes. He described scientific experiments on thought control and impact of music on living beings in Soviet Russia, and spoke at length about their methods of torture. Someone in Soviet Russia explained to him how to perpetrate painless instantaneous deaths. 'I asked him how many times he had to do it to be able to understand.' With horror he described the application of methods to make one forget one's identity completely. 'If you ask him about the past he will keep staring blankly at your face,' said the man who knew. 'Some even go mad passing through this method. Stark mad.'

He wouldn't discuss in detail what he went through but would only leave hints, as when he told Pabitra that in the beginning the Russians didn't treat him like a son-in-law (an idiomatic reference to the special affection shown to sons-in-law in Bengali households). We get a validation that he mentioned his imprisonment and torture from a letter written by Shiva Prasad Nag. Nag could extract only part of the narrative from Kamala Kanta Ghosh who had heard about Bhagwanji's travails directly from him: *I heard from sadhak* [Kamala Kanta Ghosh] *that the Red forces had imprisoned Mahakal* [Bhagwanji] *for about ten years and nearly finished him. I heard the story of rescue from him.*

In fact, Subhas Bose's wife believed in such a scenario. In the words of Subhas's Germany-based grand-nephew Surya Bose, sometime in the early 1950s, his grand-aunt Emilie Schenkl was told by Raimund Schnabel, a well-known German journalist who had settled down in East Berlin after WWII, 'that he had been informed that Netaji was in the

Soviet Union after 1945'. Schnabel, citing his KGB sources, said that Subhas 'was being slowly poisoned and was losing his mind'. Consequently, Emilie never believed the air crash theory despite our Government's attempts to convince her.

He surely did not die, but Bhagwanji was no longer the man he used to be. Intriguingly, Bhagwanji remained aware of the problems stemming from this debility, even if the symptoms manifested only occasionally.

Think of it. Could anyone else survive even one per cent of what 'this body' has endured?

This awareness and his apprehension about the possible consequences of the psychological problem might have stopped him from coming out. It is possible that his intense spiritual practices helped him overcome the problem, but the web of other deterrents too came in his way of reappearing. This is the long and short of his tragedy, the tragedy of India.

TWELVE

WHY THE GOVERNMENT IS SILENT

TWO ISSUES REMAIN to be addressed at the end. Why is our own Government, the one being led by Narendra Modi, not stating the truth about Netaji, and what can be done now for justice?

Before we address this issue, we must state our view that successive central governments have been aware of the existence of Bhagwanji/Netaji. They figured out his location after the demise of Pt Nehru in early 1964. Since they knew he could not come out and was posed no threat to the powers that be, they did not touch him. They kept an eye on him, and possibly sent representatives to him. Perhaps on some specific occasions, he was briefed about official matters and that might explain Bhagwanji's insights, including his vivid description of the state of affairs in the FATA region of Pakistan during the first Afghanistan Jihad of the late 1970s.

Of course, we cannot explain everything due to paucity of information, as both the government and Bhagwanji's followers prefer secrecy over disclosure.

Now, to get to answers to the main question, we need to go back to the British Raj era. There is so much riding on the truth that there will be massive implications if it's accepted. The government, no matter which party is in power, is wary of those implications. What is chiefly at stake is the State-sponsored narrative being promoted for last several decades with all the public resources available to our Government. So many in and outside the Government have benefited from it and continue to benefit from peddling it.

This is the history you were not taught at school. When WWII ended in 1945, people in the West were feeling victorious and overjoyed. On the other hand, Indians were wallowing in despondency and defeatism. Three years had passed since Quit India movement was launched, but there was no sign of independence. When the All India Congress Committee met in late September. Sardar Vallabhbhai Patel summed up the mood of the nation in the resolution moved by him:

Neither the end of the War nor the change of Government in Britain appears to have resulted in any real change in British policy towards India, which seems to be based on delaying every advance and in attempting to create new problems and fresh complications. It is significant that there is no mention in these [British] broadcasts of the Independence of India.

In clear words, the AICC resolution tells us what our Government won't. Leave everyone else aside, Prime Minister Narendra Modi has himself repeatedly claimed that the Quit India movement of 1942 led to independence in 1947. The truth is that the Quit India movement wound up long before the AICC resolution was moved by Patel. So what led to independence?

There is no denying that Mahatma Gandhi did wonders for our freedom struggle and that he was one of greatest Indians ever. His memories and legacy therefore must be treated with utmost reverence. But from all accounts available now, the man whose efforts had biggest impact in the freedom struggle was Subhas Chandra Bose. 'Mass movements by the Congress between 1920 (when Gandhi arrived on the scene) and 1947 were niggardly, and hardly upset the British,' wrote former R&AW official Colonel RSN Singh on *Sify.com*.

When Gandhi launched the Quit India movement in 1942, he in a sense accepted Bose's 1939 suggestion to serve a six-month ultimatum on the British government. Prior to this, Gandhi was, as Bose himself stated repeatedly, most reluctant to launch a movement. Bose accused him of compromising with the colonial rulers.

But when the war started in 1939, Gandhi had met Viceroy Linlithgow and issued a statement that 'India should cooperate with Britain in her hour of danger'. Subhas Bose wrote in his book *Indian Struggle* that 'this statement came as a bombshell to the Indian people' who had for years been 'taught by the Congress leaders to regard the next war as a unique opportunity for winning freedom'. However, due to pressure put by Bose and others, the Congress Working Committee (CWC) resolution of 15 September stated that 'India cannot associate herself in a war said to be for democratic freedom, when that freedom is denied to her'.

In January 1940, Gandhi wrote in *Harijan* that he was 'not spoiling for a fight' with the colonial rulers. 'I wholly endorse Subhas Bose's charge that I am eager to have a compromise with Britain if it can be had with honour.' In June, Subhas met Gandhi and beseeched him to start a civil-disobedience movement as such an opportunity would not come again. Gandhi said the time was not right. Jawaharlal Nehru, a former close friend of Bose who was now in the Gandhi camp, said on September 10 that India should not take 'advantage of Britain's difficulties'. At the AICC meeting of September that year, Gandhi stated that he did not want 'England to be defeated and humiliated'. If there was any chances of Great Britain taking a kinder view, it was totally gone as by now pathological India hater and Hinduphobe Winston Churchill had taken over as the Prime Minister.

All the same, the Quit India movement was launched. Bose, who had by this time escaped out of India and was in Germany, praised Gandhi's stirring speech on 8 August

1942. This was despite his reservations expressed earlier: 'Every show of strength and defiance that Gandhi puts up is always followed by an attempt at a compromise.'

As it happened, the Quit India movement turned out to be a non-starter. 'Immediately, the entire top leadership of Congress was taken into custody. Leaderless and rudderless, the movement died in a year's time, but the Congress leaders remained in prison till the rest of the war. This served the interest of the British as well as the reputation, prestige and political prestige of Congress leaders,' commented Col Singh.

Author-journalist Khushwant Singh put it more bluntly in *Hindustan Times*. In 2003, he wrote that the movement was 'crushed within three weeks'. Singh was far from being an admirer of Bose.

'It was during this period, when the Congress leaders were ineffective, that Subhas Chandra Bose was exerting himself for India's independence,' Col Singh underlined.

'By the end of 1942, the British had definitely come out victorious in their immediate total confrontation with Indian nationalism, and the remaining two-and-a-half years of the war passed without any serious political challenge from within the country,' summarised noted historian Sumit Sarkar in his book *Modern India.* Like late Khushwant Singh, Sarkar is not a big fan of Netaji's. In fact he publicly made fun of his mysterious disappearance when the Mukherjee Commission was formed.

Unknown to most Indians today, beginning late 1943, Gandhi wrote several letters to Viceroy Linlithgow, explaining his position with regard to the 'August disturbances' (as the Quit India movement was called in those days). In declassified Home Department files available at Delhi's National Archives, the term used for Gandhi's action was 'apologia'.

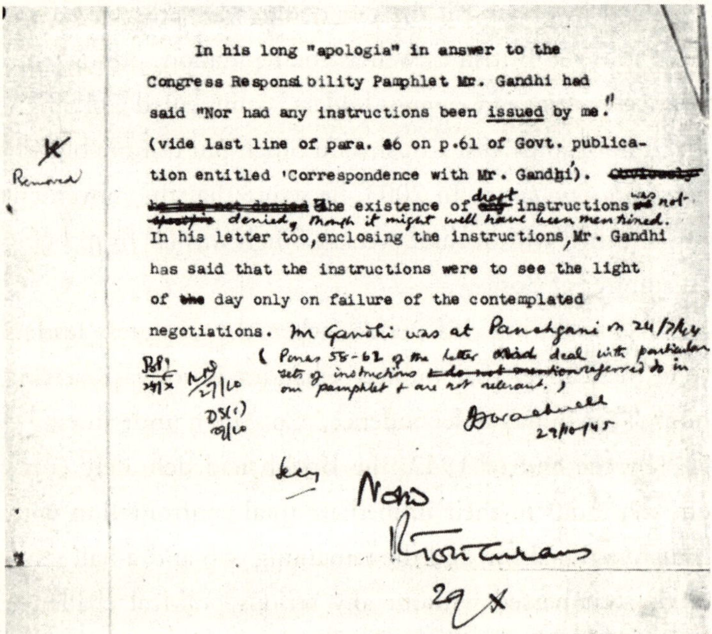
Removed

In his long "apologia" in answer to the Congress Responsibility Pamphlet Mr. Gandhi had said "Nor had any instructions been issued by me." (vide last line of para. 46 on p.61 of Govt. publication entitled 'Correspondence with Mr. Gandhi'). The existence of draft instructions was not denied, though it might well have been mentioned. In his letter too, enclosing the instructions, Mr. Gandhi has said that the instructions were to see the light of day only on failure of the contemplated negotiations. Mr Gandhi was at Panchgani on 24/7/44

(Paras 58-62 of the letter deal with particular sets of instructions referred to in our pamphlet & are not relevant.)

29/10/45

29 X

[National Archives, New Delhi]

Noted historian Dr RC Majumdar was of the view that 'far from claiming any credit for achievements of 1942, both Gandhi and the Congress offered apology and explanation' for the violent acts of those who carried on with the movement after the arrest of Gandhi and other senior leaders.

Indeed, Gandhiji wrote to the Viceroy that it was not the Quit India resolution but the British Indian government's actions which led to the acts of violence. It was the government which 'goaded the people to the point of madness', he added. In February 1943, then Congress president Maulana Azad wrote to the Viceroy to deny the charge that Congress was responsible for acts of sabotage during the Quit India movement. 'You say you have ample information that the campaign of sabotage has been conducted under secret instructions circulated in the name of AICC. But we do know and can state with authority that AICC at no time contemplated such a campaign and never issued such instructions, secret or other.' In September 1945, Nehru, Patel and GB Pant issued a statement on behalf the Congress. It read: 'No movement had been officially started by the AICC or Gandhiji.'

This was the backdrop against which the Congress party geared up to go to the general elections in the winter of 1945-46, as announced by the Clement Attlee-led new Labour government in London as a precursor to reaching an agreement about the question of India's freedom. The British were insisting on substantial agreement between the Congress and the Muslim League before considering giving independence. The Congress' inclusive election manifesto would go on to articulate that the only thing which mattered was the independence of India. The party was all for secularism in contrast to the League's claim that it alone had the right to represent the Muslims of India. At this crucial juncture, the Red Fort trials commenced against the INA soldiers. They represented Indians of all hues—including Anglo-Indians. Subhas Bose was able to unite Indians like never before in history.

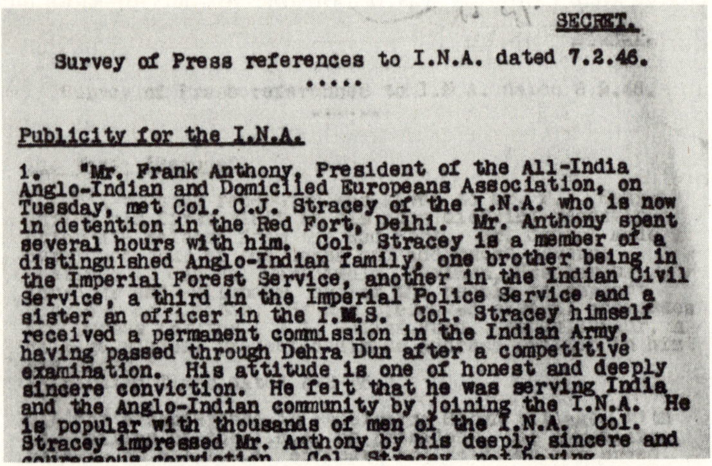

SECRET.

Survey of Press references to I.N.A. dated 7.2.46.

.....

Publicity for the I.N.A.

1. "Mr. Frank Anthony, President of the All-India Anglo-Indian and Domiciled Europeans Association, on Tuesday, met Col. C.J. Stracey of the I.N.A. who is now in detention in the Red Fort, Delhi. Mr. Anthony spent several hours with him. Col. Stracey is a member of a distinguished Anglo-Indian family, one brother being in the Imperial Forest Service, another in the Indian Civil Service, a third in the Imperial Police Service and a sister an officer in the I.M.S. Col. Stracey himself received a permanent commission in the Indian Army, having passed through Dehra Dun after a competitive examination. His attitude is one of honest and deeply sincere conviction. He felt that he was serving India and the Anglo-Indian community by joining the I.N.A. He is popular with thousands of men of the I.N.A. Col. Stracey impressed Mr. Anthony by his deeply sincere and

[National Archives, New Delhi]

The Congress party to made the best of this opportunity. So, there was a major shift in the party's stance. At the September 1945 AICC meeting, a backhanded compliment was paid to the INA soldiers—hitherto dubbed 'misguided' by the party leaders. From this point on, Congress leaders also started branding the failed 1942 movement as 'August revolution'.

Thanks to records declassified by the UK Government, we now have a more granular insight into why Congress leaders came around to backing Bose's INA in the course of the Red Fort trials, even though violence against the colonial rulers had no place in their worldview. Military Intelligence figured out that before taking a stand on the INA issue, the Congress high command sent a top leader out on a recce mission to gauge public feeling. He travelled across India and discovered that people were overwhelmingly in support of the INA. The MI's final assessment sent to the Secretary of State for India in London was that 'political expediency' was the reason for Congress' backing of INA and Bose.

There were multiple such reports from different authorities. Commander-in-Chief of British Indian armed forces, General Claude Auchinleck, wrote to Viceroy Field Marshal Viscount Wavell in November 1945 that the INA trials 'provided the Congress with an excellent election cry'.

These facts expose the fantasy interpretation of history fed to us over the decades. In August 2006, while defending his rejection of the Mukherjee Commission report, Home Minister Shivraj Patil proclaimed in Parliament that Jawaharlal Nehru had 'donned the black coat and gown and gone to the Red Fort to defend' the INA men. The real story was somewhat different.

According to KK Ghosh, who was the first to write an authoritative and comprehensive account of the INA, the Congress 'had no political programme ready at hand to rejuvenate' the dull political atmosphere. The 'ready-made issue' the cause of the INA officers offered the Congress 'an opportunity to organise an all-India nationalist front against the British', Ghosh wrote in his book *The Indian National Army*.

From 21 to 24 November 1945, street protests broke out in Calcutta, followed by riots in Bombay, Karachi, Patna, Allahabad, Benaras, Rawalpindi and other places. By this time, Auchinleck had received many disturbing reports. On 19 November, he received a letter from British Indian Army Colonel KS Himatsinhji (a scion of the Jamnagar royal family and later Major General) apprising him of the fear of an armed revolution in India if the INA men were executed. In December, the Governor of Punjab wrote that Indian Army had 'a very considerable degree of sympathy' for the INA. Himatsinhji (the first Lieutenant-Governor of Himachal Pradesh) again wrote to Auchinleck in February 1948 that India was 'in a very hostile mood towards the British Government' and that most regarded INA as an army of liberation, and that this is the only point on which the Congress and the Muslim League had the same view.

Consequently, Auchinleck was compelled to explain to his top military commanders on 12 February 1946 through a 'Strictly Personal and Secret' letter the reasons why the military had to let the INA 'war criminals' and 'traitors' go off the hook:

Having considered all the evidence and appreciated to the best of my ability the general trend of Indian public opinion, and of the feeling in the Indian Army, I have no doubt at all that to have confirmed the sentence of imprisonment solely on the charge of 'waging war against the King' would have had disastrous results, in that it would have probably precipitated a violent outbreak throughout the country, and have created active and widespread disaffection in the Army, especially amongst the Indian officers and the more highly educated rank and file.

Many luminaries watched events unfold in those days, but only a few articulated their honest views publicly in later years. On top of the list was Dr Bhimrao Ambedkar, who had no special bonding with Bose—and hence his words carry all the more weight. Speaking to the BBC in February 1955, Ambedkar wondered, 'I don't know how Mr Attlee suddenly agreed to give India independence. That is a secret that he will disclose in his autobiography. None expected that he would do that.'

In October 1956, two months before Dr Ambedkar passed away, Clement Attlee himself disclosed in a confidential private talk that very secret. It would take two decades for Phani Bhusan Chakravartti, Chief Justice of Calcutta High Court and acting Governor of West Bengal, to muster the courage to divulge what the former British PM had told him in the Governor's mansion in Kolkata in 1956:

The INA activities of Subhas Chandra Bose, which weakened the very foundation of the British Empire in India, and the RIN mutiny which made the British realise that the Indian armed forces could no longer be trusted to prop up the British.

Justice Chakravartti, first Indian to become permanent Chief Justice of India's oldest court, also asked Attlee what was the extent of Gandhi's influence upon the British decision to quit India. In Chakravartti's words: *Hearing this question, Attlee's lips became twisted in a sarcastic smile as he slowly chewed out the word, 'm-i-n-i-m-a-l'!*

In 1960, in Nuffield College, Oxford, Sir Attlee reiterated his position to historian Prof Barun De—a much respected name in Leftist-Congress circles. In 1967, at a New Delhi seminar to mark the 20th anniversary of Independence, then British High Commissioner and famous broadcaster John Freeman opined that 'independence became certain after the 1946 revolt of the Royal Indian Navy'. Among those who heard Freeman speak was Swaminathan Aiyar, brother of Congress leader Mani Shankar Aiyar.

One of the most respected columnists in India, Swaminathan wrote in *The Economic Times* in 2007 that Freeman's admission 'astonished many youngsters in the audience, including me' for they 'had never been taught about the naval revolt'. This was the extent to which the

Government propaganda had brainwashed even highly educated people after independence.

The Royal Indian Navy (RIN) revolt was a watershed event in Indian freedom struggle. Its leader BC Dutt stated during an interview with the University of Cambridge in 1970 that the sailors (ratings) who caused the RIN mutiny 'were unaffected by the "Quit India" ultimatum of the Indian National Congress in 1942'. But 'there was a tremendous upsurge in the country when the men of Subhas Chandra Bose's Indian National Army were brought to India in 1945'. Dutt said the trial of the INA soldiers made Naval ratings 'restless'.

Dr Ambedkar would not have been surprised with any of these details, especially Attlee's admission that Bose's struggle had to do with his decision to free India. He told the BBC (which recorded the interview for posterity) that from his 'own analysis' he had concluded that the reason for India's freedom lay in the fight put up by the INA of Subhas Bose.

The British had been ruling the country in the firm belief that whatever may happen in the country or whatever the politicians did, they could never be able to change the loyalty of soldiers. That was one prop on which they were carrying on the administration. And that was completely dashed to pieces.

Explaining it lucidly in 1964 was British historian Michael Edwardes. He wrote in his book *The Last Years of*

British India: 'It slowly dawned upon the Government of India that the backbone of the British rule, the Indian Army, might now no longer be trustworthy. The ghost of Subhas Bose, like Hamlet's father, walked the battlements of the Red Fort, and his suddenly amplified figure overawed the conference that was to lead to Independence.'

Some thirty years after independence, Lt Gen SK Sinha came out with an astonishing insight in an op-ed article in *The Statesman*. The would-be Assam and J&K Governor, as a young captain along with fellow Lt Colonel Sam Manekshaw and Major Yahya Khan, were the only natives posted to the hitherto exclusively British Directorate of Military Operations in 1946. Sinha wrote: 'There was considerable sympathy for the INA within the Army. ...I am convinced that well over 90 per cent of officers at that time felt along those lines.'

In 1946, I accidentally came across a very interesting document...prepared by the Director of Military Intelligence. It was a classified document marked 'Top Secret. Not for Indian Eyes.' ... The paper referred to the INA, the mutinies at Bombay and Jabalpur and also to the 'adverse' effect on the Indian officers and men of the humiliating defeats inflicted by the Japanese on the white nations in the early days of the war. The conclusion reached was that the Indian Army could no longer be relied upon to remain a loyal instrument for maintaining British rule over India.

Of course, none of this is reflected in history of freedom struggle as projected by our Government—right to this day. What happened in and after 1947 is heartbreaking. Having granted India dominion status (which is what Gandhiji wanted and Bose opposed), the British transferred power to Congress party leaders. After having come to control the official apparatus, the leaders of free India started using it to glorify their non-violent struggle, pushing everyone else into near oblivion. The official narrative was immortalised through an all-time hit 1950s Bollywood song—*De di hame aazadi bina khadag bina dhal. Sabarmati ke sant tune kar diya kamaal.*

This view of India winning freedom without taking recourse to violence cast the colonial British in favourble light—as large-hearted, democratic people who yielded to peaceful persuasion. The heart-wrenching accounts of ruthless suppression, brutal torture and killings of freedom fighters including INA men were whitewashed overnight. 'The British withdrawal is one of the noblest acts,' Gandhi declared.

From Day One of independent India, Subhas Bose's memories and his role in the freedom struggle were downgraded and pushed to the periphery. Congressmen who in 1946 raised the cries of *Lal Quile se ayee awaz, Sehgal, Dhillon, Shah Nawaz. Inqlab zindabad* in favour of INA heroes switched to *Mounbatten ki jai ho* in 1947. It did not matter to them that the man they had selected to be free India's first Governor General was responsible for the defeat of the INA as former supreme Allied commander for South East Asia. Lord Louis Mountbatten chose to free India on 15 August 1947 as it reminded him of his great victory against Japan, and the INA if you please, in the war two years earlier.

An average Indian's perception of Independence Day—the Union Jack going down and the Tricolour coming up—is so remarkably different from the real event that it will sound fanciful to him if he was told that the Union Jack did not disappear that day. Mountbatten himself recorded that he disapproved of a ceremonial lowering of the British flag and Nehru agreed with him, not wanting to offend British sensibilities.

Mountbatten even wanted the Union Jack on the upper canton of the Indian Tricolour—a proposition that Gandhi supported to the hilt. Gandhi actually took a swipe against those who were opposed to it. 'But what is wrong with having the Union Jack in a corner of our flag? If harm has been done to us by the British, it has not been done by their flag and we must also take note of the virtues of the British. They are voluntarily withdrawing from India, leaving power in our hands,' he said at his prayer meeting of 19 July 1947.

The British couldn't have asked for a more honourble exit from India after having reduced her to one of the poorest nations in the world from being one of the richest.

Consequently, for them to tacitly support the official India government narrative is perfectly understandable.

Since power was concentrated in the hands of Gandhians, frcc India's government put the Mahatma on the pedestal reserved for God. Carrying out the politicians' wish were cunning bureaucrats, most of whom had loyally served the British Raj and then flourished in free India.

To take one name, there was Sir Chandulal Madhavlal Trivedi, who became Governor of Punjab and Andhra Pradesh after retirement and was conferred the Padma Vibhushan. As revealed by a declassified record in the National Archives, Trivedi was a loyal servant of the Raj in whose eyes the INA men were 'traitors and rebels'.

Confidential.

WAR DEPARTMENT.

I have spoken to Mr. Lal about the press cuttings below. Our definite view is that officers and men of the Indian Army who joined the so-called Indian National Army have not, in law, the status of combatants or belligerents and that they are traitors and rebels. We shall undoubtedly hear more of this in the Press and the competence of Courts-Martial to try these persons will probably be challenged. We should be most grateful for an exposition of the law on the subject.

Sd/- C.M. Trivedi.
1.9.45.

Legislative Deptt. (Mr. Lal).
W.D. U.O. 4628-S/WI dated 1.9.45.

Innumerable people like him and their offspring became the ruling elite of free India. If the father was a Rai Bahadur in the Raj era, the son became a top official in free India—both united by their deep attachment to everything English—later on the larger West. Every evening they would strut around the clubs in big cities vacated by the British, aping their former masters in mannerism, thoughts and accent. The *brown sahibs* had evergreen memories of their good old days of toadying under the *gora sahibs*, and dreams of settling their children in the West. This in turn shaped much of their view of Subhas Chandra Bose at least. Their legacy continues till date.

Precisely this was the slave mentality which enabled free India to give pension benefits to those 'Indian' soldiers who had, without batting an eye, opened fired in Jallianwalla Bagh when ordered to do so by their foreign master. This was the mentality which allowed snooping on people linked to Subhas Bose and sharing intelligence with MI5 in London without any qualm. This very slave mentality allowed lowering of the tricolour on government buildings and paying of glowing tributes on All India Radio in 1965 on the demise of Winston Churchill, responsible for millions of death in India. And this very mentality prevented the Narendra Modi government from renaming Andaman and Nicobar islands as Subhas Bose had done. This very slave mentality is coming in the way of telling the truth.

Paul Johnson noted in *The New York Times* of 6 February 1977 that there was 'a sizeable Gandhi industry' in India, 'complete with innumerable foundations, museums, colleges and other hagiographical institutions'. Since that time, this 'industry' has expanded manifold, not just in India but also abroad, especially in the West, much of it using the Indian exchequer.

The BJP-led government is taking it to a different level. India missions are constantly engaged in the propaganda—which Government itself doesn't believe in when it comes to the crunch. For instance in Chicago on 2 October 2015, the Consul General of India told a gathering of Americans that the principles of 'Gandhism' 'basically focused on fighting against the negative forces with the blunt weapon of peace, perseverance and non-violence as opposed to waging of wars'.

India is the third largest military spender in world, which is absolutely essential as it is in our national interest.

Now, since innumerable highly-placed people—historians, bureaucrats, politicians, foreigners, journalists—have benefitted from this state-funded, gigantic exercise revolving around empty talk of ahimsa costing millions to the people of India each year, everyone's happy. Why should anyone complain? Governments come and go. Politicians support whatever clicks, never mind what they personally feel or what they opine when they are not in power.

In their previous incarnation, in numerous RSS *shakhas*, BJP leaders used to give speeches about revolutionaries—but now they sing the Gandhi *dhun* (tune). 'Mahatma Gandhi is an idol for us, he was our guiding light and will remain so,' asserts Defence Minister Rajnath Singh in a video posted on BJP's YouTube channel. In the *CNN-IBN* debate where the DNA fraud over the Bhagwanji matter was exposed, the BJP spokesperson, defending the Sahai Commission report, candidly admitted that the party had no qualms about being engaged in 'Gandhi Bhakti'.

The admission of truth about Subhas Bose's fate will cause this grand edifice of Gandhi bhakti to implode. The sheer sensational value of the admission that Netaji was alive after his reported death will, in this age of uncensored free flow of information, cause such an upheaval that acrimonious debates will break out in every fifth home, among kin and friends. The media will rush to dig out facts, give space to those who are denied it otherwise—resulting in guilt, anger and searing feeling of having been betrayed by those in power.

It will not be long before Subhas Chandra Bose's sterling role in making India free would start coming into the spotlight. That's where the real trouble will start. Those who have everything to gain by peddling the make-believe ahimsa theory will use every iota of their considerable influence to maintain the status quo.

As the Government comes under increasing pressure to either dismiss or accept the truth about the freedom struggle, it would be guided by several considerations—the topmost of which would be the fact that the truth won't be saleable in the West, where the souls and children of India's elite reside. Because the official non-violence fiction casts the white man in flattering light, the idea has great appeal in the West. Watch again Richard Attenborough's 1982 masterpiece *Gandhi*, funded by our Government, to understand this underlying subtext. The West defines our world and no one knows it better than our ruling and the elite class. 'Modi government ministers prefer Oxford, Harvard for their children's education and not IIT, IIM,' was the headline of a story in *The Print* in March 2020. 'Of the 56 ministers in Modi council, 12 have sent their children to foreign varsities.'

Lest our argument is misunderstood, it is perfectly fine for anyone to aspire for good life in the first world. The authors are unflinching in their admiration for Western civilisation overall. Britain is great for us for so many things—from savouring the best literature to fish and chips, enjoying best TV series, songs, or rides on the Tube. The list is endless. In our research, we were always treated with consideration by officials of archives and governments in these countries. We have received so much support from Persons of Indian Origin (PIOs) in the US and the UK. They remain attached to India even as they are totally loyal to the countries that have given them a new life.

The simple point we are making as Indians is that it is not fine for Indians and PIOs to view their foremost freedom fighter with the prism of others. It is an open secret that a big chunk among the Indian elite class consider Bose 'misguided' because this is how things would appear to average Westerners. 'Bose's role in the freedom struggle is well known. But history often forgets his connection with the likes of Hitler and Mussolini,' read the blurb of an article in *The Hindu* on 4 September 2020. Uday Balakrishnan, its writer, a former fellow at NIAS, CEU Budapest and at CCS-IISc, wrote pieces titled 'Being Nehruvian in these difficult times', 'He [Gandhi] lived and died for dignity in diversity', 'Gandhi, through his writings', 'Taking an objective view of the Raj', 'Let's admit it, China is not our enemy', 'Dangerous deification of the armed forces'. Phew!

The stark truth is, that all nations and their leaders pursue nothing but their national interests. In doing so, they often set aside moral considerations. Nelson Mandela, touted as a Gandhian, explained this in plain language. In the summer of 1990, at the City College of New York, Mandela was interacting for the first time with American people in a town meeting. He was bombarded with questions about his dealing with leaders of certain nations not approved by America. In response, Mandela asserted the following amid a standing ovation from the audience:

One of the mistakes which some political analysts make is to think their enemies should be our enemies. Our attitude towards any country is determined by the attitude of that country to our struggle. Yasser Arafat, Colonel Gaddafi, Fidel Castro support our struggle to the hilt. There is no reason whatsoever why we should have any hesitation about hailing their commitment to human rights as they're being demanded in South Africa. They do not support [the anti-apartheid struggle] *only in rhetoric; they are placing resources at our disposal for us to win the struggle.*

Mandela's response to the executive director of the American Jewish Congress, was more pointed. 'Firstly, we are a liberation movement which is fully involved in a struggle to emancipate our people from one of the worst racial tyrannies the world has seen. We have no time to be looking into the internal affairs of other countries. It is unreasonable for anybody to think that this is our role,' he was quoted as saying by *The Washington Post*.

At home, haven't the followers of Mahatma Gandhi taken the same approach since 1947? Pandit Nehru himself told noted activist Balraj Puri that India had 'gambled on the international stage on Kashmir' and consequently till things improve, democracy and morality can wait. National interest is more important than democracy. What was India's main national interest in 1940s—to be free or to preach virtues of non-violence to mankind? Much as our hearts go out for the victims of holocaust in Europe, we cry first and foremost for millions of Indians lost to the Bengal famine and other man-made disasters our nation faced.

On the foreign front, New Delhi has extended a friendly hand to all sorts of leaders reviled, especially in the Western world, as the worst dictators and tyrants. The list includes Libyan leader Muammar Gaddafi, Nicolae Ceausescu of Romania, Robert Mugabe of Zimbabwe, and Kim Jong-Un of North Korea.

It is not Aung San Suu Kyi, the winner of the Nobel Peace Prize and the Jawaharlal Nehru Award, but the Burmese military junta which received most support from the land of Gandhi when they were in charge. Cut to our times—India has virtually turned a blind eye to the allegations that the Burmese under Suu Kyi's leadership are engaged in 'ethnic cleansing' of the Rohingyas. All we are hearing from our Government is that we have our own security concerns first. Ignoring street protests, India actively backed and even assisted militarily the Mahinda Rajapaksa regime in Sri Lanka as it was being accused of carrying out war crimes against the Tamils.

While the Western nations regarded him as a monster in the league of Adolf Hitler, for India Saddam Hussein was a most trusted friend. Iraq did not denounce but supported India's right to possess nuclear bombs. 'Saddam was a dictator but remember he was on our side when it came to Kashmir,' former Prime Minister IK Gujral, an ex-diplomat, underlined in an interview with the *Indian Express* in April 2003.

Pakistani dictator Pervez Musharraf, directly responsible for the deaths of so many Indians, including the soldiers we lost during the Kargil war, was given a ceremonial Guard of Honour by the Indian armed forces upon his arrival in New Delhi in 2001. How many times did the Americans accord such an honour to Fidel Castro, or the British to Russian heads of governments? And if making our armed forces salute Musharraf was a triumph of Indian diplomacy, how come Subhas Bose's reaching out to Hitler, who had not caused even a single Indian death and actually aided our freedom struggle, became a cause to beat one's chest in the name of morality?

Put another way, Western sensibilities are perfectly understandable in view of the trail of destruction left behind, in particular by Adolf Hitler in that part of the world. But the Indian attitude has been hypocritical, coloured by pro-Western outlook of the elite in India. Isn't it a plain fact of history that Great Britain, for all her goodness, was not willing to free India even as she and the United States waged war against Hitler in the name of liberty? It was not Hitler but Winston Churchill who used filthy words for Indians. And yet, Nehru and others treated him with deference. Not a single Indian diplomat ever squeaked a single word to Churchill or others that they owed India an apology.

Indians need to see Netaji and his actions to make India free from their very own Indian eyes. When he was in Germany in the 1930s, Bose became friendly with Kitty and Alex, a sensitive, newly married Jewish couple in Berlin. After being advised by Bose, the couple went to the US, and from her Massachusetts home in 1965 Kitty Kurti wrote her tribute for 'Netaji'—a book titled *Subhas Chandra Bose As I Knew Him*. In it she wrote that Bose 'did not attempt to hide' from her his deep contempt for the Nazis. In the same vein, he cited India's exploitation by British imperialism and explained why he had to do business with the Nazis. 'It is dreadful but it must be done. India must gain her independence, cost what it may,' he told the couple after a meeting with Hermann Göring.

So, for the Government of India to accept the truth about Netaji would mean to sabotage their own narrative, propagated for generations with countless backers and converts all over the world, especially in the West. All those who have benefitted from this state-sanctioned hoax, and even their families, are not going to allow it all to be frittered away. Therefore, the entire system is loaded against the truth. This is the biggest stumbling block in unravelling the Netaji truth today. Even if all that Bhagwanji said was true about his engaging in a covert war against the Anglo-Americans, the passage of time has removed all sensitivities. Records declassified in the UK in 2018 show that Great Britain was considering reconciling with Netaji's legacy in 1993 during the India visit of Prime Minister John Major. 'We are quite happy to rehabilitate other ex-colonial leaders who fought us. Aung San had a comparable career to Bose but that is forgotten. Mr Mandela is forgiven for his armed struggle,' wrote Alan Rosling, special advisor in Downing Street. The proposal, however, was shot down by the Foreign Office. High Commissioner to India 'strongly' advised against the attempt at 'retrospective reconciliation with Bose, a controversial figure in Indian history'.

Assuming the top men in the system decide to go ahead and tell the truth despite everything, there would be another factor to consider. As things stand today, no specific political dividends can be reaped from stating the truth. Subhas Chandra Bose's legacy, unlike some other national icons, does not translate into a vote-fetching proposition even in his home state of Bengal, what to speak of the rest of the country. Netaji doesn't enjoy iconic status in his home state comparable to, say, Sardar Patel in Gujarat. Most Bengalis elites, the ruling class and the intellectuals in particular, do not think much of Subhas Bose.

In a 2001 Op-ed piece in *The Statesman*, Soumitra Das mocked Netaji in these words. 'After having been marginalised in the Congress and in the independence struggle by Gandhi and Jawaharlal, Bose was looking for a role to play commensurate with his ambition of being a leader of the Indian people. Since he could not do it in India, his best bet was to strike an extreme nationalist posture even if that meant ignoring larger historical, ideological and moral issues, in the hope that his countrymen would focus on his heroism and his sacrifice and forget the rest. They have.'

Similarly, Sumit Mitra's diatribe in *The Telegraph* in April 2005 was brazen. Netaji was charged with pioneering 'Bengal's trademark factionalism in Congress politics', sitting 'in the lap of Hitler when the air of Auschwitz was acrid with the smell of the gas chamber' and losing a 'clumsy war against the British'. It also poked fun at him: 'He hated Gandhi and non-violence, but asked his countrymen to unite under Gandhi.'

Post-1947 Bengal was ruled by Congress and Communist parties, both of which were hostile towards him. They have been successful in downgrading his legacy in the state. The annual ritual of paying lip service to Netaji in Bengal on his birth anniversary will also vanish if the holiday to mark the occasion is withdrawn.

All the same, among the common people of Bengal and other parts of the country, and especially among the youth, Netaji remains popular. In Bengal, his memories and afterlife as Bhagwanji, have been revived/reinforced by the hit movie *Gumnaami,* in whose making the authors were involved throughout. People in theatres cried upon seeing it. And this holds out the hope for what we can do now for justice.

The template we need to follow is the one used previously by the followers of Dr Ambedkar and Sardar Patel. Not long ago, their memories were also pushed to the sidelines, in fact they were not more than footnotes in history when most of us were growing up. Then came the remarkable concerted efforts by their followers, which have resulted in the proper positioning of these national icons in present-day India. This has happened because the political class realises that public sentiments are linked to these icons. Their chances of winning elections increase as they pander to these sentiments.

For the truth about Netaji to be manifested, the matter needs to be politicised. This is a sword that can cut through the cobwebs created by those who do not want it out. Dangle the carrot of electoral advantages and politicians will do whatever is expected of them.

Given the fact that despite everything, the highest number of Netaji's followers are in Bengal, this efforts must start from there. A pressure group may perhaps be formed, comprising politicians and others.

This pressure group, or caucus in American terminology, should ideally comprise MPs from all parties. These MPs can, in Parliament and outside, corner the Government on the issue of Netaji's role in making India free, and the issue of his disappearance. They can employ tactics which are used for other political issues. They can seek full details of intelligence records and operations related to Netaji and those linked to him. They can demand that heads of intelligence should be asked to come to parliamentary committees to answer questions. They can ask the Government to free all serving and retired intelligence and other officers to from provisions of the Official Secrets Act so that they can speak freely about Netaji in national interest. There are one hundred things that can be done if a group of ten MPs are willing to speak for Netaji.

In August 2005, Shivraj Patil dismissed the findings of the Nanavati Commission that had probed the 1984 anti-Sikh violence. As reported in *Indian Express,* the 'action taken report' in this instance said that the Commission was itself not certain of the involvement of Congress leaders in the genocide and therefore 'any further action will not be justified'. Then, the Opposition members and the people of Punjab lunged at the throats of ruling party leaders and there was this complete about-turn. Patil went on to assure the Lok Sabha that 'all the recommendations' of the Commission would be implemented by the Government 'as it is'—reported *The Tribune* of Chandigarh. The same Government, the same Shivraj Patil got away with blatant dismissal of the Mukherjee Commission report because people, especially in Bengal, took it lying down.

It is a matter of great shame that thus far we haven't seen even a single politician from Bengal of consequence

to announce the decision to release many of these files.

Q: But Netaji's daughter wants a DNA test of his remains kept in Tokyo's Renkoji temple, which is most logical thing to do. Why haven't you discussed it in this book?

A: The issue of DNA testing of the presumptive remains of Netaji in Japan has been discussed in detail in our previous books, lectures, Facebook posts, etc. Our intention in writing this book was to convey the basic truth in concise form. Since we have proven that Gumnami Baba was Netaji, obviously the remains in Tokyo cannot be his. The Mukherjee Commission report establishes that the remains are of a Japanese solider, whose body was passed off as that of Netaji as per the escape plan. The Commission wanted to get the DNA test done but our Government did not cooperate.

Anyhow, we are all for a DNA or any other scientific test on the Renkoji temple remains as we are sure that their outcome would support our finding. Our demand is such a test must be carried out by the Federal Bureau of Investigation. If India could seek FBI's expertise in resolving death mysteries of Bhanwari Devi and Sunanda Pushkar, what prevents us from approaching the American agency over this matter?

Recent statements from the Bose kin about the DNA test of Renkoji remains (which many of them now claim are of Netaji's) were made with a view to divert public attention from the raging Gumnami Baba controversy. The idea was to give people an impression that on one hand there were people peddling

APPENDIX

Frequently asked questions

Q: Netaji's daughter has publicly stated that she supports the air crash theory. Why should we not believe her?

A: Views of three members of the Bose family count the most over the issue of his death. Elder brothers Sarat and Suresh and wife Emilie Schenkl. All three rejected the air crash theory. Netaji's daughter Dr Anita Pfaff was just three years old when her father reportedly died in Taipei. Her outlook about this matter has been influenced by the views of some of her close relatives in India linked to the Congress party. We expected her to be the foremost supporter of the demand for declassification of the Netaji files. But she was not supportive of the idea when it took shape with the approval and support of the majority of her kin. She was conspicuous by her absence when Prime Minister Narendra Modi called the Bose family, Mission Netaji members and others to his official residence in October 2015 in the last few decades stating publicly that Netaji was No. One reason for India's freedom. On the other hand, there is virtual competition among the parties in the state in our times to prove who is a bigger Gandhi *bhakt*.

This must change if the truth about Netaji is to emerge. Just as they led the freedom struggle, the people of Bengal must take a lead and send signals to their leaders that their prospects in the elections are going to hinge on what they do about Netaji-related issues. The battle will be half won the day Bengali politicians get the message. It will be a matter of time before politicians from other parts of the country join in.

a 'nonsensical' holy man theory, on the other, these family members were 'sensible' enough to adopt a scientific approach.

The cold fact is that Dr Anita Pfaff herself opposed the DNA test when she was first approached by the Government in 1995. You can see this in the following relevant portion (point 12) of a declassified MEA memo signed by then Foreign Secretary Salman Haidar:

VIEWS OF NETAJI'S DAUGHTER

12. Ms. Anita Pfaff, Netaji's daughter from his German wife, had visited Delhi for discussions with other members of the family and been in touch with the Japanese Ambassador in Delhi in February 1995. She had also written to some associates of Netaji, including Hayashi. EAM met her in Germany in October 1995. During discussion with EAM, she expressed her willingness to go along with the proposal of bringing back the ashes to India but did not approve of the DNA test.

VIEWS OF OTHER IMPORTANT MEMBERS OF NETAJI'S FAMILY

13. While Dr. Sisir Bose supports the idea of bringing back the ashes, Late Amiya Nath Bose, Netaji's nephew had been the most vociferous skeptic of the air crash episode and had opposed any proposal of bringing back the ashes.

14. This issues with the approval of the External Affairs Minister.

S. Haidar

(Salman Haidar)
Foreign Secretary

[National Archives, New Delhi]

Q: London-based senior journalist and Netaji's grandnephew Ashis Ray has also written a book and given public statements that Subhas Bose died in Taipei. He researched this matter for a long time. What do you say to that?

A: In 2016, several close relatives of Ashis Ray issued a public statement calling him a Congress agent. Ray himself makes no bones about his leanings towards the party. In January 2019, Ray organised Congress-backed 'EVM Hackathon' in London, which made big news in India. In this event, claims were made that the 2014 general elections in India were rigged and that Union minister and senior BJP leader Gopinath Munde was murdered because he knew about it. These revolting conspiracy theories were floated with the aim of giving the Narendra Modi-led government a bad name, and, in the process, boosting the prospects of Rahul Gandhi. This is the level at which Ray operates.

Ray claims to have all the evidence to prove Netaji's death. However, he was nowhere to be seen when the Mukherjee Commission was functioning. He surfaced when declassification of Netaji files became a big issue. He and other members of his family linked to Congress employ a standard operating procedure of cherry-picking data and dishing it out to the unsuspecting public to convince people that the air crash theory was true.

Q: People say you are BJP agents. What about that?

A: This allegation owes its origins to disgruntled elements in Bengal—those who have for generations supported Congress and Communist parties and do not approve of what we are doing. The manner in which we have highlighted the fact that India became free because of Netaji and not Gandhiji has not been taken kindly by them. Hence the smear campaign against

us. We have been objective in our approach and blunt in stating facts. BJP and Congress both have engaged in cover-up.

Q: But you have referred to Bhagwanji's RSS links! Aren't you saffronising Netaji?

A: That RSS chief Madhav Golwalkar was in contact with Bhagwanji is proven by his letter found among Bhagwanji's belongings. It is listed on the inventory prepared on the order of Allahabad High Court in 1986. That former RSS chief KS Sudarshan repeatedly stated that Bhagwanji was Netaji was reported by many newspapers. If someone doesn't like these details and blames us for citing them, probably they are shooting the messengers who brought them 'bad' news.

Q: Netaji's family says he was secular and we should follow him.

A: Of course. Refer to our previous books. Many of these kin are of Congress and Communist orientation and their statements must be viewed in that context. They won't tell you that Netaji was a devout Hindu. He led a struggle for organising Durga Pujain the prisons in Burma and Kolkata. He carried a copy of Bhagavad Gita all the time. Being secular doesn't mean one should forsake one's religion.

Q: What would you say to those who say that since the Netaji matter is so old, it's better to put the past behind us and just move on?

A: In October 2010, an ex-IG in Kochi was found guilty of gunning down a Naxalite in a fake encounter. The case was reopened forty years after the incident. Special CBI Court judge's observations were widely reported in media. It is instructive to quote from them:

Truth by its very nature does not yield to be kept hidden forever. Truth which has been hitherto hidden as covered by the glitter of golden plate, has by now, though belatedly, been discovered. Truth triumphs; truth alone.... The offence of custodial murder, be it of an extremist, terrorist or Naxalite, in the hands of the police whose duty is to produce him before a court for trial, does not get wiped off merely by efflux of time, be it decades... cannot be justified in a society like ours....

Q: There are media reports that Netaji was present in Tashkent when Lal Bahadur Shastri signed the accord with Pakistan. What is your take?

A: Bhagwanji was in India when the Tashkent summit took place.

Q: How can ordinary people help you in your quest?

A: By picking up this book and going through it carefully, you have rendered us support. People must know facts and take an informed stand. And they should help disseminate them in national interest. So we request you to tell your near and dear ones about this book. We would like you to look for us on YouTube, Facebook and Twitter and promote our views wherever you agree. In future, you can organise lectures by us.

PAPERBACK ISBN: 978-9386473578

HARDBACK

ISBN: 978-9380828695

PAPERBACK

ISBN: 978-9382711469

NETAJI 125
MISSION NETAJI
END THE SECRECY